THE
MONEY
GAME

THE
MONEY
GAME

'Adam Smith'

VINTAGE BOOKS
A Division of Random House
New York

FIRST VINTAGE BOOKS EDITION, September 1976

Acknowledgment is hereby made to Harcourt, Brace & World, Inc., Macmillan & Co. Ltd., The Macmillan Company of Canada Ltd., and The Trustees of the Estate of the late Lord Keynes for permission to reprint from *The General Theory of Employment, Interest, and Money*, by John Maynard Keynes.

Some portions of the book previously appeared in *West*, *The Atlantic Monthly*, and the *World Journal Tribune*. Copyright © 1966, 1967 by World Journal Tribune, Inc.

Library of Congress Cataloging in Publication Data

Goodman, George J   W
  The money game.

  1. Stock-exchange—United States. 2. Investments—United States. I. Title.
[HG4910.G64 1976]   332.6'78   76-10592
ISBN 0-394-72103-9
C9 8 7 6

For Sallie Brophy
Kinswoman and friend

CONTENTS

III. THEY: THE PROS

IV. VISIONS OF THE APOCALYPSE: CAN IT ALL COME TUMBLING DOWN?

V. VISIONS OF THE MILLENNIUM: DO YOU REALLY WANT TO BE RICH?

PREFACE TO THE
VINTAGE EDITION

It is now a decade since *The Money Game* was written. Ben Graham, the classics scholar who was the dean of security analysis, started his text with a quote from Horace: "Many shall come to honor that now are fallen, and many shall fall that are now in honor." That is certainly true for the players of the money game over the decade, as it probably will be in any decade. Not only did some of the players fall, but the names of some of the companies in *The Money Game* have become one with those of the harness makers and the locomotive kings. Any book written in the sixties is going to have some images that become the nostalgic amber of old tintypes.

This edition of *The Money Game* is the same as the first —not a word changed, as they say. There are other conventions which could be brought up-to-date, should the author choose to meddle. For example, Cassius Clay has become Muhammed Ali, and so on. But the book stands as it did.

For *The Money Game* is not, first and primarily, about money. It is not a compendium of techniques, nor even something that could be filed under "microeconomics." Such a book would have dated more. *The Money Game* is, it says, "about image and reality and identity and anxiety and money." That seems still the proper order. The money which can preoccupy so much of our consciousness is an abstraction and a symbol. The game we create with it is an irrational one, and we play it better when we realize that, even as we try to bring rationality to it. "New Book That Views Market as Irrational Is a Hit on Wall Street," the *Wall Street Journal* headlined, in some wonder.

Irrational? When its language was built upon numbers, the very essence of rationality? It did seem an odd idea, even as the accounting boards worried about all the dialects that could be created out of that language of numbers, so that clarity became elusive. But the false rationality of numbers was not the only symbol that was not what it seemed. Another was the image of the banker, the Prudent Man, the Steward of Capital. For behind the funds which described themselves as virtue engendered—that is, Prudent and Faithful, usually in the more Latinate form, and American and Growth-Seeking—there operated a new generation of professional money managers, unscarred by depression memories, whose efforts were bent not toward the stewardship of capital but toward its increase—and incidentally making a record for the fund, which could then be sold to more investors. The ebullient sixties—so they seem, after half a decade of the gravest economic dislocation since the great world depression of the thirties. There were cities burning, civil disorders, an unpopular war, campuses torn apart, Presidents driven from office—but also a sense of excitement that contrasted with the gray fog which was to follow. The markets churned, but the times were good. "You and I know," says one of the characters in *The Money Game*, "that one day the orchestra will stop playing and the wind will rattle through the broken window panes." I must have liked the image; I used it again after *The Money Game* appeared but before the market fell apart: "We are all at a wonderful party, and by the rules of the game we know that at some point in time the Black Horsemen will burst through the great terrace doors to cut down the revelers; those who leave early may be saved, but the music and wines are so seductive that we do not want to leave, but we do ask, 'What time is it? what time is it?' Only none of the clocks have any hands."

So we knew it was going to happen, and it did. The Black Horsemen came and cut down the revelers, even those with the names of virtue engendered like Prudent and Faithful and American and Growth. If you entrusted your money to them at the end of the sixties, you were lucky to keep half. That went, too, for banks whose headquarters were vaulted like cathedrals. Not only did the market go down, it kept going down—the popular averages disguised the extent of the decline. Another day it would come back, but not until the unscarred generation, so bold without memories, had become scarred like its predecessor.

Probably the biggest error in *The Money Game* is an implicit one. The small investor is a lovable fool, and the professional manager is a worldly riverboat dealer; find smart people, the small investor is told. Very good. That is like Ben Graham saying, "Many shall be called to honor that now are fallen." But how do you find smart people? Those who have just finished being smart are sometimes the dumb ones in the next part of the cycle. The scarred sit, frozen by memories, through the ebullient markets, and the unscarred are sliced apart by the Black Horsemen of greed at the end. Only a longer time span reveals the truly Prudent Man, who knows that the first rule of making money is not to lose it. The implication in *The Money Game* is that the professional investors, who have access to all the information, whose computers can churn out ratios at fingertip touch, are smarter than the small investor. They are not smarter, they merely have more information. That does not protect them from the compulsions of theology; witness the wonderful Two Tier market of the seventies, with the so-called Nifty Fifty growth stocks selling all by themselves, supported by the religion of the managers, until they collapsed. The small investors without theology fared better.

There were two legal changes—strokes of the pen on a law—that were to change the theater or stadium in which the game was played. When the brokers first met under the buttonwood tree in 1794, a kind of club was formed, with the members agreeing on the fees or commissions to be charged to those outside the club who wanted to use the facilities to trade. That fee was the same for each share, whether you were buying one share or a million. If you were buying a million shares, the commissions were quite large, though it cost the broker no more for the pencil and pad to write the order. As the institutions—pension funds and mutual funds—grew in size, sometimes there actually were million-share orders, and frequently orders in the hundreds of thousands, but the cost of making the trade involved no more people than a few shares would have.

But by the early seventies, the fixed-fee system had been broken. The institutions bargained for—and got—reduced

rates on their commissions. For the brokers who had set
their costs on the old, fixed rate of commissions, the result
was loss, and many of them did not survive. Here is a
paragraph from an essay I did at the time, called "The End
of the Buffalo Days":

> Up and down the Street, various entities are waking to
> the possibility of their own extinction. It is an extra-
> ordinary time. There have been periods of consolida-
> tion in American industrial history before, of course.
> But the financial community has been built along the
> same lines, and with almost the same customs and
> mores, for the better part of 200 years. Of course, time
> is no guarantee. The livelihood, the customs and
> mores, the rhythm of life of the Sioux were centered
> around the buffalo. Standing on a hill, looking over a
> mass of hundreds of thousands of buffalo, it must have
> been out of the realm of consciousness that anything
> could ever happen to so many buffalo, and when
> something did, all the trusted actions of the shamans
> and the ghost dancers were of no avail.

Diminished commissions meant that the river of income
for research and for all those brokers calling customers
with tips dried up. Not so many friendly voices on the
telephone.

Five million small investors cashed in their chips—if
they had any left—and departed the marketplace. Most
of them left because they lost money. But many of them
also left because the brokerage firm they dealt with was out
of business, and their broker had become a short-order
cook, a ski instructor or a junior vice president in his
uncle's pants factory.

That was one result of the legal action that changed the
fees. The other legal action was more complex. It involved
pensions. American industry grew, the work force grew,
wives went to work, more than eighty million people were
at work—most covered by pension plans—and the pension
money grew until it was the biggest factor in the marketplace.
Then came a law which allowed investors—and pensioners
—to sue their managers for improper investments. Personally. The stocks go down, you ask the court for the manager's

car and his house. That certainly diminished some of the
enthusiasm for managing pension money. The trustees of
the pension fund turned the money over to the banks.
Banks have always run pension money, protected by their
corporate form. They also know that a Prudent Man is one
who does what everybody else is doing—"as would any
Prudent Man," said the 1831 decision. If the top six banks
in the country all buy the same stock, that must have been
prudent, even when the stock goes down. The result was
that the top six banks—and the top thirty banks—got more
and more money to manage.

More and more money in fewer hands. If Rodney at the
Morgan Bank wanted to get out of a stock before lunch,
the stock could be down 50 percent by the time you heard
about it, even supposing you spent all your time listening.
There is, in *The Money Game*, an institutional buying panic,
when Poor Grenville tries to spend $25 million by lunch
and fails. That still goes on—only more so. The market
motion is more violent, not really conducive to serenity,
and yet, as one wise investment counselor says, the end
object of investment ought to be serenity.

Which brings us back to what *The Money Game* is about
—image and reality and identity and anxiety and money,
in that order. "If you don't know who you are, this is an
expensive place to find out," the book says. That had to do
with people who want to lose, people who want to play out
life scripts in the marketplace, old tapes in their heads.

I was to get some remarkable reactions to *The Money
Game*. One visitor from India brought a beautifully bound
volume of *The Life Divine*, by Sri Aurobindo, an Indian
saint. He said *The Money Game* was a yoga, or had elements of yoga—not the breathing and stretching of hatha
yoga, which we see sometimes on television or at the local
Y—but an exercise called Fair Witness. Mr. Johnson says,
"The first thing you have to know is yourself. A man who
knows himself can step outside himself and watch his own
reactions like an observer." Mr. Johnson had read a lot in
Eastern literature and his daughter was a serious practitioner, so perhaps that was not as coincidental as it seemed.
(The Indian visitor, incidentally, said I had been influenced

by Sri Aurobindo. I said that while I looked forward to learning more, I was not familiar with that master. The Indian visitor smiled mysteriously and said that was all right, the influences didn't always work the way you thought.)

Then there was the visiting Zen practitioner, disciple of a famous master, who said the axioms of detachment were appropriate to his own discipline. "The stock doesn't know you own it," he said. "Prices have no memory, and yesterday has nothing to do with tomorrow. If you really know what's going on, you don't even have to know what's going on to know what's going on." Detachment from the consequences of actions were part of his mode, as was self-observation. The visitor was himself writing a book on Zen and business management. If you were centered, he said, you performed better at whatever the task. Golf pros know that too, he said.

The point of this is not to dignify *The Money Game* by analogy or to make it seem exotic. Observations about behavior, arrived at pragmatically, can extend beyond their immediate scene, and they can even find a resonance in other disciplines from other cultures.

When I reread the parts of *The Money Game* that have to do with behavior, I do not have the same itch to meddle and correct that I do when going over the nuts-and-bolts marketplace stuff. They seem all right, and I will stick by them. When you read that the gunslingers at the banks believe in concentration and turnover, you should know that so many of them tried it that that portfolio theory became disastrous, and now the mode is for non-concentration and non-turnover. Enantiodromia, the tendency of men to swing to their opposites. Any remarks about portfolio theory are an attempt to freeze some pattern into rationality, and Lord Keynes rightfully said that there is nothing so disastrous as a rational policy in an irrational world. But you are well served to know that a stock is going up as long as it is going up, or that a stock doesn't know you own it.

So, in the sense that *The Money Game* is about money, it it certainly not a how-to-do-it book. Any book that is merely about some technique for manipulating securities can be expected to fade once that technique is popular. We have had books that say, Buy assets. That worked for a time. Books that say, Convertible bonds. Fine until collapse. Books that say (even as this one does), Find rapidly growing companies. That is still a good philosophy, if you think of yourself as a partner in a growing business, but you must be sure that the price does not outrun the growth, and that the growth continues. No, oddly, the how-to-do-it, if there is such, is all about behavior. You don't have to worry about it. Enjoy the stories, they always teach more than the rules.

If the years since *The Money Game* have been financially somber, remember enantiodromia, and Ben Graham's classical axiom from Horace. When J. P. Morgan was asked what the market would do, he said, "It will fluctuate." The moment of this new preface is one of rising euphoria in the marketplace, in which the money game is once again the dictionary definition of a game—sport, frolic, fun and play. New players, new profits. Now it may indeed be that the money game is not the highest order of game. One of my correspondents, the author of a mystic book called *The Master Game*, said it was only one game, amid that of Fame and Householder and Art and Science, all subservient to the Master Game. But the Swiss psychiatric pioneer Carl Jung wrote, "One of the most difficult tasks men can perform, however much others may despise it, is the invention of good games, and it cannot be done by men out of touch with their instinctive selves." It may be that a hundred years from now, or even less, the money game played in the securities markets may be seen as a passing phase of capitalism. It may even be seen as Keynes saw it, as a game of musical chairs. Great rewards accrue to the successful, and even though, he said, there will be some without chairs when the music stops, all the players can still play with zest and enjoyment.

Adam Smith
February 1976

I

YOU

Identity
Anxiety
Money

1. WHY DID THE MASTER SAY "GAME"?

The world is not the way they tell you it is.

Unconsciously we know this because we have all been immunized by growing up in the United States. The little girl watching television asks will she really get the part in the spring play if she uses Listerine, and her good mother says no, darling, that is just the commercial. It is not long before the moppets figure out that parents have commercials of their own—commercials to keep one quiet, commercials to get one to eat, and so on. But parents—indeed all of us—are in turn being given a whole variety of commercials that do not seem to be commercials. Silver is in short supply, and the Treasury is running out and begins to fear a run. So the Treasury tells the *New York Times* that, what with one thing and another, there is enough silver for twenty years. Those who listened to the commercial sat quietly, expecting to get the part in the spring play, and the cynics went and ran all the silver out of the Treasury and the price went through the roof.

This is a book about image and reality and identity and anxiety and money. If that doesn't scare you off, nothing will. It isn't really that serious and there is a message in here from Lord Keynes to that effect. You already know about image and reality, and you probably already know all about identity and anxiety, and everybody knows about money, so all we are doing is stirring them up together. In this introduction, I have two things to tell you. One is who I am not and the other is the single sentence, the *illumine*, the apple falling on the head, that led me to the attitude expressed in the first sentence, that the world is not the way they tell you it is.

I am not, of course, Adam Smith. Mr. Smith lies in the churchyard at Canongate, his tombstone, written by himself, identifying him as the author of *The Wealth of Nations*, and he has been there since he died in 1790, rich in respect and honors, having made himself immortal as the first great free-market economist in all the texts of economic history. Mr. Smith did not think of himself as an economist but as a moral philosopher. "To what purpose," he asked in *The Theory of Moral Sentiments*, "is all the toil and bustle of this world? What is the end of avarice and ambition, of the pursuit of wealth, of power, and pre-eminence?" I like that, but it wasn't because of it that I picked the name Adam Smith as a pseudonym. That was a happy accident.

Not so long ago I was asked to write something about Wall Street in a new publication, and I had what I thought was a bright idea. There is not very much written about Wall Street that Wall Streeters themselves believe. (The Street runs on oral-aural communication anyway, like Mc-Luhan's global village.) The reason for this is that the writers about the Street are Outside, and Wall Street tells them more or less what it wants. Wall Street is well paid, and the writers aren't, and when the writers learn enough they get offered jobs in Wall Street and off they go, perhaps satisfying their creative urge by working on a black comedy on the weekends. Then they are Inside and rich and don't write about Wall Street any more. Writers who really want to write would rather ride with the President in Air Force One, or sit in the Polo Lounge of the Beverly Hills Hotel with some movie star. Such writers are heroes at the next dinner party. Wall Street writers are never heroes at dinner parties because any broker or fund manager knows as much Street gossip as they do.

There are, of course, Wall Street writers, as opposed to writers on Wall Street, and some of them are essayists as good as Addison, Steele, and writers writing anywhere. Bradbury Thurlow, for example, writes a weekly market letter which has the grace of a Mozart sonata. But these essays are musings on the scene related to particular stocks; the coda of the essay is a *therefore*, as if the essay were an argument: therefore should we now buy Telephone, Q.E.D., so have I proved.

What is really going on is very difficult to report except for an insider. (B.C. Forbes, the founder of the magazine of that name, knew this. He noted that reporters with notebooks and pencils had to wait by the kitchen of the old Waldorf, so he got himself top hat, striped pants, and circulated with the tycoons.) But for an insider, there are problems, namely, how do you keep your friends from getting irritated if you are putting the Breughel scene to paper?

My bright idea was to use a pseudonym and to change the names and numbers of my friends, the players. A fund manager will tell another fund manager the innermost state of his emotions, the condition of his marriage, and even his purchases and sales, but he will not tell a broker or a magazine or any outsider who is likely not to understand him completely. I figured if we were not too solemn, everybody at Oscar's, off Wall Street hard by Lehman Brothers, would get into the spirit of the game.

Pseudonyms are not much used in this country. Mr. George Kennan, upon leaving the State Department, did sign his famous article on containment in *Foreign Affairs* as "Mr. X." But then he went right back to being George Kennan again. In England, where on some levels literacy seems to arrive at birth, the business of pseudonyms has gone on quite a long time. In the early nineteenth century, if something in the marketplace was bugging a merchant banker, he did not hire a P.R. man but wrote his own polemic, signed it "Cato" or "Justinian" and dispatched it. If a governor of the Bank of England wanted to loose a salvo at his opponents, he could sign it "Plautus" or "Seneca" and be as acid as he wanted. He knew he would get rapt attention, because his expertise was so obvious. Some of this still survives in England, but often it is just so that "Justinian" can be several people. (I am not saying he is, and for all you know, six of us are Adam Smith.)

So I had "Procrustes" all picked out. Procrustes, as you remember, was a highwayman of Attica who placed his victims on a bed of iron. If they were too short, he stretched them, and if they were too long, he chopped off their feet. It seemed appropriate for Wall Street.

The new publication did not come to pass, and the editor of *New York* magazine, in the Sunday *World Journal*, scooped up my sample and ran it. (The *World Journal* was a newspaper in New York which has since joined its ancestors.) "I had to change your name," said this editor on the phone. "They wouldn't believe here that anyone was named Procrustes; just plain Procrustes sounds too much like a pseudonym, and we don't use pseudonyms. So I put down the first name I could remember that would fit. I think it was Adam Smith."

So then there was Adam Smith, my Sunday recreation, and it all became too much fun to stop.

First of all, when the situations I described were successful, Wall Street filled in all the details of my sketches. Take Poor Grenville, a fund manager I described who bet the wrong way. He had just gotten himself a nice $25 million cushion of cash in his fund when the market turned around and ran away without him. Everybody knew Poor Grenville, only—it was pointed out to me—Poor Grenville wasn't caught with $25 million but with $19 million or with $33 million and his hair wasn't blond, it was red or it was brown. Otherwise it was Poor Grenville all right. I have since met six Poor Grenvilles and there are more coming into town all the time.

Then there were the Lamont Cranston aspects of it all. (If you don't remember Lamont Cranston, the Shadow, and the secrets he learned in the Orient which enabled him to pass invisibly among men, we must not be in the same generation.) I was at a cocktail party once and I joined a respectful circle listening to a *New York Times* reporter I had never met. The reporter said he knew Adam Smith well and had for years, and he told us all about him. I listened raptly. In another instance, my seat-mate on a cross-country jet introduced himself, and we got to talking, and he told me about Adam Smith. When I seemed to be impressed, he said he *knew* Adam Smith but he couldn't tell me who he was, because Smith had sworn him to secrecy.

It's great. It's like being the Fugitive with nobody chasing you.

You will notice all through this treatise a leitmotif of observations by John Maynard Keynes. This use of Keynes has very little to do with Keynes the economist; it has rather to do with Keynes the writer and speculator. Keynes the economist is simply *there*, like Darwin and Freud and

Adam Smith of Kircaldy, County Fife, a part of history. I bring this up because Keynes the economist still elicits an emotional reaction from many readers. Having, in publications, quoted Keynes a few times, I began to receive mail from gentlemen whose phrasing is generally found in more right-wing publications, the gentlemen implying that if I had any truck with Keynes, I was a dupe of the internationalist bankers and the British, and that I was probably rejoicing in the disintegration of the dollar and the, therefore, inevitable disintegration of American moral character. I wrote a long paper on Keynes in graduate school which I found recently while cleaning out a file. It is amazing how stupid one can be in graduate school, because while I was puzzling through $L_1 (Y) = \dfrac{Y}{V} = M_1$, the income velocity of money, I missed all the fun.

Here is an economist with a sparkling style, something rare enough in itself. But more than that, here is a man with a great sense of life and of living. Keynes was a great speculator, and made a fortune not only for himself but for his college, Kings College, Cambridge, and he did it in half an hour a morning from his bed. I believe that Keynes' participation in markets as an investor led him to some of the observations in the "Long-Term Expectation" parts of his General Theory. They are throw-away *aperçus*, secondary to the main points, but they are the sharpest things around. I wish he had written more. No one has ever been more perceptive on markets than Keynes, and I don't think he would have had this "feel" without himself being a participant; academic economists just haven't.

We are taught—at least those of us who grew up without a great deal of it—that money is A Very Serious Business, that the stewardship of capital is holy, and that the handler of money must conduct himself as a Prudent Man. It is all part of the Protestant ethic and the spirit of Capitalism and I suppose it all helped to make this country what it is. Penny saved, penny earned, waste not, want not, Summer Sale Save 10 Percent, and so on. Then I came across this sentence in "Long-Term Expectation" of Keynes' General Theory:

The game of professional investment is intolerably boring and overexacting to anyone who is entirely exempt from the gambling instinct; whilst he who has it must pay to this propensity the appropriate toll.

Game? Game? Why did the Master say Game? He could have said business or profession or occupation or what have you. What is a Game? It is "sport, play, frolic, or fun"; "a scheme or art employed in the pursuit of an object or purpose"; "a contest, conducted according to set rules, for amusement or recreation or winning a stake." Does that sound like Owning a Share of American Industry? Participating in the Long-Term Growth of the American Economy? No, but it sounds like the stock market.

Let us go one step beyond. Drs. John von Neumann and Oskar Morgenstern developed, some years ago, a *Theory of Games and Economic Behavior*. This game theory has had a tremendous impact on our national life; it influences how our defense decisions are made and how the marketing strategies of great corporations are worked out. What is game theory? You could say it is an attempt to quantify and work through the actions of players in a game, to measure their options continuously. Or, to be more formal, game theory is a branch of mathematics that aims to analyze problems of conflict by abstracting common strategic features for study in theoretical models. (You can tell by the phrasing of that last sentence that I have the book before me, so let me go on.) By stressing strategic aspects, i.e., those controlled by the participants, it goes beyond the classic theory of probability, in which the treatment of games is limited to aspects of pure chance. Drs. von Neumann and Morgenstern worked through systems that incorporated conflicting interests, incomplete information, and the interplay of free rational decision and choice. They started with dual games, zero sum two-person games, i.e., those in which one player wins what the other loses. At the other end you have something like the stock market, an infinite, *n*-person game. (*N* is one of the letters economists use when they don't know something.) The stock market is probably temporarily too complex even for the Game Theoreticians, but I suppose some day even it will become a serious candidate for quantification and equations.

I bring this up only because I think the market is both a game and a Game, i.e., both sport, frolic, fun, and play, and a subject for continuously measurable options. If it is a game, then we can relieve ourselves of some of the heavy and possibly crippling emotions that individuals carry into investing, because in a game the winning of the stake is clearly defined. Anything else becomes irrelevant. Is this so startling? "Eighty percent of investors are not really out to make money," says one leading Wall Streeter. Investors not out to make money? It seems almost like a contradiction in terms. What are they doing then? That can be a subject for a whole discussion, and will be, a bit later.

Let us go back to the *illumine,* that the investment game is intolerably boring save to those with a gambling instinct, while those with the instinct must pay to it "the appropriate toll." This really does say it all. We have more than twenty-six million direct investors in this country, i.e., people who have actually bought stocks. (I say direct investors because indirectly, through insurance companies and pension plans, we have more than a hundred million investors, which is just about everybody except children and the truly poor.) Not all of the twenty-four million are fiercely active, but the number grows all the time, making the stock market a great national pastime. Active investors do not pursue bonds (except convertibles) and preferreds (except convertibles). It isn't that one can't make money with these instruments, it's that they lack romance enough to be part of the game; they are boring. It is very hard to get excited over a bond basis book, where your index finger traces along a column until it gets to the proper degree of safety and yield.

Sometimes illusions are more comfortable than reality, but there is no reason to be discomfited by facing the gambling instinct that saves the stock market from being a bore. Once it is acknowledged, rather than buried, we can "pay to this propensity the appropriate toll" and proceed with reality.

I mean here no more than recognizing an instinct. Dr. Thomas Schelling, a Harvard economist and the author of a number of works on military strategy, goes a lot further. Writing on "Economics and Criminal Enterprise," Dr. Schelling says:

> The greatest gambling enterprise in the United States has not been significantly touched by organized crime. That is the stock market. . . . The reason is that the market works too well. Federal control over the stock market, designed mainly to keep it honest and informative . . . makes it a hard market to tamper with.

Sentences like the first one in that excerpt must make the public-relations people at the New York Stock Exchange wake up screaming. For years the New York Stock Exchange and the securities industry have campaigned to correct the idea that buying stocks was gambling, and while there may be some dark corners of this country that persist in a Populist suspicion of Wall Street, by and large they have succeeded. Dr. Schelling's phrasing has to be counted as unfortunate, and in no sense is the stock market a great gambling enterprise like a lottery. But it is an exercise in mass psychology, in trying to guess better than the crowd how the crowd will behave. Sometimes the literature which was produced in order to dispel the pre-1929 suspicions can get in the way of seeing things the way they are.

All this is simply leading up to a pragmatic observation. It has been my fate to know a number of people in and around markets: investment bankers, economists, portfolio managers of great institutions. I have been through the drill of security analysis—that set me back quite a bit—and in a minor way through portfolio management. (I haven't ever been a broker or sold securities; that is another talent.) During lunch at my own house I have seen "random walk" theoreticians grow apoplectic over their dessert at the thought that there were people who called themselves "technicians" and believed that prices forecast the future, and I have known technicians, backed by computers, who got themselves so wound up into their own systems they forgot what they started with.

It has taken me years to unlearn everything I was taught, and I probably haven't succeeded yet. I cite this only because most of what has been written about the mark t tells you the way it ought to be, and the successful investors I know do not hold to the way it ought to be, they simply go with what is. If thinking of this fascinating, complex, infinite, *n*-person process as a Game helps, then perhaps that is the way we should think; it helps rid us of the compulsions of theology.

If you are a player in the Game, or are thinking of becoming one, there is one irony of which you should be aware. The object of the game is to make money, hopefully a lot of it. All the players in the Game are getting rapidly more professional; the amount of sheer information poured out on what is going on has become almost too much to absorb. The true professionals in the Game—the professional portfolio managers—grow more skilled all the time. They are human and they make mistakes, but if you have your money managed by a truly alert mutual fund or even by one of the better banks, you will have a better job done for you than probably at any time in the past.

But if you have your money managed for you, then you are not really interested, or at least the Game element—with that propensity to be paid for—does not attract you. I have known a lot of investors who came to the market to make money, and they told themselves that what they wanted was the money: security, a trip around the world, a new sloop, a country estate, an art collection, a Caribbean house for cold winters. And they succeeded. So they sat on the dock of the Caribbean home, chatting with their art dealers and gazing fondly at the new sloop, and after a while it was a bit flat. Something was missing. If you are a successful Game player, it can be a fascinating, consuming, totally absorbing experience, in fact it has to be. If it is not totally absorbing, you are not likely to be among the most successful, because you are competing with those who do find it so absorbing.

The lads with the Caribbean houses and the new sloops did not, upon the discovery that something was missing, sell those trophies and acquire sackcloth and ashes. The sloops and the houses and the art are all still there, but the players have gone back to the Game, and they don't have a great deal of time for their toys. The Game is more fun. It probably does not make you a better person, and I am not sure it does any good for humanity; the best you can say is what Samuel Johnson said, that no man is so harmlessly occupied as when he is making money.

The irony is that this is a money game and money is the way we keep score. But the real object of the Game is not money, it is the playing of the Game itself. For the true players, you could take all the trophies away and substitute plastic beads or whale's teeth; as long as there is a way to keep score, they will play.

2. MISTER JOHNSON'S READING LIST

"... the dominant note of our time is unreality."

Since wealth awaits those who can play this game well, it is not surprising that there is a large body of serious literature devoted to telling you how. There is first the whole literature of economics, business, and business cycles. If you want to sound learned on these subjects, there are shelves full of high-priced paperbacks, some of them excellent. Then there are money-rate books, i.e., those that attempt to chart the course of the market by attention to interest rates and hence to what has always been the classic teeter-totter between stocks and bonds. All of this involves paying close attention to what the Federal Reserve is up to and adjusting your course appropriately. Burton Crane's *The Sophisticated Investor* is one readable account. Finally there are books of security analysis, led by Graham and Dodd's *Security Analysis*. (Any true student of Graham and Dodd can spot an undervalued utility with one whisk of a slide rule.)

However, one thing should be apparent to you. The field of *rational* study is becoming very well worked. When the New York Society of Security Analysts was founded in 1937, it had twenty members. Today it—together with all the associated chapters of the Financial Analysts Federation—has more than sixteen thousand members. This does not mean automatically that there are sixteen thousand millionaires right there.

For a generation, Wall Street was relatively unpopular; that generation's working years run from 1929 to 1946. In 1937, the year the first lonely band of security analysts huddled together, only three members of the graduating class of the Harvard Business School braved the wrath of their families and friends to enter the Street of iniquity. The very next year, Richard Whitney, ex-president of the

21

New York Stock Exchange, paused to be photographed on the steps of Sing Sing, his new home. It was not a good time for the money business.

Now we have had twenty years of rising markets and Wall Street respectability, and not only are the security analysts pouring forth their handiwork but the universities are flush with graduate students and grants, and the graduate students get time on the local IBM 360 to relate every number and price and trend they can think of to every other number they can think of, and a few nanoseconds from the 360 gives everybody a few months' more work after that.

So let us heed, for a moment, Mr. Gerald Loeb, long-standing champion tape-reader and author of *The Battle for Investment Survival:*

> There is no such thing as a final answer to security values. A dozen experts will arrive at 12 different conclusions. It often happens that a few moments later each would alter his verdict if given a chance to reconsider because of a changed condition. Market values are fixed only in part by balance sheets and income statements; much more by the hopes and fears of humanity; by greed, ambition, acts of God, invention, financial stress and strain, weather, discovery, fashion and numberless other causes impossible to be listed without omission.

Hopes, fears, greed, ambition, acts of God—it would be hard to put it more succinctly. It is very hard to program these into anything as unforgiving as an IBM 360. There is a school that says all these things are in the numbers already, but actually the study of numbers is rational, a search for some shining inner Truth called Value. Value is there, like Bishop Berkeley's tree that made a noise when it fell in the forest whether or not anybody heard it fall, only, as Mr. Loeb says, value is only one part of the game.

The one thing we have, whether or not we ever find true Value, is liquidity—the ability to buy and sell momentarily and relatively effortlessly. Liquidity is the cornerstone of Wall Street. It is what makes it the financial capital of the world, for it is, except for rare, odd moments of panic, a truly liquid market. It is liquid and it is run honestly, and there are so few places like that in the world that if you are a rich foreigner who wants to be able to cash in on any given day and yet wants to make capital gains, you have virtually only one place to go. London is liquid and honest, too, but those are British securities and the choice is much more limited, and restricted by the current horizons of Britain itself.

I am not putting down the study of economics, business cycles, and even security analysis. But knowing them does not guarantee success, and if you haven't a clue about them, there may be hope for you yet. Before we go on, let us hear from one of the deans of money management. Mister Johnson runs a group of funds called Fidelity, and Fidelity has been the Green Bay Packers of the fund league for some time now. The Packers do not win every year by any means, but they are the team to beat. A number of fund managers I know describe their jobs very simply, all in nearly the same way. "My job," they say, "is to beat Fidelity." General Montgomery used to keep Rommel's picture in his tent, so they said. I don't think any of the professional money managers have tacked up Mister Johnson's picture. What they do is tack up his portfolio and look for the sections they can beat.

When I came back to New York from lunching in Boston with Mister Johnson, it was so late in the afternoon that I went straight to Oscar's, a well-frequented restaurant and bar off Wall Street. I wanted to find out what had happened that day. There is one table at Oscar's where you can learn why a lot of money changed hands that afternoon, why the stocks that are moving are moving. It is a table populated by some martini-oriented performance fund managers and their friends, not your average customer's men, but the guys running hundreds of millions of dollars with a lot of pressure on them to be right. Show performance, as they say. I knew this was sophisticated money because there was no confusion when I said I had had lunch at the Union Club with *Mister Johnson,* no cracks about beagles, Texas, and the most recent White House alumnus. The boys wanted to know what *Mister Johnson* thinks now, and suddenly there was a certain amount of respect floating in the air which usually does not hang over the cynical tables. The net effect was like coming to a rehearsal if you are an actor and telling the cast that you have just been playing tennis with Mister Abbott at the River Club and Mister Abbott saw the run-through yesterday and had a few thoughts. Guaranteed to bring hushed attention.

Come to think of it, nobody in the theater calls Mister Abbott "George," and I never heard anybody call Mister Johnson "Edward." But Mister Johnson is not in the public eye; he does not have his name on a fund like Jack Dreyfus, and even the average Wall Streeter draws a blank. My friend Charley with a go-go fund of his own has to be reassured that there *is* a Mister Johnson. The name "Mister Johnson" brings up an image to him as remote and distant as Kilimanjaro behind the clouds, as the guru in Tibet who gave the guy in *The Razor's Edge* the Secret.

Other people have companies that control a lot of money, so it is not just the $4.5 billion that Mister Johnson's funds swing. Part of the reason is that one of Mister Johnson's funds, Fidelity Trend, managed to justify its label as a "performance" fund, coming in with the top track record of all major funds in the first half of this decade. And then two of Mister Johnson's funds, Fidelity Capital and Fidelity Trend, managed to hold up well against the bear markets. Since then they have not done so well, but the fidelity image continues undimmed.

Another part of the aura is that Mister Johnson's boys are out in the world garnering a lot of attention. Some people think Mister Johnson must have run an academy for money managers. Two years ago Gerry Tsai was in all the papers because he started a new fund and the people sent in $274 million, the all-time record. "I wanted to have a little fund of my own," Gerry said, when he left Mister Johnson's Fidelity Capital. Now he has $450 million, but he still says *Mister Johnson* in the same tone the other Old Boys do. Then Roland Grimm left to start a little outfit of *his* own. Roland's first client was Yale, which handed him its $500 million endowment. Pretty soon you begin to picture the Fidelity Group as a bunch of medieval buildings with the fellows all toasting their buttered scones in front of the crackling fire while the wind whistles outside, glad that

Mr. Chips made them learn Greek so well because now they can really appreciate the nuances of the Euripides he is reading to them.

What hooks me about Mister Johnson is that he does not talk about the stock market in terms of GNP and tax cuts and automobile production. He talks about whether reality and time are coexistent at the moment, about whether there is anything in Alan Watts' *The Wisdom of Insecurity* that is relevant, whether the hemlines of women's skirts really mean anything, and he is deadly serious; he had his analysts check out whether hemlines were a true indicator.

"The market," says Mister Johnson, "is like a beautiful woman—endlessly fascinating, endlessly complex, always changing, always mystifying. I have been absorbed and immersed since 1924 and I know this is no science. It is an art. Now we have computers and all sorts of statistics, but the market is still the same and understanding the market is still no easier. It is personal intuition, sensing patterns of behavior. There is always something unknown, undiscerned."

To me this is Mister Johnson's appeal: he talks as though he were on a quest for truth, and this is dignity in an industry that Norman O. Brown, if he carried the Freudian analysis of money in *Life Against Death* a bit further, would have to describe as shifting piles of, well, dirt from one place to another. Some of this is the way Walter Gutman used to write in his market letter, and up and down Wall Street there are other people hypnotized by The Witch of markets, some of them well psychoanalyzed. The difference is that Mister Johnson has read all the books. Mister Johnson is going to be seventy-one, and Mister Johnson has $4.5 billion. Maybe Mister Johnson has a reading on The Witch. *Maybe Mister Johnson knows.*

Boston has not been run by the Mister Johnsons since before George Apley, but you can almost forget how the Irish and Italians took it over if you walk only around Devonshire and Congress and the Old State House where there are plaques on every corner saying Paul Revere hitched his horse here, John Hancock dropped his pen here. Mister Johnson walks to the Union Club by the same route his father took. His father was in the dry goods business and actually had to walk a bit further, but the route was the same. In the elevator at the Union Club there are some young fellows and some not so young fellows and they all say "Good day, Mister Johnson." I don't think it could happen in New York, walking the same route to the same club where your father lunched. In New York they would have torn down the club and replaced it with a giant glass slab, and then put the club back on the forty-sixth floor, and the club would have P.R. men maneuvering to make sure the maître d' remembered their names.

Mister Johnson smiles when he talks about the market, a warm smile, and says "Gee." A little like the Prof in the movies where they used to come just before the big number and say, "But, Prof, if you don't pass good old Tank he can't play against State on Saturday." That is, Mister Johnson has the perky polka-dot bow tie and the horn-rimmed glasses and the red suspenders and the iron-gray short haircut, like Prof, and three pens in the shirt pocket. Slight, and full of animation.

Mister Johnson went to The College, which is how they refer to Harvard, and The Law School, and when he left Cambridge he went to work for Ropes Gray, the biggest Boston law firm, and got intrigued by The Witch on the side. He didn't get into the fund business except as a lawyer until 1943. "The fellow who was running Fidelity couldn't support his family on it, so I took it over," says Mister Johnson.

"It had three million dollars. Gee, it's nice to see something grow geometrically. The last ten years have been the best, because I could interest myself in the managers. You can't just graduate an analyst into managing funds. What is it the good managers have? It's a kind of locked-in concentration, an intuition, a feel, nothing that can be schooled. The first thing you have to know is yourself. A man who knows himself can step outside himself and watch his own reactions like an observer. Gee, I don't think I did a thing to develop good managers. It's just that I was oriented to a big law firm and in a law firm every associate handles his own clients. So I let the managers develop and handle their own funds. Each one had his own responsibilities. He could walk down the hall for a chat if he wanted to consult, but the show was his own. Positive decisions have to be made by an individual; groups can't do it. And I think a lot of the investment business was committee-oriented. Then you know a man is really at his best, his most fulfilled, when he's on the way to becoming what he's going to become. After he's become it, he loses an infinitesimal bit of sharpness, like a star after his best role, and we've been lucky enough to hit a couple of fellows like that. With the good men, you can see the learning juices churning around every mistake. You learn from mistakes. When I look back, my life seems to be an endless chain of mistakes."

I told Mister Johnson what interested me was his concern with the mass-psychology aspects of the market.

"As a lawyer," Mister Johnson said, "I had no time to check individual companies; it was a matter of trying to sense behavior patterns. The market is a crowd, and if you've read Gustave Le Bon's *The Crowd* you know a crowd is a composite personality. In fact, *a crowd of men acts like a single woman.* The mind of a crowd is like a woman's mind. Then if you have observed her a long time, you begin to see little tricks, little nervous movements of the hands when she is being false.

"You know, I've talked to a lot of psychiatrists. I wanted them to do some work for us because the market is a composite personality, sometimes manic, sometimes despairing, sometimes overcome in lassitude. But the problem with the psychiatrists was they worked on *a priori* reasoning, and it won't work. Good market work, I think, like successful psychiatry, has to work on emotional rapport. You can have no preconceived ideas. There are fundamentals in the marketplace, but the unexplored area is the emotional area. All the charts and breadth indicators and technical palaver are the statistician's attempts to describe an emotional state.

"I once thought maybe these fellas that have worked on the Eastern sense of consciousness—you know, Alan Watts' studies of Zen—I thought maybe there would be some answers there."

Maybe Mister Johnson knows. The Zen Buddhist approach to the market!

"Oh, gee, no. There are individual perceptions. If you

remember *The Wisdom of Insecurity*, you know we need obstacles. We need toughness for the extra reach. Something is going to be lost in this national obsession for security when you have full employment, even overemployment. But Zen, I am just a reader, not a student, and *the market is too complex for Zen.*

"I think the dominant note of our time is unreality. The thin air of the music we all heard has died away. It lasted a long time, certainly several decades, but the best rule is: *When the music stops, forget the old music.* Why unreality? Times of crusading spirit are times of unreality. In much of history the crusading spirit is a subject of lampoon, *Don Quixote*, but now we have mass emotion moving, trying to change the folkways of the world. The Vietnam war and the civil rights movement are both examples. I am not making judgments on these things. I am just saying that the attitude of mind in approaching these problems is a crusading attitude, and crusades do not have the elements of durability. In good times it's not hard to make money, but in times of unreality the market is saying, 'You don't understand me any more; don't trust me until you understand me.'"

By the time the coffee came, Mister Johnson and I were talking about Sherlock Holmes and the stock market, and Sigmund Freud and the stock market, and *The Ordeal of Change* and Marcus Aurelius.

At Oscar's there was silence and furrowed brows. "Marcus Aurelius," says my friend the gunslinger from the hedge fund. "I bet he says Marcus Aurelius to some of his slow-witted dealers from the hinterlands and they fall down."

"It was one of Mister Johnson's funds had the Stukas out over Fairchild that day, got even the SEC mad," says another wise man. "Where are the Stukas going next?"

Charley's lips were moving over the edge of his glass. "The Vietnam war is a crusade and LBJ is Louis the Ninth," he murmured. "A crowd of men is like a single woman. The thin air of music has died away."

Now Charley's voice grew louder. "This guy has lunch with *Mister Johnson!* And he comes back with *questions.* Questions! What is the sound of one hand clapping? What

are the answers? What is Mister Johnson doing? I can't
stand it! Don't tell me about Jung and the bear market!
*What three stocks does Mister Johnson like best? What's
going to happen next?"*

"Δουὸς πεσούσης, πᾶς ἀνὴρ ξυλεύεται,
φταν δὲ δαίμων ἀνδρὶ πορσύνη κακά, τὸν νοῦν ἔβλαψε
πρῶτον," I told him.

Mister Johnson has a great gift of phrase, and now you
begin to get the idea: ". . . this is no science. It is an art.
Now we have computers and all sorts of statistics, but the
market is still the same and understanding the market is
still no easier. It is personal intuition, sensing patterns of
behavior. . . ."

Personal intuition does not mean that you can translate
last night's exotic dream into some brilliant choice in the
market. Professional money managers often seem to make
up their minds in a split second, but what pushes them
over the line of decision is usually an incremental bit of
information which, added to all the slumbering pieces of
information filed in their minds, suddenly makes the picture whole.

"What is it the good managers have? It's a kind of
locked-in concentration, an intuition, a feel, nothing that
can be schooled. The first thing you have to know is yourself."

It sounds simplistic to say the first thing you have to
know is yourself, and of course you are not necessarily out
to become a professional money manager. But if you stop
to think about it, here is one authority saying there are
no formulas which can be automatically applied. If you
are not automatically applying a mechanical formula, then
you are operating in this area of intuition, and if you are
going to operate with intuition—or judgment—then it follows that the first thing you have to know is yourself. You
are—face it—a bunch of emotions, prejudices, and
twitches, and this is all very well as long as you know it.
Successful speculators do not necessarily have a complete
portrait of themselves, warts and all, in their own minds,
but they do have the ability to stop abruptly when their
own intuition and what is happening Out There are sud-

denly out of kilter. A couple of mistakes crop up, and they say, simply, "This is not my kind of market," or "I don't know what the hell's going on, do you?" and return to established lines of defense. A series of market decisions does add up, believe it or not, to a kind of personality portrait. It is, in one small way, a method of finding out who you are, but it can be very expensive. That is one of the cryptograms which are my own, and this is the first Irregular Rule: *If you don't know who you are, this is an expensive place to find out.*

It may seem a little silly to think that a portfolio of stocks can give you a portrait of the man who picked them, but any tuned-in stock-picker will swear to it. I know a private fund where there are four managers, each with one section—$30 million or so—to run. Every three months they switch chairs. "In three months," says my friend, "Carl's portfolio will have little Carlisms creeping in. Maybe Carl is skirting the high fliers too much—he never has liked them. Maybe there are a couple of real Carl-y ones in there that he gives too long to ripen. So when I move into his chair, I have no trouble dialing out the stuff that is too Carl-y. Meanwhile Teddy is doing the same thing in my chair. It hurts me when I look over and see what he is doing, but that's the way it works best."

Back to Mister Johnson:

"You can have no preconceived ideas. There are fundamentals in the marketplace, but the unexplored area is the emotional area. All the charts and breadth indicators and technical palaver are the statistician's attempts to describe an emotional state."

After my first lunch with Mister Johnson, I felt the way Robert Ardrey did when Professor Raymond Dart showed him the jawbone of the *Australopithecus Africanus*. What got Robert Ardrey so excited was that this ancient ape had evidently been bopped in the jaw, and that set him rounding up the story that man's ancestors were real-estate-loving killers, a theme that in *African Genesis* and *The Territorial Imperative* caused convulsions in the world of speculative anthropology. It was just as if Mister Johnson and I had been walking through the African veld, there, and I had said, "What are these, Mister Johnson?" and Mister Johnson had said, "Sir, they are the footprints of a gigantic Hound!" The emotional prowlings of the market-place have left their tracks, all right, but unfortunately no one has found the key jawbone that unlocks the puzzle.

Even without a jawbone, I tried. If the emotional area is the unexplored area, and the statistical area is being so thoroughly explored, why not explore the unexplored area? Unhappily, such a study seems to require a cross of disci-plines. I set out after market people who had occasionally used a term such as "mass masochism" in a sentence such as "Everyone knows that odd-lot purchases demonstrate mass masochism on the part of the public." But when I talked to them, all that appeared were the usual generaliza-tions about markets, buttered lightly with a few cocktail party psychiatrisms. Then I began to correspond with a few psychologists and social scientists. Here, in an area where, if there is any Truth to be found, there is certainly a commercial application, only a handful of people were even interested. Twenty thousand psychologists were writ-ing papers on what made call girls take up their trade, and all the social scientists were busy flying to Vietnam on Government contracts and writing up what Vietnamese so-ciety ought to be, since we have to build it from scratch.

I did meet two brokers who had formerly been psychol-ogists, and three university professors working in psy-chology or social sciences who had formerly been brokers. All five seemed unwilling to remember their previous ex-istences, at least not to the point of articulating anything. Finally I did meet a couple of helpful psychiatrists. They weren't really interested in mass psychology, but they wanted to know should they buy a little more Com Sat and would I sell Xerox here, and so I traded them gossip for time and the access to a few patients whom we will come to a bit later.

I do have to tell you about one psychiatrist I met while searching for my own *Australopithecus* jawbone. This good doctor was introduced to me as the one man who really knew both the stock market and the human mind. He was an investor himself and interested in the market. He had made a lot of money in the market. He had a lot of patients who were investors.

The good doctor didn't want to tell me too much, he said, because he was planning to write a book himself and he didn't want to give away any of his ideas. He was, he admitted, absolutely spectacular as an investor.

"Why are you holding your hands like that?" he asked suddenly. "Were you ever afraid of fire as a child?"

It's amazing how big your hands can suddenly feel. I said I didn't think I'd been afraid of fire as a child, but even now, I'm not quite sure.

"You're supposed to know so much about the market," said this learned psychiatrist. "I have put all my money into one stock. That's the only real way to make any money. The stock has already come from ten to thirty, but it's going to two hundred. You still have time to load up."

I wanted to know why the stock was going to 200.

"Take my word for it," he said. "I know the market and I know mass psychology. This is it. I understand what makes a stock go."

An eager student, I said I would like to know this secret, but the learned psychiatrist wasn't telling. "How can I tell you?" he said. "I have had years of training, medical and psychiatric. I have written books. I have spent thirty years in the labyrinth of the human mind. And in a few sentences, you want me to tell you what I know? Why are you so arrogant?"

This story has a happy ending. I went and looked up the stock the learned psychiatrist had picked as the summation of all of his years of study, but I couldn't get with it. The earnings were growing beautifully, but they seemed stuck together somehow. I just didn't understand the company. The stock went on, and when it was 50, the learned psychiatrist wanted to know whether it was hostility that had prevented me from buying it.

The name of this stock was Westec. It went from 5 to 60, and at about that level, trading in it was suspended. There were, apparently, irregularities and misstatements so great that the stock has never been permitted on any exchange again. There are dozens of suits and countersuits, and it will take the courts and the receivers years to straighten out the mess. Creditors put the company into bankruptcy, and if, when they are satisfied, there is anything left for the stockholders, it will not likely be much. But worst, for the unlucky stockholders, was that there was no way, once the bombshell burst, to sell the stock. It is almost impossible to lose *all* your money in the stock market, because—remember liquidity—you can always sell, any hour, any day. The learned psychiatrist had picked, out of all the thousands of stocks, the one that permitted him to lose every penny.

The happy ending is that we may all learn something, because he is still writing his book. It will be out next year, and I can hardly wait, since he saved his insight for publication.

I have one footnote on psychiatrists and the market. This footnote is a popularly told story, and I haven't checked it, for fear the symmetry of the story might be spoiled by a fact somewhere. Jack Dreyfus, founder of the Dreyfus Fund, also thought of the value of studying unconscious motives in the marketplace. Dreyfus built a fund with an outstanding record, bringing the sensibilities of a superb bridge player—which he is—to the market. For many years, Dreyfus had had an emotional rapport with a particular psychiatrist, and finally he decided that the psychiatrist should have an office at the Dreyfus Fund, just to see whether the managers were functioning at peak efficiency.

A portfolio manager of my acquaintance was called in one day. All prepared, he loosened his tie, took off his jacket, and lay down on the couch. The psychiatrist sat in his psychiatrist's chair, and the portfolio manager waited for the probing question.

"Polaroid," said the psychiatrist.

"Polaroid," repeated the portfolio manager.

"It's awfully high here, don't you think?" suggested the psychiatrist.

The portfolio manager mulled over the possible unconscious implications of this.

"I have a lot of Polaroid, personally," said the psychiatrist. "It's come up awfully fast. Should I hold it?"

The portfolio manager sat up. "It's going to be all right," he said, in soothing tones. "It's going to work out just fine."

The psychiatrist slid into a more relaxed position. "I worry about Polaroid," he confessed.

"Let's examine this," said the portfolio manager, "and see why you're so worried. I think I can be of some help. . . ."

There is work to be done here, as you can see, but so far none of the appropriate people have taken mass psychology and the marketplace as an area for study. Part of the reason, in scholarly circles, is that the pursuit of Truth in such a direction has an application too commercial and not relevant enough to the main problems of society. Perhaps that is true. But while the mass aspects of the animal are unexplored, the first hypotheses about successful individuals have been postulated.

3. CAN INK BLOTS TELL YOU WHETHER YOU ARE THE TYPE WHO WILL MAKE A LOT OF MONEY IN THE MARKET?

The social scientists may be too busy reconstructing Vietnamese society along their own lines to pursue the elusive *Australopithecus* of a market animal, but one psychologist of my acquaintance has at least begun to ask some questions and to make the first hypotheses. The hypotheses are not on mass psychology but on individual psychology, so we will have to come back to the crowd in the next chapter. Some of my Boston fund-managing friends put me onto Dr. Charles McArthur at Harvard, since their funds were using him as a consultant to scout out prospective security analysts. Usually Dr. McArthur sits in the splendid Jose Maria Sert building testing Harvard students, and then a couple of the Bostonians figured that if you could spot a dropout with multiple choices and ink blots, maybe the same thing would work for money men. One thing led to another, and now Dr. McArthur spends part of his time firing ink blots at guys who think they can manage a hundred million dollars.

That is how I found myself slicing into the horse steak at lunches at the Harvard Faculty Club. If the President ever appoints you liaison to the intelligentsia or if you find yourself at the Harvard Faculty Club for any other reason, you will be well advised to order the horse steak. That shows you are one of us. The horse steak has been on the menu since the World War II meat shortages, and the Harvard cognoscenti, always alert for new taste thrills, found it gamier and more interesting than plain old cow steak, especially when washed down with an amusing little Australian Pinot Chardonnay. So it stays on the menu, a permanent fixture. Horse steak is the symbol of the open, questing mind, which is how Harvard likes to think of itself.

35

Anyway, Dr. McArthur is slicing his way through his own horse steak, modestly pointing out that his samples are too small to be sure. That means if he published this as a scholarly paper with a colon in the middle of the title, the academic psychologists and social scientists might jump all over him. They would probably jump all over him anyway for the very idea of searching for anything so sordid as the type of personality that makes money. Money is anathema in the groves of Academe unless it comes from foundations or the Government, especially the Government.

One thing Dr. McArthur's probings outline is that there is a personality difference between the people who are good at finding stocks and the people who call the shots on the timing and manage the whole portfolio. Security analysts dog down information and come up with an idea about what should be bought or sold, but they do not necessarily make good conductors for the whole orchestra. If they are woodwind players to start, they tend to hear the whole orchestra as woodwinds, and it takes another type to keep the woodwinds and brasses and strings in line.

How is a good security analyst spotted? The first thing the testers give you—and the potential conductor too—is a Strong test, named after the Stanford psychologist who devised it. Somewhere along the line you have already taken a vocational preference test, so this one will be familiar to you. It is designed to tell you what you like, just in case you have been conning yourself. The questions are multiple choice, like this:

> Tomorrow is a holiday, and you can do anything you want. Would you rather
> a) fly an airplane
> b) read a book
> c) catch up on some sleep
> d) go down to your neighborhood tavern and mix it up with the boys
> e) work in your garden cutting flowers

That's the kind of thing. When the test gets going, you can really get involved.

An expedition is announced to explore the danger-ous upper reaches of the Amazon, where piranha fish rule in the water and vicious headhunters on land. Would you rather

   a) lead the expedition
   b) raise the money for this scientific endeavor
   c) go along and write up the story when you get back
   d) just as soon not go

You see yourself leading an expedition up the Amazon? That may seem pretty glamorous, but maybe you have dangerous fantasies and almost certainly you are going to get an itchy bottom sitting at a desk reading stock market reports. If you pick *c*, we might let you write our weekly stock market letter, but you had better be able to do some other things, too.

   You are coming home from a party, and you are having a fight with your wife. The fight is about

      a) what time you finally got her to leave
      b) how much she (you) had to drink
      c) what she was (you were) doing with that fel-low (lady) on the couch
      d) money
      e) the children

   In this fight, it is more efficient to

      a) say nothing and let her talk herself out
      b) make sure she understands your point of view, for her own good
      c) establish who runs things, quickly and firmly
      d) keep peace any way you can

If you wanted to leave before your wife did, if she had more to drink than is good for her, if the fight was about money and the children, you are right along with 81.1 per-cent of all our testees, and welcome to our organization. You do know better than your wife and you want to be sure she understands that and we like that attitude here.

Preference tests have been given for years and by now they have revealed patterns—on punched cards, at that—

which group various occupations together. Analysts end up in Groups V and IX on the Strong test. Group V is social services, telling people what to do for their own good. Group IX is sales, extroverted, common sensical, and "people-centered atheoretical." It won't do you any good to dig up the good idea if you can't put it across.

The portfolio manager is another animal, currently in the process of escaping from Group VIII, office detail. Portfolio managers used to have the same sort of profile as a CPA, because portfolio managers were usually trust officers, safe, sound Prudent Men who wore green eyeshades, sleeve garters, and said "My good man." But the really swinging managers, portfolio as personality, out running super-aggressive funds, have profiles much more like the entrepreneurs who like to get an idea, round up people, and start a business or a project. The trust officer portfolio manager tolerates detail; the aggressive fund manager can barely stand it. All portfolio managers are supposed to be physically vigorous, but the aggressive portfolio managers play squash, tennis, and row, so that they don't have to be on anybody's team. Presumably the CPA-type manager would run best on a relay team or play soccer, or do something where the whole team would be in on the scoring. (The new, itchy, aggressive manager is a breed lately arrived. We do not have much of a dossier on him and we will come back to him in a later chapter.)

Other tests with pen and pencil peel away other veils. John has four apples, Mary has three oranges, and they both get on a train that is going forty miles an hour which left the station at 2:10. When the train arrives, John has two apples and Mary has six oranges. What time is it?

The analyst is inductive. He will break the problem into its components and work away at each, building up to the answer. The old portfolio manager will settle happily into the problem; he loves it. The aggressive portfolio manager says, "What the hell kind of stupid question is that, and how is that going to make me any money?" and goes into the same kind of rage he did when his wife wouldn't leave the party. He has to get the Concept in one fell swoop or he is very restless.

While the analysts can do the problems, they make a lot of arithmetic errors, unlike the accountants, who get everything right to the decimal point. But good analysts have high aptitude with both words and numbers. They shine best in Vocabulary. It is when the functioning gets abstract, both numerically and verbally, that they begin to fade.

Everybody in the whole field is very smart. The bottom IQ is 130, so if you're dumb, better stop right here—all the other people are too bright. The range is from bright to near-genius. Are you ready for the blot? A sample blot is on the next page.

What do you see in the blot? How many things did you see? Is it the whole blot, or only part of the blot? How quickly did you see it?

If it will make you feel any better, a lot of other people have seen those bugs, animal hides, and outstretched hands. But you have to do better than that, since you are only seeing what everybody else sees. You had better find something of your own within the first twenty seconds.

The point of the blots is not what you see in the blots, but your response pattern to them. How high is your evidence demand? That is, how much do you have to see before you will commit yourself?

Again the analyst is building inductively, but the real gunslinger of a portfolio manager can't stand second thoughts. He bounces with the stimulus, is enthusiastic, almost overresponds. The analyst really wants to be right, his ego needs the pleasure of being right, and he would almost rather be right than make money. The aggressive portfolio manager doesn't really care about being right on each judgment, as long as he wins when you tot up the score. He has to be right more than wrong, naturally, but he tends to go in white-hot streaks and hope that his decisions add up more right—and so weighted—than wrong. What he is really doing is testing—quickly and unconsciously—each stimulus against the "apperceptive mass" of his own intuition, his intuition including all the "cognitive perception" he has used for years.

This portrait of an aggressive portfolio manager is not one that will make ancient trustees in paneled board rooms feel secure. But, as we have said, there are not many such; the portrait is really of a handful of hedge fund and

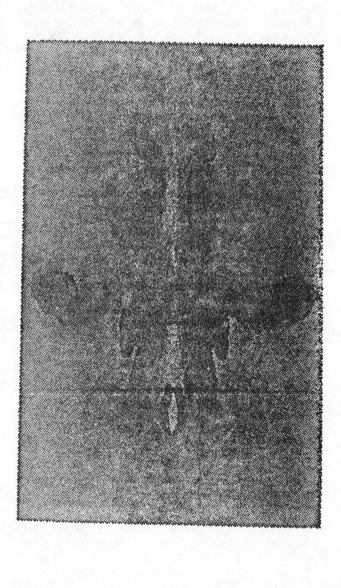

mutual-fund managers, not that of trust officers or the managers of large institutions.

These performance-oriented managers are new enough that their game is still on trial, but they have already weathered some of the bumps. What distinguishes this kind of investing—the quick reaction to the information— from that of the small investor who hears a tip and rushes out and buys? The small investor has the reaction without the knowledge. He has no "aperceptive mass" behind the reaction; the portfolio manager, quite simply, can remember the profit margins of a hundred companies, how the stocks react to a variety of situations, and where in the spectrum of managers he himself fits. If he knows these things, he can be away from the market and still know where its rhythm and his are meshing. In short, *if you really know what's going on, you don't even have to know what's going on to know what's going on.* All you need is a hell of an aperceptive mass, an IQ of 150, and a dollop of ESP, and you can ignore the headlines, because you anticipated them months ago.

There is one requirement that is absolute in money managing, and you have already learned it with the first Irregular Rule: *If you don't know who you are, this is an expensive place to find out.* The requirement is emotional maturity.

"You have to use your emotions in a useful way," says Dr. McArthur. "Your emotions must support the goal you're after. You can't have any conflict about what you're after, and your emotional needs must be gratified by succeeding at what you're doing. In short, you have to be able to handle any situation without losing your cool, or letting your emotions take over. You must operate without anxiety."

The psychological tests can't really tell you whether you are going to be an ace at making money; they are descriptions of existing groups, some of them followed up with later tests for incumbency (how long in the job), contentment, and success. You may be out of the patterns and still succeed, or the world may change to the point where these are not the successful patterns. But given the world as it is, this is the way the Game goes. Some analysts should not manage their own money, some portfolio managers should be running funds with other characteristics, and some investors should be cutting flowers in their garden and letting smart people run the money.

You may even come out a fine fellow on tests, but the real test is how you behave when the crowd is roaring the other way. We know a little about some individual types, but the crowd, the elusive *Australopithecus*, is still largely an unknown, an exercise in mass psychology still not accomplished. But is the market really a crowd?

4. IS THE MARKET REALLY A CROWD?

"The crowd always loses," wrote Mr. Fred C. Kelly in a noted work on the stock market in 1930, "because the crowd is always wrong. It is wrong because it behaves normally."

What the crowd—or the public—or the market is up to is always a subject of speculation, for the crowd, according to investment mythology, must always be wrong. (The believers in this rule are numerous enough to constitute a crowd, but of course anyone speaking of the crowd believes himself to be outside of it.) In 1841 David Mackay published what is supposed to be the first good book on crowds, *Extraordinary Popular Delusions and the Madness of Crowds*. Mr. Mackay's book, said Mr. Bernard M. Baruch, helped him to make his fortune, and one Wall Street investment house sends the book out as a Christmas present. If any of its clients read the book, they probably felt superior, because those Dutchmen who kept bidding the prices of tulip bulbs higher and higher a couple of centuries ago now seem sort of silly. Unfortunately, it is quite possible to read about Dutchmen thinking that the world had an infinite hunger for tulips, and then to go right out and buy some very snazzy computer stock because the world has an infinite hunger for computers. There must always be a rationale, and if the computer rationale is easier than the tulip rationale, it may just be that we do not know the whole story on tulips.

Every investor at some point hears, if only from his broker, that things are still a buy because the crowd has not awakened yet. Is the market really a crowd? Obviously there is no collected mass in the central courtyard chanting *Duce* or Yankee Go Home. All you have is a ticker tape recording market actions, and a certain number of board rooms all over the country with people watching this movement. There are a far greater number of people who do not even watch this motion but find a few minutes' sport each morning with the price changes in the paper. Doctors, merchants, lawyers, chiefs—can all these scattered people really constitute a crowd?

At the end of the nineteenth century a French physician called Gustave Le Bon published his *Psychologie des Foules,* translated as *The Crowd.* Le Bon spent a good deal of his other writings on generalizations about the characteristics of races, and these have not held up so well, but *The Crowd* seems absolutely prophetic—in 1895 —long before the world knew the kinds of crowds a Hitler or a Mussolini could assemble and manipulate. To Le Bon, a crowd was not merely a number of people assembled in one place; it could be thousands of isolated individuals. These he called a psychological crowd, subject to "the disappearance of conscious personality and the turning of feelings and thoughts in a different direction." The most striking peculiarity of a crowd, said Dr. Le Bon, was that

> whoever be the individuals that compose it, however like or unlike be their mode of life, their occupations, their character, or their intelligence, the fact that they have been transformed into a crowd puts them in possession of a sort of collective mind which makes them feel, think, and act in a manner quite different from that in which each individual of them would feel, think, and act were he in a state of isolation.

By this definition we do indeed have at the least the material for a psychological crowd in all those scattered number-watchers. And what, then, do we know about a crowd? The first thing we know, says good Dr. Le Bon, is that an individual in a crowd acquires—just from being in a crowd—"a sentiment of invincible power which allows him to yield to instincts which, had he been alone, he would perforce have kept under restraint. . . . the sentiment of responsibility which always controls individuals disappears entirely."

The second element in Le Bon's crowd was *contagion,* the communication of feeling—"not easy to explain," he wrote—and "which must be classed among those phenomena of a hypnotic order." And the third element in Le Bon's crowds was *suggestibility*—"the state of fascination in which the hypnotized individual finds himself in the hands of the hypnotizer." Once we have dissolved responsibility, we are ripe for contagion and suggestibility and acts of "irresistible impetuosity."

Plainly, Le Bon did not think of a crowd as something one should spend one's time in; an individual, he wrote, upon becoming a member of a crowd, "descends several rungs in the order of civilization" because the mind of the crowd is not an average but a new common denominator, mindless in the sense that it has surrendered to its own unconscious impulses. While the crowd would be "intellectually inferior to the isolated individual," the crowd could be better or worse than an individual, depending on the nature of the suggestion to which it has been exposed.

Is all this really relevant? Remember, we have here a field—securities and their price movements—which is being avidly studied by sixteen thousand rational security analysts, any number of fervent students and graduate students, and a whole slew of computers. Fifty thousand rational brokers—registered representatives, as they are called—dispense information to twenty-six million investors. The whole process is rife with statistics, tables, mathematics, and dazzling reasoning.

And yet stocks that go up do come down again, very smart investors are mousetrapped, and every year some group of stocks heads for the moon with its propellants believing the destination is gold and not green cheese. In 1961 the whole world was going to go bowling, but in 1962 Brunswick managed to make it from 74 to 8 with scarcely a skid mark. In 1965 the whole world was going to sit and watch color television, but shortly thereafter Admiral, Motorola, Zenith, and Magnavox collapsed like a soufflé on which the oven door has been untimely slammed. It will happen again.

The collapse of these groups—and I am sure that of future groups—is marked by a further outpouring of tables, numbers, and statistics. Motorola's dive from 233 to 98 was punctuated by reports, some of them over one hundred pages long, full of analyses of inventories, total demand, supply, cost structure, discretionary income, and consumer intentions. I still have them in my files. They say—at 212, and 184, and 156, and 124, and 110—that *now* the stock is a buy. To me these reports are far more illuminating than David Mackay's essay on the tulip madness in seventeenth-century Holland. All the orders for these stocks, both on the way up and on the way down, go through those brokers, fifty thousand of them, and public madness does not happen all by itself.

There is no substitute for information. The market is not a roulette wheel. Good research and good ideas are the one absolute necessity in the marketplace, and until someone can better define this *Australopithecus* of a market animal, they will be the best tools. But perhaps there is something else going on here. Let us go back to Dr. Le Bon, although his usefulness is about to veer away from us.

"Crowds," says good Dr. Le Bon, "are everywhere distinguished by feminine characteristics." And now we remember hearing Mister Johnson saying that *a crowd of men acts like a single woman.* (I know one distinguished senior partner who believes that the study of women is the best preparation for the market. It ought to be easy to recruit apprentices for a serious study.) The crowd, says Dr. Le Bon, does not reason, it only *thinks* it reasons; what it does actually is to accept a series of images, not necessarily connected by any logical bond of succession, and this explains why contradictory ideas can occur simultaneously. The crowd is suggestible to images, and what produces these images is "the judicious employment of words and formulas. Handled with art, they possess in sober truth the mysterious power formerly attributed to them by the adepts of magic." What Dr. Le Bon has in mind are words like "liberty" and "democracy" and "fifty-four forty or fight," but perhaps "growth" and "Xerox" will do just as well. All that is necessary is to recognize "the magical power attached to those short syllables, as if they contained the solution of all problems. They synthesize the most diverse unconscious aspirations and the hope of their realization."

All of this will be no news to many of the players of the Game. Wall Street unconsciously accepts this; the "image" that a company or a stock presents helps its price, and can keep it up long after the rational factors of earnings and return on invested capital have begun to deteriorate. If a company has a reputation for "continuous innovation" or "creating its own market," that is exotic fuel. The whole process keeps a lot of public-relations firms in business. "Crowds," says Dr. Le Bon, "are somewhat like the sphinx of ancient fable: it is necessary to arrive at a solution of the problems offered by their psychology or to resign ourselves to being devoured by them."

Or, as Kipling might have said, "If you can keep your head when all about you are losing theirs, maybe you haven't heard the news."

Sigmund Freud was so impressed by *The Crowd* that he used it as the take-off point for his *Group Psychology and the Analysis of the Ego.* (I have always like the German title, *Massenpsychologie Und Ich-Analyse,* because it sounds like Hans and Fritz, the Katzenjammer Kids.) Freud also examines *The Group Mind* by Dr. W. McDougall, who said that the chief characteristic of the crowd was "the exaltation and intensification of emotion" produced in every member of it. Freud pointed out that this same intensification of emotion occurred in dreams and in children, where the adult repressive tendencies couldn't get at it.

(If you think Dr. Le Bon was down on crowds, listen to Dr. McDougall: the crowd is "excessively emotional, impulsive, violent, fickle, inconsistent, irresolute and extreme in action. . . . extremely suggestible, careless in deliberation, hasty in judgment, incapable of any but the simpler and imperfect forms of reasoning. . . . like an unruly child.") However, Dr. McDougall's crowd begins to stray from all our board room watchers, because here we need an organized structure within the crowd and maybe even a rival crowd.

The force in the crowd, wrote Dr. Freud, not surprisingly, is libido, the energy of the instincts that go under the name of "love." Love here is not only for valentines, it is all forms of love—Eros, the force that holds things in the world together, and hence can also include the devotion to concrete objects and abstract ideas. In Freud's crowd, the individuals fasten on an object, substitute it for their ego ideal, and all those with the same ego ideal identify themselves with each other in their ego. Remove the object, and you get anxiety. The suggestion is that in the fusing of the ego and ego ideal, "the person, in a mood of triumph and self-satisfaction, disturbed by no self-criticism, can enjoy the abolition of his inhibitions, his feelings of consideration for others, and his self-reproaches." Freud then goes on into the primal crowd, with the hero leader, and the sons who kill the hero leader, and it gets rather hard to make any neat application. The group, Freud concludes, is the "inherited deposit from the phylogenesis of the human libido." Don't worry about it. We are not through with Dr. Freud, but that is all the further he can lead us here.

No one, after these few remarks, will ever want to be part of a crowd again, and yet the fact is that it is really quite comfy to be part of the crowd. (It has to do with individuals being part of a multicellular mass that the commentators on Freud go into and that we need not.) And it is certainly better to be comfy, everybody will agree, than not to be.

Outside of New York there is an aggressive fund housed in pastoral surroundings, run by a man who won't go into New York. It is not only that he considers New York a sink, which he does, but that "all those fellas ride into New York on the same train and read the same things and talk to each other all the way in." This captain of money management doesn't talk to anybody and doesn't read anything. "All that is all in the price," he says. "Eighty percent of the market is psychology. Investors whose actions are dominated by their emotions are most likely to get into trouble." He has a good record, this urbanthrope, but then so do many of the readers, talkers, and riders of the Penn-Central.

There is, one has to conclude, a kind of crowd there, and it is well to be aware of it. If the crowd is so fickle, feminine, and irrational, then does success follow from simply staying out of the crowd? Perhaps sticking to one's

knitting, the rational following of rational choices? **Here**
are the pithy comments of Lord Keynes:

> . . . Americans are apt to be unduly interested in
> discovering what average opinion believes average
> opinion to be; and this national weakness finds its
> nemesis in the stock market. . . . if the reader inter-
> jects that there must surely be large profits to be
> gained from the other players in the long run by
> a skilled individual who, unperturbed by the pre-
> vailing pastime, continues to purchase investments
> on the best genuine long-term expectations he can
> frame, he must be answered, first of all, that there
> are, indeed, such serious-minded individuals and that
> it makes a vast difference to an investment market
> whether or not they predominate in their influence
> over the game-players. But we must also add that
> there are several factors which jeopardize the pre-
> dominance of such individuals in modern investment
> markets. Investment based on genuine long-term ex-
> pectation is so difficult today as to be scarcely prac-
> ticable. He who attempts it must surely lead much
> more laborious days and run greater risks than he who
> tries to guess better than the crowd how the crowd
> will behave; and given equal intelligence, he may
> make more disastrous mistakes.

That is why, even at the most sophisticated levels, the
crowd rationale is heard. "My biggest customer has just
taken down a large chunk," says the salesman, "and I understand on very good authority—don't tell anyone—that
Fidelity is looking very hard at this one."

5. YOU MEAN THAT'S WHAT MONEY REALLY IS?

"The very bright people," says one of my Wall Street philosopher friends, "know how to worm their way around the Street, and they do very well. And the ones who just buy the stock and put it away probably do all right. But the investors who really follow the market, the ones who call up all the time, ninety percent of them really don't care whether they make money or not."

We will come back to what these eager investors *do* care about, but first, this business about all the investors not wanting to make money; it may just be the healthiest thing we have heard in a long time, if we can believe what money *really* is, at least unconsciously. If the sixteen thousand security analysts, the fifty thousand brokers, and all these programs in the IBM 360s are busy looking for the right set of rational numbers, perhaps we can sneak around the flank for a look at what money may mean to you. If we knew that, we might be able to step outside ourselves, as Mister Johnson said, and look back, and if we know something about ourselves and money, at least we can be conscious of the instincts toward it which influence our actions.

The reading list on mass psychology and markets may be brief, but the list on men and money is endless. Norman Brown, whose *Life Against Death* is one of the most brilliant critiques extant, has to run through Alfred North Whitehead, Émile Durkheim, Claude Lévi-Strauss, Marcel Mauss, Freud, Marx, M. J. Herskovits, Laum, Ruskin, and Nietzsche just to get warmed up. All of these learned scholars think money is more than just that green stuff in your wallet. Money has a mystical quality; the markets of antiquity were sacred places, the first banks were temples, and the money-issuers were priests and priest-kings. Gold and silver held a stable relationship through antiquity, based, says one authority, on the astrological ratio of the cycles of their divine counterparts, the sun and moon. (This is in a book called *Wirtschaftsgeschichte des Altertums,* if you want to look it up. I don't. I am reporting this at second hand, and anyway we have busted the old sun-moon business by pegging gold and letting silver go through the roof. There are those that think gold is due to go up—whether or not because of the influence of the sun—but that is another story.)

The point all these learned scholars make is that money is useless; that is, it must literally be useless in order to be money, whether money is the stone cartwheels of Yap island, shells, dogs' teeth, gold stored in Fort Knox, or East African cattle which can't be eaten because that would be—literally—eating up capital. The thread of thought here goes directly against that of Adam Smith the First, who postulated that money was useful and men rational. The invisible hand of the market brought the cobbler's boots to market in exchange for the farmer's cabbages so that, efficiently, the cobbler did not have to farm nor the farmer to cobble. Adam Smith the First's economic man was a rational man, and much of economics assumes that men will always go in the direction of the maximization of profit or of production. But since we are skittering over the idea that men are not always rational, we have to see where the idea that money is useless, or why it is useless, will lead us.

At the root of the impulse to pile up this useless money is "the compulsion to work." (Norman Brown here.)

> This compulsion to work subordinates man to things.
> . . . it reduces the drives of the human being to greed and competition (aggression and possessiveness) . . . the desire for money takes the place of all genuinely human needs. Thus the apparent accumulation of wealth is really the impoverishment of human nature, and its appropriate morality is the renunciation of human nature and desires—asceticism. The effect is to substitute an abstraction, *Homo economicus,* for the concrete totality of human nature, and thus to dehumanize human nature.

Wealth is useless stuff that can be condensed and stored. Sandor Ferenczi, a member of Freud's Wednesday Evening Psychological Association, went about as far as you can go in an essay called "On the Ontogenesis of the Interest in Money," in which he equates money with body wastes—"nothing other than odorless dehydrated filth that has been made to shine"—presumably gold, in this case. (Before hooting, remember that we are groping for something on the nonrational level. Aristotle said money-making was an unnatural perversion.) Money has always had overtones of the mystical; for Luther this becomes secular, and therefore demonic—Satan's work.

Why pile up this useless stuff? The surplus labor that produces surplus wealth is from the dammed-up or mis-channeled libido (Freud again). Norman Brown goes Freud one further: "The whole money complex is rooted in the psychology of guilt," and gold is the absolute symbol of sublimation. Money is "condensed wealth; condensed wealth is condensed guilt. But guilt is essentially unclean." Thus Christmas gift-giving is a partial expiation for piling up all that condensed guilt during the year. Guilt here is not for anything in particular; it is part of the personality structure. Back to Freud: "One must . . . never allow oneself to be misled into applying to the repressed creations of the mind the standard of reality; this might result in underestimating the importance of fantasies in symptom-formation on the ground that they are not actualities . . . one is bound to employ the currency that prevails in the country one is exploring; in our case it is the neurotic currency." To which Norman Brown adds, "all currency is neurotic currency."

Now it may seem a far cry from the kind of money being cited here to the total wealth of all those liquid pieces of paper, say some $700 billion in common stocks and $600 billion or so in bonds. That money, clearly, is not useless, it is out there building new plants and paying payrolls and producing widgets and so on. But Norman Brown, trying to work interest (i.e., return on capital) into his scheme, even covers this: "Things become the god (the father of himself) that he [man] would like to be; money *breeds* . . . thus money in the civilized economy comes to have

a psychic value it never had in the archaic economy."
And this is a true infantile wish: to become a father to
oneself. All of this leads Norman Brown on into a discussion of the city as related to all that piled-up wealth,
and the city as an attempt at immortality, an attempt to
beat death. (The inability to accept death is the woof of
Brown's fabric.)

All this may seem like peculiar stuff, especially taken
cold, but I find it provocative. I have been a bit terse
with it, and perhaps have not done it justice. Perhaps our
whole Game is outside the realm of money as condensed,
useless, and guilt, for if it is a Game, then it is "sport,
frolic, fun and play," and presumably on the Life side,
not the Death side. (Norman Brown does make me feel
sometimes that the only way to spend an afternoon is
drinking beer and fishing, so as to escape the accusation
of compulsive, guilt-ridden work, but I have the sneaky
feeling that while I am fishing he is working on another
book.) It is true that you have to work long enough to acquire a surplus enough to buy some chips for the Game,
but the money you make playing the Game isn't work, it's
play—or are you making it seem like work?

What seems to me missing from Norman Brown is not
only the idea of the Game but any concept of the paper-
ness of our paper markets, what we all learned in basic
economics as the multiplier. Grant all that compulsive
work to make the compulsive money on a one-for-one
basis, we slave one hour, we get one white chip for the
Game. But three of us form a little company, create stock
(paper), earn $50,000, and our public liquid market will
give us not $50,000 but a million if we can convince it
that the piece of paper is worth twenty times earnings. That
is really effortless wealth, and we live in one of the only
countries where this can be done.

Come to think of it, the Federal Reserve Board creates
money all the time. It just waves its wand of bill purchases and sales, and presto, there is money where there
was none before. This is called regulating the money
supply, but it works exactly the same as printing bright
new greenbacks, and the Fed doesn't even have to take
the money from somewhere else in order to put that

money into the banking system. On the other hand, maybe the members of the Federal Reserve Board feel guilty as hell.

So, in a logical sense, perhaps all these investors who come to the marketplace *not* to make money are free from the guilt and anxieties of money-making, and that's why they set out not to make money. No? I don't believe it either. If they were really free, they wouldn't have even shown up for the Game. Something else must be bugging them.

I suppose there does have to be a balance in time, so that we do not have, as Keynes said, quoting *Alice*, "a case of jam tomorrow and never jam today," or in Norman Brown's words, "the dynamics of capitalism is postponement of enjoyment to the constantly postponed future." And it is true that many of our most adept Game players never get around to spending the money they have made. But if they had escaped the guilt and tension necessary for the first white chip, they would never have had all the fun of the Game.

6. WHAT ARE
THEY IN IT FOR?

"Ninety percent of investors don't *really* care whether they make money or not," I postulated to my friend Harold the Psychiatrist. "They say they do, and that, of course, is the name of the game, but my downtown savants say that they don't. What do you suppose they are in it for?"

"I haven't a clue," said Harold the Psychiatrist, over his corned-beef sandwich at lunch. Harold the Psychiatrist and I occasionally retire to a little coffee shop near his office on the West Side of Manhattan. "Practically all of my patients are in the market, and it means something different to each of them. They're not seeing me because they're in the market, but people who can afford a psychiatrist can also afford a broker, and money is part of the *Geist*. I'm working on their personal problems. Why don't I lend them to you, and you can talk to them about the market."

So still pursuing the elusive *Australopithecus* jawbone, I began going to lunch with some of Harold the Psychiatrist's patients, and eventually with some of their friends—also patients somewhere—until I was the lunchtime Boswell of the set that takes taxis in midday to see their doctors. First they would talk to Harold—or whomever—for an hour, and then they would come to the coffee shop and talk to me. I would like to be able to report some learned conclusion, but when I group my notes they begin to take on a strange tone, as if Danny Kaye were attending Freud's Wednesday Evening Association: "Und zo, zen I began to notice in zis patient strange symptoms: ven she took off her chooze . . ." Therefore I will let you come to your own conclusions.

55

A. CUDDLING COMSAT

"I don't really know anything about stocks," said the bright-eyed pretty thing across the table. "But I love the market. All the men I know love to talk about the market, and if a girl can listen to them about the market, it makes them feel good."

"So you talk to the men you go out with about the market," I said. (I picked up this technique from Harold. You never really have to say anything, you just agree gently with what was just said and maybe form a question a tiny step forward from that.) "That's where you find out what to buy."

"Sometimes," said the bright-eyed thing across the table. "I came out about even in those. Some of them went up and some of them went down. Right now I only have one stock, and I thought of that one all by myself."

"You thought of that one all by yourself." (You begin to see the technique. It helps if you have a pipe and go *mmmm* as well.) "And what is the stock you had yourself?"

"Comsat," said the bright-eyed thing. "What do you think of Comsat?"

"What do *you* think of Comsat?" I said, with the proper turn-back technique.

"I just love it," said this pretty girl. "I got it, well, right when it started, practically the first day. And it's grown and grown. I just love it."

I wanted to know what was so lovable about Comsat.

"It's satellites, you know," said the girl, stirring her Tab. "And rockets, and the *future*. I got it when it was twenty-two and now it's seventy, and it was all my idea, by myself. Every time they fire off one of those satellites, I think, that's mine, that's my baby!"

"Do you know anything about the prospects for Comsat? What kind of money it's making, or could make?"

"No. I don't care. I don't understand that anyway. I just love Comsat, and I'll never sell it. I don't care if it goes down."

"You don't care if it goes down?"

"No, I wouldn't care. I won't ever sell it. Some day it would come back up. It's too well behaved to stay down;

whenever it goes down it comes back up, anyway."

"The men you go out with—what do they think of your Comsat?"

"Oh, they all have other stocks, but you know, Comsat is really something you can't disapprove of."

"A noble institution."

"Yes, and it was all my idea."

About a month after this lunch—which I had mentioned to him—I got a call from Harold.

"I thought you might like to see her again," Harold said. "She just had another one."

So the bright-eyed girl and I met again at the coffee shop.

"McDonnell Douglas," she said. "What do you know about McDonnell Douglas?"

"What do *you* know about McDonnell Douglas?" I said.

"I think it's very exciting. They're in missiles and jets and things like that."

"What happened to Comsat?"

"Nothing happened to Comsat. I still love Comsat. I always will. But you know, you don't want to have just one, all alone."

B. I WANT TO BE LOVED FOR MYSELF

I didn't meet Edward in the coffee shop, I met him at his club in midtown. Edward has a management consulting business that does very well, and whatever he was seeing a doctor about has no relevance here, or at least I never found it out. Edward was interested enough in the market and in the vocabulary everyone picks up from those taxi trips to the shrink to explore his own market experience.

"I started with a big problem," he said.

"You started with a big problem," I went along.

"Yes, you see, I inherited a couple million dollars' worth of Avon Products."

"I can see where that would be a problem."

"I haven't told you the problem yet."

"Sorry."

"I knew I was going to inherit this money, so I went to work at a bank, to learn how to handle money. I was quite young, just out of college, and just learning the securities business. And Avon had had a big run, and all I had was Avon. I got very nervous. Against the advice of the bank, and of the investment counselor who handles the family's funds, I sold out a big chunk of it. You know what happened then."

"I know it went up tenfold, probably, since you sold it."

"I felt very dumb about that, and I felt bad because it was the family stock, my grandfather was in the company."

"You could have bought it back."

"That never occurred to me. I don't think I ever even thought of it. You see, Avon is the family stock. But it isn't mine. I found one while I was working at the bank, in fact, I found a couple. Schering was one, in the fifties. I took it to all the members of my family, but none of them would buy a share. I bought a big chunk of it, and I did very well with it, very, very well. And I've had others."

"You've done just as well with your own choices as you would have holding the Avon," I suggested.

"I don't know," Edward said. "I never totaled it up. I don't want to. The point is, somehow there was no way of *me* participating in Avon. It was already there. What I really enjoyed was doing the work on a company, checking with the management, finding out all about the company and its problems, making up my mind, and then telling everybody about it. That way, it would be my stock."

"Do you still do this?"

"No, I don't really have time. I do dabble just a bit here and there, but mostly the bank does it for me. They've come up with some real winners this year. They had Leasco at thirty and Mohawk Data in the twenties."

"Don't you get a kick out of that?"

"It's nice to have the money, but my business is doing very well and I really don't care—at least I don't care the way I did when I picked them myself and convinced people to do the same and then watched them go up."

Later, over dessert, Edward said, "You know, if you

meet a girl and she's ready right away to hop into bed
with you, you might as well be some sailor ashore from
Venezuela, she doesn't even know who you are. You want
to take her out to dinner, to talk to her, to have her get
to know you. You want at least a little give and take,
a little resistance. Then it means something. Right?"

The bright-eyed girl might not have been conscious of
what Comsat meant to her, but Edward was more perceptive about what the market had been to him. Maybe that is
why he got out of it.

C. WAS I DUMB! WAS I DUMB! KICK ME!

You would never have known it, but Arthur actually
did very well in the market, I suspect over every vibrating
impulse in his body.

"Are you in Solitron?" he asked me.

"Are *you* in Solitron?" I asked him back, using Harold's
stone-wall questioning technique. It's quite amazing, but
almost no one questioned the stone-wall technique.

"I am," Arthur said. "I bought it at sixty on the old
stock, so that's thirty on this stock."

"Brilliant," I said. "You made eight times your money."

"Yeah," Arthur said sadly. "I remember the day this
guy called me up about it. I was going to buy three hundred shares, but it looked too high. So I only bought two
hundred. Was I dumb!"

"You're doing all right," I said.

"Every time it goes down, I feel better," Arthur said.
"Isn't that silly? I get nervous when it goes up, and I feel
better when it goes down."

"But you don't sell from nervousness," I said.

"I can't," Arthur said. "My Solitron is margined to buy
my Ling-Temco-Vought. I bought that around fifty."

"Fantastic," I said. "You almost quadrupled your
money on that one."

"Yeah, but I did something really stupid," Arthur said.
"I sold half of it at one hundred. Somebody should kick
me. I'm so dumb I make myself sick sometimes. I just got
too nervous watching it go up, and it never went down
enough so I could relax."

"Too bad about that," I said.

"Did you catch Burroughs?" Arthur asked.

"Did *you* catch Burroughs?" I asked.

"I missed it completely," Arthur said. "I was in my broker's office, and he told me to buy it. It was around fifty then, so it's more than doubled. And I didn't buy a single share. Boy, did we miss a good one there."

"Why didn't you buy Burroughs?"

"I don't know," Arthur said. "I already had a computer stock, and I thought another one would be too much. I was going to buy five hundred Burroughs, too. I remember, I wrote a note to myself, Buy five hundred Burroughs. Just think, I lost a profit of eighty points on each one hundred, eight thousand dollars. Incredible! I lost forty thousand by not buying Burroughs!"

"What was the computer stock you had?"

"Oh, I bought some Control Data just before that."

"But Control Data tripled! It's tripled since then!"

"How could I have missed that Burroughs when I was so close to buying it?" Arthur mourned. "I'm so stupid! Somebody ought to kick me!"

Arthur, as you can see, had all the winners in the market, and had probably seen his money increase 500 percent. But he didn't feel very good about it. If the stock went up, he should have bought more, so he was stupid there, and if it went down, that proved he was stupid there. Some people go to all the trouble of actually losing the money just to have that sheer wallowing joy of losing, but Arthur only talked it.

"When a stock goes down, I feel that's where it probably *should* go," Arthur said, "and when it goes up, the higher it goes, the more I feel it's going against its natural tendency."

"You've done very, very well," I said, "so you must be under a terrible strain."

"It's terrible," Arthur agreed. "I don't think I can stand it much longer."

I suppose some people are only really happy with motherly sympathy, and sometimes it gets hard to find a reason for Mother to be sympathetic. Happily for Arthur, there is always stock somewhere that is going up more than the one you just bought.

D. IBM AS RELIGION: DON'T TOUCH, DON'T TOUCH

Here are some short notes from a broker who happens to be on Harold's circuit, all sworn and attested to be true.

Once upon a time there was a very astute gentleman we will call Mr. Smith. Mr. Smith was so astute that many, many years ago he invested in a company called International Tabulator, which was a predecessor of IBM. Mr. Smith had great faith in the company, which in due course became IBM, waxed fat, and prospered. Mr. Smith and Mrs. Smith had issue, and the children grew up to be nice children. Mr. Smith said to them, "Our family owns IBM, which is the greatest growth company in the world. I invested twenty thousand dollars in IBM and that twenty thousand has made me a millionaire. If something happens to me, whatever you do, don't sell the IBM." Mr. Smith himself never sold a share of IBM. Its dividends were meager, naturally, and so Mr. Smith had to work hard at his own business to provide for his growing family. But he did create a marvelous estate. Eventually he became a grandfather, and he made gifts of the stock dividends of IBM to his grandchildren. And at family Thanksgivings, he counseled: "If anything happens to me, whatever you do, don't sell IBM."

Mr. Smith died; the IBM was divided among his children. The estate sold only enough IBM to pay the estate taxes. Otherwise the children—now grown, with children of their own—followed their father's dictum, and never sold a share of IBM. The IBM grew again, made up for what had been amputated to pay estate taxes, and each of the children grew as rich as Mr. Smith had been because the IBM kept growing and growing. They had to work quite hard at their own businesses, because their families were growing and their only money was in IBM. Only one of them even borrowed on his IBM, to get the down payment for a heavily mortgaged house. And the faithful children were rewarded by seeing IBM multiply and grow. Mr. Smith's original $20,000 has become millions and millions.

The Smiths are now in their third generation of IBM ownership, and this generation is telling the next, "Whatever you do, don't sell IBM." And when someone dies, only enough IBM is sold to pay the estate taxes.

In short, for three generations the Smiths have worked as hard as their friends who had no money at all, and *they have lived just as if they had no money at all,* even though the various branches of the Smith family all put together are very wealthy indeed. And the IBM is there, nursed and watered and fed, the Genii of the House, growing away in the early hours of the morning when everyone is asleep. IBM has been so good to them that even after divisions among children and rounds of estate taxes they are all millionaires or nearly so.

Presumably the Smiths will go on, working hard, paying off their mortgages, and watching their IBM grow with joy, always blossom, never fruit. It is a parable of pure capitalism, never jam today and a case of jam tomorrow; but as any of the Smiths will tell you, anyone who has ever sold IBM has regretted it.

E. THE BROKER AS WITCH-DOCTOR

"You get into some strange situations," said Harold's friend the broker. "The customers who don't get involved themselves and don't understand anything about the market think you can actually make them money by some sort of mystical power if you really want to.

"I met a girl at a party, and when I told her what I did for a living she got quite interested. I met her for a drink the next day.

" 'I want you to make me fifty dollars,' she said. 'In the market. Just pick something that's going to go up fifty dollars.'

"I said I thought we could do better than that, that the commissions would probably take away that first fifty dollars.

" 'You don't understand,' she said. 'I love my husband, that's why I'm meeting you here. I want to get him a jacket for his birthday, but I don't have any money and I can't ask him for money to buy him a present for himself. So could you make me fifty dollars?'

"I said again we'd have to try for a little better than

that—and that I had no objections to trying—but she was adamant.

" 'I only want fifty dollars,' she said, 'and I don't want any more than fifty dollars.'

"I suppose I should have just taken her phone number and then sent her fifty dollars later, saying I had made it in the market, but when I wanted to do better than the fifty dollars she finished her drink, said good-bye, and left.

"Then I have a client who is a surgeon. He's been in some good long-term stocks and he's done quite well. One day he came in and said he wanted me to take part of the account and trade it, every day. I wanted to know why.

" 'I ride home on the train at night,' he said, 'and everybody else turns to the stock page to see what happened that day. I don't have anything to watch in the market.'

"So I opened another account for him and he watched it every night and it did well, so he had happy watching. They were pretty wild, swinging stocks, though, and that made him a bit nervous. He used to call me in the mornings.

" 'My God, I have to go in and operate in about ten minutes and all I can think about is California Computer,' he said. 'It went down yesterday. Will it go up today?'

"So I calmed him down and he went in and operated on a patient. The trading account did well and he said he wanted to send me a present. I told him I didn't want a present, the commissions were quite enough. He said he wanted to send me a present anyway, and he did. It came in a little box, and it was a gland, a gland he'd cut out of some guy that he thought was the best job he'd done, and he wasn't kidding, either. You know anybody wants a prostate gland in a little box?"

F. CAN I TELL ROSALIND? CAN I TELL HARRIET?

The gentleman who supplied this one works in the Street and trades actively.

"My grandmother," he said, "is the very picture of a Norman Rockwell sweet old lady. Gray hair and little old glasses and a black dress and those little old-lady shoes. As you know, my grandfather was in the Street and he left my grandmother well provided for with trusts and whatnot. In spite of having been married to my grandfather for fifty-two years, she really doesn't know a stock from a bond. One night she tells me she wants to open an account with me. I tell her I am not in her kind of stocks—she must own Jersey at one dollar a share—but she wants to do it anyway. I tell her she mustn't tell anybody—the other members of my family certainly wouldn't approve.

"So we open an account, and I tell her the next swinging stock I am about to buy. She gets a very conspiratorial air about her. 'Wonderful,' she says. 'Can I tell Rosalind?' Rosalind is her buddy. Grandma is seventy-nine, Rosalind is eighty-one. I tell her sure, she can tell Rosalind. 'Can I tell Harriet?' Harriet is her other buddy—Harriet is eighty-three. All these ladies are well provided for, the Morgan bank is managing the trusts their husbands left, their children are well provided for, the grandchildren come to see them on Sundays sometime, and here they all are chasing hot computer leasing stocks.

"Well, things roll along and the ladies do very well. Then I come across a real find. It's a small electronics company with good earnings, not much stock out, and for some reason nobody has found it. 'Oh, how exciting,' says my grandmother, when she buys the stock. Grandma is now used to making five for one on her money. 'Can I tell Rosalind?' she says, with that secret, conspiratorial air. I picture these sweet old ladies in Schrafft's, having an afternoon soda in their black dresses and black shoes, and I say she can tell Rosalind.

"As I said, there isn't much stock around, and all of a sudden I find it hard to buy. The stock is twenty-four asked and I reach for it and I get two hundred shares and it moves up to twenty-eight, zingo. I call the dealers, I scout around—the stock keeps moving away from me. Somebody else is accumulating it! Zingo, it's thirty-three! Very discreetly, on little cat feet, I pad around the Street, but nobody has heard of it, my information is very good, somebody is indeed accumulating it, but nobody knows who.

"You guessed it, it comes to me in a flash. Grandma has told Rosalind and Harriet, and each of them has told two other friends, and a bunch of sweet old ladies in Schrafft's is accumulating a massive position and upsetting my game completely. So I am quite irritated when I call her. These ladies have buying power just a bit bigger than the Bank of England.

" 'Grandma,' I said, 'I said you could tell Rosalind. One friend. *Rosalind*. You're chasing this stock away from me.'

" 'Adele and Dorothy wanted some too,' Grandma says.

" 'Lay off my stocks,' I say. 'You shouldn't even be in this kind of stock.'

" 'Why not?' Grandma says. 'I have to own growth companies. I'm getting a stake together for my old age.'

"I let the reference to old age pass. 'The Morgan bank is doing a very good job,' I said.

" 'I looked up those stocks the Morgan bank manages,' Grandma said. 'Boring. They never move.'

" 'Now listen!' I said, my voice rising. 'If you and your friends don't lay off, I'll never tell you about another stock!'

" 'Don't say that, don't say that,' says Grandma, her voice querulous.

" 'Then behave,' I said.

" 'When you're eighty,' Grandma said quietly, 'it gets lonely. I bore you all, I know that. And I want my friends to call me. This is the most fun I've had in years. Don't take my stocks away.'

"What could I say?"

G. THEY MAKE ME DO EVERYTHING WRONG

"A broker," said this Mr. Thatcher, "is a true parasite. He is the most overpaid individual in the world. He doesn't produce anything. He doesn't make shoelaces, he doesn't tell you the law, he doesn't make the traffic move. He just takes orders, like a clerk, and for this—do you see the size of those commissions? Fantastic! When trading gets light, the brokers scream, they want to raise the commissions. But when the trading goes from five to ten million shares a day, do we hear that commissions are being reduced? We do not. The brokers just sit there piling up money."

"You're not happy with your broker," I ventured.

"The one I've got now," said this Mr. Thatcher, "is no more a thief and no less a thief than the rest of them. The jails aren't big enough to hold all the brokers who should be in them. Take information. When a broker gets a piece of information, does he call me right away? No. First he buys some himself, then maybe he calls me. I always ask, when he calls up to toùt me, has he bought it yet himself. If he hasn't, I don't buy. Of course, when I want to talk to the bastard, half the time I can't get him on the phone."

"He's busy."

"He's busy all right, the lousy tout. And take selling. You think they tell you when to sell? Never. First they sell themselves, then you watch the stock going down day after day, you can't get them on the phone, finally you get them, they say, 'While the outlook near term is uncertain, long-term holdings need not be disturbed.' They suckered me in with that a couple of times, but no more. That means, 'I sold last Tuesday, Charlie, and I forgot you were still in that dog.' You know how long that long term they talk about is? Five hundred years. Maybe seven hundred years. But whatever happens, they make it, coming and going. You make money, they take those commissions. You lose money, they take commissions. You leave your account alone, they call you up and tout you, they don't make any money when it's sitting still. It's got to keep moving, or they starve to death. That's what's wrong with the system. They have to keep pushing. They don't get rewarded for doing a good job, like a brain surgeon. They could put you in some stock that would go up ten times, but then they would starve to death, they only get the commissions when you buy and sell. So they keep you moving. The other thing wrong with the system is the type of person who becomes a broker. Who would stand to sit and watch numbers all day, making unconscionable amounts of money from touting on the telephone? A bookie maybe, or a thief. They're all thieves."

"You haven't done too well in the market, I gather."

"I've done just as well as anybody else, you can't believe half of what people tell you. Especially brokers. Did you ever hear a broker say 'I don't know' when you ask him a question? No. He's always got an answer. 'Why is my stock going down?' Profit-taking, he says. 'Why is the market going down?' Taxes are going up, he says, or the President is having a press conference this afternoon, or there is a war somewhere. They can never tell you anything straight, they're so used to lying.

"Take my Syntex. I should have sued the lousy thief who put me into that. This was on the last swing. The stock has a good move, from eighty to one hundred ten. I tell this lousy tout, I say, I want to sell if it's going down. He says the future looks good. The stock drops to seventy, I'm actually losing money. At seventy all of a sudden he sees the problems, the stupid lousy tout. He wouldn't let me sell at one hundred ten, but at seventy he makes me sell.

"Well, naturally, I canned that guy. But the next broker was no better. First he touts me into a couple, they barely move, he touts me out again. Then I give him one I heard at the country club, United Fruit isn't making bananas any more, something like that. The stock is twenty-eight, at thirty-five the lousy tout makes me sell. The stock goes right on to fifty-five, but the lousy tout makes me sell. Then he makes me buy some piece of junk he's touting."

"It sounds like you need a better broker."

"There's no such thing. They're all lousy touts hustling commissions. If there was a good one, he wouldn't stay. Saint Peter would grab him, an honest broker makes a marvelous example for the angels. Believe me, I've had half a dozen brokers. They're always touting, and they're always right a little, and then they tout you out of what you know is right."

"You ought to follow your own impulses."

"That's all very well, but I'm a busy man, I could beat these touts seven ways from Sunday, but I don't have time, I have my own business to take care of."

"It sounds like you ought just to use a broker to execute orders, not for any kind of advice."

"I should. I should. I'd be a rich man today if the lousy touts didn't always make me sell at the wrong time, or buy the wrong stock."

The list of roles investors play could go on and on, but the *Australopithecus* jawbone is still missing. Perhaps, as the savants say, the investors are in the market for something else. I have a friend who runs a small clearing-house shop, and this is what he says: "I don't care whether they're big investors or little investors. If they make a little money, they're happy, if they lose a little money, they're not too unhappy. What they want to do is to call you up. They want to say, 'How's my stock? Is it up? Is it down? What about the earnings? What about the merger? *What's going on?*' And they want to do this every day, they want a friend, they want someone on the telephone, *they want to be a part of what's going on,* and if you gave them a choice between making money, guaranteed, or staying in the game, and if you put it in some acceptable face-saving form, every last one of them would pick staying in the game. It doesn't make sense, or the kind of sense you expect, but it makes a nutty kind of sense if you see it for the way it is."

7. IDENTITY
AND ANXIETY

An Anthem From
George Frederick Handel:
When I Am Rich
Then Shall All Things Change,
and My Life Be Different

The absolute mobility in this country is wonderful, but it does leave its mark in pressures. For if our neighbors are growing rich, then should we not also? And if we are not, why are we not? It would be nice to say *imshallah*, Fate, buddy, or that's show biz, but it doesn't work quite that way, for we do believe in the ability of things to change, and in the Manifest Destiny of continual progress.

We have seen, in the scientifically selected samples just presented, that markets can mean different things to different people, that they present a kind of stage on which roles can be played.

But for the serious players of this game, there are more serious dangers. These are not new, and in fact they are probably inherent in a work-oriented society where identities are supposed to come from occupations and senior identities from achievements. If the occupation is money-making in its pure raw white form, then anxiety must always be present, almost by definition, because there is always a threat that the money which represents the achievement can melt away. You do not have to read so recent an author as David Reisman to get this. You can find it, although the author did not quite intend it so, in *The Romance and Tragedy of a Widely Known Business Man of New York* by Himself, himself being a man called William Ingraham Russell, and the year of publication being 1905. Mr. Russell's story, in one form or another, has recurred since the Protestant Ethic and the Spirit of Capitalism first touched these shores. Mr. Russell thirsted not only for money, but for the approbation of having it. He made it, he lost some, he made it again, he built himself a fine house with a magnificent library, then he lost it, and finally he lost it to the degree that his friends deserted and no one would even put up bail when he was sued over some relatively ordinary transaction. Sheer Hogarth. With his last energies Mr. Russell wrote the book, wishing to pay tribute to the "fine little woman" who had stood by him through it all.

The harsh jungle edges of laissez-faire capitalism have been blunted since Mr. Russell's day, and for all we know his friends deserted because he became impossible to get along with. Some things are not quite the same as they were in Mr. Russell's day. Markets are more honest, and friends do not desert in quite that Dickensian way. On the other hand, the "fine little women" are rarely as stalwart as Mrs. Russell, for imperfect samples show that current-day Mr. Russells find it easier to hang on to friends and to bail bondsmen than to wives, but maybe that is so much a part of the times that it has nothing to do with money.

The strongest emotions in the marketplace are greed and fear. In rising markets, you can almost feel the greed tide begin. Usually it takes from six months to a year after the last market bottom even to get started. The greed itch begins when you see stocks move that you don't own. Then friends of yours have a stock that has doubled; or, if you have one that has doubled, they have one that has tripled. This is what produces bull market tops. Obviously no one rationally would want to buy at the top, and yet enough people do to produce a top. How do they manage it? It must be that element of contagion from Le Bon's crowd, from the unwillingness to be out of step. It is really quite amazing how time horizons and money goals can change. Investors can start out tentatively after a market bath, and they buy something they hope will go up 50 percent in eighteen months. But as the pace accelerates, 50 percent in eighteen months seems much too slow, when there are stocks around—owned by somebody else—that are going up 100 percent in six months. Finally it all turns into a marvelous carmagnole that is great fun if you leave the party early.

The same thing happens in reverse. When stocks start down, the tendency is to wait until they come back a little before lightening up. They head down further, and the idea that you have made a mistake, that you have been betrayed by your own judgment, can be so paralyzing that you wait a little longer. Finally faith evaporates entirely. If stocks were down 10 percent yesterday, they may be down 20 percent today. One day, when all the news is bad, you have to get rid of the filthy things which have treated you so cruelly. Again, it all ends in a kind of paroxysm that is no fun unless you have anticipated it.

No matter what role the investor has started with, in a climax on one side or the other the role melts into the crowd role of greed or fear. The only real protection against all the vagaries of identity-playing, and against the final role of being part of the crowd when it stampedes, is to have an identity so firm it is not influenced by all the brouhaha in the marketplace. Mr. Linheart Stearns, a New York investment counselor now deceased, wrote a very interesting essay on investing and anxiety, for anxiety is the threat to identity. Mr. Stearns evidently had some clients who were every bit as wacky as the ones we have just met. One of them wouldn't buy bonds because bonds reminded him of death, an observation perhaps not so far wrong in the light of the discussions of Freud's Wednesday Evening Psychological Association in Vienna. A dress manufacturer insisted stocks were no different from dresses, to be sold at a profit if possible, but "marked down and sold regardless before the end of the season." Mr. Stearns must have been a soothing investment counselor to know, for his thesis is that the end object of investment is serenity, and serenity can only be achieved by the avoidance of anxiety, and to avoid anxiety you have to know who you are and what you're doing.

You can see that all this is leading to another of Smith's Irregular Rules, this one that the identity of the investor and that of the investing action must be coldly separate. It can be granted right away that if you have been a brilliant decision-maker, over a long enough period of time, maybe that's who you are, and it won't hurt you to walk around feeling brilliant. But it is a dangerous procedure, for the market has a way of inducing humility in even its most successful students. It is dangerous because to know what you're doing, you do have to be able to step outside yourself and see yourself objectively, and this is very tough if you think of Comsat as your baby, or even think "That's mine, and I bought it a lot lower."

A stock is for all practical purposes, a piece of paper that sits in a bank vault. Most likely you will never see it. It may or may not have an Intrinsic Value; what it is worth on any given day depends on the confluence of buyers and sellers that day. The most important thing to realize is simplistic: *The stock doesn't know you own it.* All those marvelous things, or those terrible things, that you *feel* about a stock, or a list of stocks, or an amount of money represented by a list of stocks, all of these things are unreciprocated by the stock or the group of stocks. You can be in love if you want to, but that piece of paper doesn't love you, and unreciprocated love can turn into masochism, narcissism, or, even worse, market losses and unreciprocated hate.

It may sound a little silly to have a reminder saying *The Stock Doesn't Know You Own It* were it not for all the identity fuel provided by the market these days. You could almost sell these identities as buttons: I Am the Owner of IBM, My Stocks Are Up 80 Percent; Flying Tiger Has Been So Good to Me I Love It; You All Laughed When I Bought Solitron and Look at Me Now.

Then there is a great big master button called I Am a Millionaire, or I Am So Shrewd My Portfolio Has Gone into Seven Figures. The magic of this million-dollar number, and of its accessibility to Everyman, is so great that books sell with titles like *How I Made a Million* or *You Can Make Millions*, with very little content at all. They are the most dangerous of all the things written on the market because (and I collect them as a hobby) inevitably there is some mechanical formula somewhere within. Never mind who you are or what your capacities and abilities are, just charge in with the book open to chapter three.

If you know that the stock doesn't know you own it, you are ahead of the game. You are ahead because you can change your mind and your actions without regard to what you did or thought yesterday; you can, as Mister Johnson said, start out with no preconceived notions. Every day is a new day, providing, in the Game, a new set of continuously measurable options. You can live up to all those old market saws, you can cut your losses and let your profits run, and it doesn't even make your scar tissue itch because, being selfless, you are unscarred.

It has been my fate to know people who have made considerable amounts of money, sometimes millions, in the market. One is Harry, who made it and blew it and made it again. Harry really wanted to make a million dollars, and he did. I think Mr. Linheart Stearns had a very good point when he said the end object of investment ought to be serenity. Now if you think making a million dollars will give you serenity, there are two things you can do. One is to find a good head doctor and see if you can discover why you think a million dollars will give you this serenity. This will involve lying on a couch, remembering dreams, talking about your mother, and paying forty dollars an hour. If your course is successful, you will realize that you do not want a million dollars but something else which the million dollars represents to you, such as love, potency, mother, or what have you. Released, you can go off about your business and not worry any more, and you will be poorer only by the number of hours you spent in accomplishing this times forty dollars.

The other thing you can do is to go ahead and make the million dollars and be serene. Then you will have both a million dollars *and* serenity, and you do not have to deduct the number of hours times forty dollars unless you feel guilty about making it.

It seems simple, and there is indeed a catch. What do you do if the million dollars arrives and serenity does not? Aha, you say, you will worry about that when you get to it, you are sure you can handle it. Perhaps you can. Money, contrary to popular myth, does help people more than it spoils them, simply because it opens up more options. The danger is that when you have your million, you then want two, because you have a button saying I Am a Millionaire and that is who you are, and there are, all of a sudden—as you will notice—so many people with buttons saying I Am a Double Millionaire.

Harry, I should tell you, is not a real person, or rather, he is a blend of observed characteristics. I mention this because when this cautionary tale first appeared a number of guesses at Harry's identity were made, using the old device that The Portfolio Is Mirror to the Man. Two different Harrys called me. One said I had gotten his stocks right but his domestic situation wrong, and the other said I was a cad to put in all his leisure-time activities and anyway he had never owned any of those stocks. Recently I was having a drink with a corporate executive in an expensive mid-Manhattan watering hole and he said, "You know, Harry's made it all back again." He had somebody else entirely in mind, but when I checked around I realized that that was what time of market it was, all the Harrys had made it all back again. There are new Harrys all the time, and the thing that distinguishes them is that their identities are the sum of a set of numbers.

The trouble with Harry is not just the trouble with one man who made and lost a lot of money, nor even that there are hatching, at this very instant, other Harrys who will play out this role next month and next year. The trouble goes beyond Harry, beyond Wall Street; it's a kind of virus in the whole country, when the cards of identity say not how well the shoe is cobbled or the song is sung, but are a set of numbers from an adding machine. Usually we hear only the triumphs by adding machine, but those who live by numbers can also perish by them, and it is a terrible thing to have an adding machine write an epitaph, either way. Perhaps measuring men by the marketplace is one of the penalties of our age, but if some scholar would tell us why this must be, we would all know more about ourselves.

I saw him sitting in the bar of the Carlton House, this fellow who was a legend of our own Wall Street generation, only he didn't look like a legend; he looked like a Dunhill-suited, balding, slim, morose man seeking truth at the bottom of a shot of Jack Daniel's. Maybe all legends have to pass through this stage, and Paul Hornung and Cassius Clay just haven't gotten there yet. Harry was pushing the ice cubes around with a swizzle stick. I hadn't seen him in a couple of years, so I went up to him and asked him how things were going. He didn't even stop pushing the ice cubes; he just said, "I did it again." I didn't get it.

He did what again? I hadn't seen him for a long time. This time he practically shouted, and the happy buzz in the bar quieted for a moment while the people stared.

"I did it again! *I did it again!*"

Harry pulled a piece of paper from his pocket, tape from an adding machine. There were a lot of little red marks and at the end it said 00.00. Then I understood, rather dimly, that what Harry had done was to part with a million dollars-plus in the market, which brought him for the second time to where he started, which was 00.00.

"I'm busted," Harry said. I was sorry to hear it, but, trying to be cheerful, I said busted is not *terra incognita;* one has been there before. I wanted to know what else Harry was doing, who was he seeing, what was he reading, what did he think about the market now. All Harry could do was slap the adding-machine tape on the bar and say "Busted." He wasn't seeing anybody, he wasn't doing anything, it took a supreme effort to throw off the covers and get out of bed in the morning. When I protested that in Wall Street the curtain goes up every day at ten o'clock on a new show, Harry shut me up and repeated "Busted." Somehow not only Harry's bank account but also Harry himself was busted, as people are when they get fired or divorced or otherwise get denuded of their identity card, when the contest between identity and anxiety has been won by anxiety, and ego is crushed to a powder. No use telling them not to be that way. You might as well tell a paralyzed man to walk by putting one foot in front of another.

"Right now I have to make one decision," Harry said, and I figured that was good, because if you can make one decision you can make the next. "The important decision is whether to live or not. Isn't that what Camus said?" Camus may have said it, but this is not something most of us debate about every day, and it is a rather frightening debating topic for somebody who has just run into somebody else in a bar, so in a sweeping affirmative action I ordered another round. Some of the names and numbers in this, as they say, have been changed to protect the innocent, but all the constants are there as they are. So, as the balladeer says, all you young gunslingers listen to my song.

I met Harry about ten years ago, when he thought Dunhill was a tobacco store and not a Fifty-seventh Street $300-a-shot tailor. Harry was working for a major downtown investment firm. The distinctions then were perhaps fewer than today; Wall Street has been a popular place for young tigers to go for ten or fifteen years, and now there are so many they have all sorts of chevrons to keep the *stratae* apart. Harry was a security analyst, such as they were then, and he had a few accounts of his own and a great enthusiasm for what he was doing. Big partners went to see big companies and got big underwritings and made big mergers. Harry went to see the little companies because that was all there was left. He had a desk in the middle of a big bullpen, surrounded by guys like himself. He was making about $11,000 a year and his wife had left him, settling for a small lump settlement because that's all she figured Harry would ever be good for. Harry went to see his little companies and he wrote reports that only sometimes did the partners let him sign with his initials. When one of Harry's reports was published he was happy, and when the partners let him put his initials on it he was very proud indeed. He didn't know it, but the clouds of fortune were gathering over his head, and being in the right place at the right time is a good part of the game.

In every cycle there is some industry whose stocks do not just rise; they go up 500, 700 percent. In the early sixties, these were airlines: Northwest, Braniff, Delta, all went up 600, 800 percent, even 1,000 percent. You don't have to hit a play like that more than once or twice in a lifetime. Figure it out.

Back in the fifties Harry had maybe $5,000 saved and a one-room apartment in the West Village. He made a little money on the stocks that everybody made a little money on, and he dated the actresses who were trying for off-Broadway shows. He swam a lot; he went to Fire Island in the summer and played chess. Life wasn't terrible. Then the Russians put up a Sputnik and Joe Alsop discovered the missile gap, and all of a sudden any company that could make an instrument or components for a computer or an exotic fuel was a lovely, nubile thing.

When I think of those stocks now they are like the faces

of girls we once took to football weekends. General Transistor, where are you now? Polycast, do you remember you went from 3 to 24? Filmohm, they brought you out at 2 and you sold at 11 the first day: have you gone to live in Scarsdale and are you happy now?

The rest of the market was old and tired; the young tigers fed on the marvels of science. It was not just that someone would say "backward wave oscillator" and a stock called FXR would go from 12 to 60. It was that everyone so busily and sincerely tried to comprehend, through a haze of high-school physics, what a backward wave oscillator *was*, and everyone was so smart because backward wave oscillators were harder to understand than, say, Fords coming out of Ford.

Harry was right there at the head of the pack. He had a scientific bent anyway, and when he began to talk about how the new transistors were going to change the world, the world began to tremble a little bit. It was not just luck with Harry; if it had been, he might have been better off. He actually did see the things about to happen. As one example, Harry said here we have all these computers proliferating; the computers will work but we are missing the link at the beginning that takes the information from everyday life and puts it into a form the computer can understand. A man buys a tank of gas and gives the attendant his Mobil card, but there are still clerks with stubby pencils telling the Mobil computer how to add up the bill. Harry set out to find the missing link that would make us all rich.

He ran into an inventor who said that at home, in his attic, he had a machine that could *read*. Harry saw right away that if the machine could really read, it could tell the computer what it was reading and all the Mobil clerks with the stubby pencils could be fired or put someplace more useful. Harry's seniors sniggered a bit about the reading machine because it didn't belong to IBM and went on about their business. Reading machines indeed! The inventor was a man named Dave Sheppard, whose uncle had invented the Hammond Organ, and when he taught his machine to read rather funny-shaped numbers he called the company Intelligent Machines and sold it to another company called Farrington, which went in one beautiful soaring arc from $10 to $260, and there was Harry with a quarter of a million dollars. Harry took his stocks to the bank and borrowed so he could buy more of them.

"Did you ever stop to think," he said, "what a million dollars is? A million dollars is five thousand shares of Polaroid at two hundred dollars a share, that's all it is. A million dollars, *a million dollars*. That could change your whole life, a million dollars." I agreed a million dollars could change your life, but I was too chicken to borrow and buy more as the stocks went up, and then borrow more on the amount they had risen. If you borrow $30 on a $100 stock and it goes down 30 percent, you can pay back the borrowing and still have some chips left. But if you take the $30 and buy more, and then borrow on *that*, and then when those stocks go up you borrow more on *them*, at the first downward bump you have no reserves and they come and take the whole pile away. Harry knew this was true, but he was measuring the risks against years of life and what you were going to do with your life. He wanted to live big or small, but not in the middle.

"What's the difference," Harry asked, "whether you have twenty thousand dollars or sixty thousand? You can buy a few more things, but it's not enough to buy freedom, not enough to change your life. You're either a wage slave or you're not. You have to go for the quantum jumps. Why are we on Wall Street? To make money. If you pick a stock that triples you're doing as well as anyone ever does. And if you start with ten thousand dollars, at the end of a brilliant record you've got thirty thousand—big deal. What have you spent your life doing! There are a lot of people down here conning themselves with little capital gains—ten thousand dollars here, twenty thousand there—feeling very wise and smug about it. One day they'll wake up and be fifty years old, with a hundred and twenty thousand in stocks, and that's all they'll have for their life; that's who they are."

Harry began to get a following, and the commissions were rolling in. He got a raise to $12,000. He went around the country making a speech about the sixties, about the wonders that were to unfold: reading machines for every transaction, computers so complex it would take other computers to design them. We were on the verge of explosions, technical breakthroughs, that would change the ways of living.

Harry took his new stocks to the bank and borrowed on them. His speech on the sixties met with a fantastic response. Harry preached and the people *believed*. They sat entranced by this Billy Graham of money. I was in an auditorium one night when Harry gave his speech, and the people went up and tried to touch his sleeve. They figured if they could get a few sentences from the master's mouth, they would have the stock that would go up enough to change their lives, to get Mother into a nursing home, to get the kids' teeth straightened, to quit jobs, to change jobs, to get married, to get divorced, to get anything they wanted. It was all within their grasp if they could just make some money in the stock market.

Every couple of days, perhaps every day, Harry added up his net worth, the value of all his stocks, less what he owed the banks. The banks had the bottom of the iceberg, but the top was growing and growing. Harry asked the adding machine, "Who is the smartest guy downtown?" And the adding machine said, "$900,000." One night Harry called me; the adding machine said he had $992,-000. "Tomorrow morning about ten-thirty if we have a good market I'll be a millionaire," he said. He repeated it softly several times, "A million dollars, a million dollars, a million dollars."

The next day at noon Harry took a taxi to Dunhill's and got measured for some suits with real buttonholes in the sleeves. Then he went to J.S. Inskip and bought a maroon Rolls Royce with a bar in the back, and a Hungarian chauffeur-butler appeared like a genie to go along with this purchase. On the driver's door of the Rolls Royce went Harry's initials in naval code, the little yachting flags. Harry wasn't a great sailor, but he had been to sailing camp one summer. He bought a forty-six-foot sloop. He moved out of the West Village into a Fifth Avenue co-op, and a couple of outrageous fag decorators made it look like the reception room of a Park Avenue P.R. agency, with glass and chrome and Barcelona chairs and Masai masks. And to the car, to the apartment, to the boat, came an endless stream of girls, airline stewardesses, nurses, sociologists, actresses; sometimes it seemed as though every girl arriving from Europe had to stop at Harry's to get her visa stamped. It was all the Gospel According to Hugh Hefner.

There is some myth afoot in this land that money ruins people, that they are happier back home in Indiana with the real folks cheering at the high-school basketball game. Bishop Lawrence knew better; he was J.P. Morgan's preacher, and of a Sunday he would look down at the assembled Wall Street tycoons in individually endowed pews and say, "Godliness is in league with riches; it is only to the moral man that wealth comes. Material prosperity makes the nation sweeter, more joyous, more unselfish, more Christlike." Of course contemporary historians snigger because that was what the boys in the endowed pews wanted to hear, Episcopal rites with a faint distillate of Calvinist salvation, Faith According to the Closing Quotations. Money may spoil some people, but in Harry's case it was just like Bishop Lawrence said: He became sweeter, more joyous and more unselfish. Harry was a soft touch for anybody who needed money. He handed it out to the artists he had known in the Village, no strings attached, just get on with their work. He started a foundation to benefit the arts.

Now all the engineers working on some tetronic hinkey-doo at RCA and Sylvania and GE would come to Harry's chrome apartment and tell him what was going on, while the Hungarian chauffeur served them a drink and the latest stewardesses browsed among the latest *objets* on the art collection. Harry started thinking: Why not back these engineers, get a little company going here and there, then take it public, be a tycoon like John Loeb or Charley Allen, not just a picker of stocks? It wasn't just the money, the second or third million. To Harry's firm, Harry was a guy making $12,000 with hot dice, and Harry wanted to be *somebody*, a father of industries, a statesman, a speech-maker, maybe the object of a modest little squib in *Who's Who*. So Harry gave money to needy engineers, became a stockholder in some infant companies.

The market started down in 1962 and Harry sold a little, but not much. How could he sell against his own fame? Then the fat profits of some of the little companies melted with competition, and there were other problems:

It isn't enough to make a beautiful widget, you have to price it right and market it right and be prepared for the bumps, and the engineers who sat with the beautiful widgets in their laps in Harry's apartment didn't know much about that. The markets in Harry's stocks were thin and a little pressure revealed air pockets in their prices. Harry's part of the iceberg melted down to the water line so quickly the whole thing seemed like a dream. The banks sold out what they could and kept the proceeds. Harry was left with 00.00 and stock in a few little companies that had just started and couldn't be sold to anybody.

Harry sat staring at the famous speech he had made about the sixties. Today, of course, imprinters record all the bills, and reading machines—optical scanners—read them, and computers are designed by other computers, just like Harry said, but people don't care about that. They only care about whether stocks go up so they can send the kids to school and get the old lady into a nursing home.

A psychiatrist bought the Rolls. In fact, as soon as Harry advertised it there were four bids, all psychiatrists, whatever *that* means. Mr. Bertram in Miami took the boat. A Greek who was later to go busted in Central America bought the apartment, Barcelona chairs and all. A couple of galleries took the paintings away. The stewardesses fluttered into the air like a flock of spring warblers frightened by a snapping twig, and alit somewhere else. Harry had left his firm to start the new ventures, so he had no job, and with the falling market, firms were cutting back. It was all like the fourth or fifth panel of a Hogarth sequence, *On the Way to Tyburn Gallows.*

Then in 1963 one of Harry's engineers called up. The product they had designed appealed to Control Data and they were swapping stock with Control Data. Harry had some chips again. The word went out, "Harry is back," but the magic was gone, and anyway there was a boom roaring like a blast furnace—you could double your money in big old General Motors. Harry edged in cautiously and when he had a little elbow room he went to the banks and the banks took the prodigal right aboard.

"Time is getting shorter," Harry said. "I'll be forty soon. You have to do what you're going to do. All professionals use leverage. You have to, or you end up just another face in the crowd, somebody who worked on the Street thirty years and saw a lot of markets and retired with a hundred and twenty thousand dollars. That's no reason to be on the Street."

This time Harry lived in one room on the West Side, a penitent for his previous exuberance. Now he was a consultant to some of his old pals, and as he checked out industries it appeared to him that one day 90 percent of the homes in America would have color TV, and only 15 percent had them so far. So there was Harry in National Video and Zenith and Admiral and Motorola, four times, five times, seven times his money.

"Who is making the greatest comeback of anybody you ever met?" Harry asked the adding machine, and the adding machine said, "$752,000." The memory of what he had felt like with a million dollars came throbbing forth, and one morning as Harry tapped out his incantation on the adding machine, *om mane padme om,* the adding machine said, "1,125,000." But Harry was reaching, trying for the last few points, a little cushion, and the great Johnson Bear Market appeared. One day in August, Wall Street was about twenty-four hours from sheer headlong panic; there wasn't any money in the banks and there weren't any bids for bonds that normally get pushed along like ratchets on an assembly line. Then came Mr. Gavin, the Motorola chairman, to the security analysts, to say the demand was there and some day everyone would have color TV, but meanwhile there was some trouble about profits. The red dog was on, q.v., and every hungry young whippet running a performance portfolio tripped over his untied shoelaces in an effort to throw the color TV stocks down the air shaft before the investment committee remembered he had bought them.

Harry was left staring at his latest report, which said that some day 90 percent of all the homes in America would have color TV, but people no longer care about that because the kids are still in public school and the old lady is still in the maid's room and the prices at the nursing home are going up all the time. When the phone rang, Harry knew who it would be: the sepulchral bankers, wondering as a matter of convenience if Harry could stop by in the morning and bring signed stock powers for everything he owned.

Harry hit the adding machine, and the machine said 00.00.

"There's always spring," I said, signaling the barman for another round.

For a moment, hope appeared to Harry like a nymph in the woods, a flash of something undiscovered selling at ten times earnings, compounding at 50 percent, to be pursued and caught and brought home in processional triumph. But the nymph flashed and was gone.

"No," Harry said. "The worst thing isn't the money. The worst thing is that I don't believe myself. I don't know what makes stocks go up any more. Things that used to be true aren't true. Everything has turned to paper.

"The woods are deep and dark and full of tigers," Harry said, and the tigers Harry was thinking of are twenty-eight and have fire in their bellies and a Billy Graham-like conviction of what is to transpire next year. All of them expect to be zillionaires, but the Witch of Wall Street is capricious, and by the rules of the game some of them must end up on a barstool with a slip of adding-machine tape in their slightly fraying $300 pockets, saying 00.00, Do Not Pass Go.

Ah, you say, gamblers must expect this. Did not Lord Keynes, himself a successful speculator, say, "The game of professional investment is intolerably boring and overexacting to anyone who is entirely exempt from the gambling instinct; whilst he who has it must pay to this propensity the appropriate toll"? Is this not the toll? But Harry was not really a gambler. You can tell those with the propensity: If the stocks are not moving they will play backgammon, and if not backgammon, they will be laying off on the football games, and if all else fails there is the gamble of which raindrop will make it first down the window. But they know themselves, and their identities are not in any one raindrop.

When the identity card says, "He had Sperry at 16," or "He made 200 thou last year," or "He is worth a mil easy," then there are the seeds of a problem. We all know what a millionaire is, and when the adding machine says, "$1,000,000," there is a beaming figure facing it. But when the machine says 00.00 there should be no one at all because that identity has been extinguished, and the trouble is that sometimes when the adding-machine tape says 00.00 there is still a man there to read it.

8. WHERE
THE MONEY IS

Before we go on to such practitioners of market diagnosis as chartists and the random-walk lads, I have to tell you a couple of things in case you think you are learning how to make a million dollars overnight. You may indeed learn this, but if you are that alert you could probably learn a lot from *Poor Richard's Almanac*, too.

Really big money is not made in the stock market by outside investors. That may come as a shock to you. You may not even care, since by "really big" I am talking about multiples of millions rather than just, say, one lousy million. It is certainly possible to make ten or twenty times your money as an outside investor in the stock market given enough time, enough intelligence, enough emotional detachment, enough luck, and somebody smart on the other end of the phone. It is possible because a lot of people have done it.

Who makes the really big money? The inside stockholders of a company do, when the market capitalizes the earnings of that company. Let me tell you a little story as an example, and for once, I am not changing the names and numbers of the players because it is such a nice story.

Once upon a time there was a little boy who lived in Chicago named Max Palevsky. His father had come to this country because the streets were paved with gold, but they weren't, and so to support his family he became a painter. Houses, not canvas. Max grew up and went to the University of Chicago and studied philosophy. His father said, "Philosophy? Max, how can anyone make a dime from philosophy?" Max didn't know, but he wanted to study philosophy, and so he went right on studying philosophy. In graduate school he was still studying philosophy, notably logic. After eleven-seven years in graduate school he got a bit fatigued with the academic environment, and so one day he went to work for Bendix as a logician. Bendix was trying its hands at computers and Max was there to tell the computer how to think, since the computer didn't know what was logical.

One day Max moved on to Packard-Bell, which was also trying its hand at computers, and one day after that Max decided to start his own company. IBM dominates the computer field, but even IBM cannot do absolutely everything well at all times, and Max thought there was a niche in the computer field that IBM wasn't covering, in the area of small computers. So Max got together with Art Rock, who had made some money and some friends at Hayden, Stone. Art had moved to San Francisco and formed a firm, Davis and Rock, to invest venture capital in ideas such as Max's. Max put up $80,000 and Art Rock's people put up $920,000, and from a sheet of yellow paper Scientific Data Systems was born.

The idea was right and the people were able and Scientific Data Systems began to make money on its small computers. A group of underwriters sold some stock to the public and the market on the first day capitalized—i.e., decided—that the earnings of SDS were worth a paper value of $50 million. That made Max's piece worth a little less than $10 million. Currently, after some notable triumphs, the market says SDS is worth about $688 million, and that makes Max's piece worth about $64 million.

You can't do that in the stock market unless you start with a hell of a lot in the first place.

The nice part of the story is still to come. One spring evening I was sitting in Max's hotel room on Central Park South and we were watching the lights go on in Central Park and I asked him what difference the $64 million made. Max thought for a minute and then he said it hadn't made any difference. He still lived in the same house and had the same friends. He did have a problem, because every once in a while his children would read in the paper that their father had roughly $64 million and he didn't want them to grow up with any false values. And of course, he did have the fun and the satisfaction of creating a company and beating IBM. Then he added one footnote.

"It has made one difference," he said. "It made my father happy. My father said, 'I did the right thing. I was right after all.' "

And Max said, "Right about what?"

And his father said, "I was right what I thought before I came, about the streets, and the gold."

So if we are talking about real big money, forget the stock market. Max's story, in varying degrees, of course, has been duplicated by the principals of a hundred other companies. That $240 million may be a paper value, but if you own a piece of it you can trade the paper in for all the nice tangible things you can think of, and even after they get the carpeting in on your boat you will still have a lot left. Engineers know this well; they follow the trail of the stock options. You have stock and as long as there are buyers for it that currency is just as good as greenbacks. You can whisk engineers out of RCA and Sperry Rand and General Electric because the engineers there are too far from the top and if they have options they are small in relation to the size of the company. So if you have a device or a process for which there is a ready market, and you can corral some engineers, that is the way to the big money.

Sometimes this process of capitalizing the earnings in a glamorous field takes hardly any start-up money at all and isn't limited to the arcane disciplines of computer technology. Let us say three fellows are working for an advertising agency on the Cosmo Hair Cream account. One is the producer of Cosmo's television commercials, one is the writer who gets the ideas, and one is the account executive, i.e., salesman and mother hen, who has the Cosmo people in his pocket. In the old days, just taking home $60,000 a year would have been enough for our three heroes. Now they meet in one of those Manhattan restaurants where the maître d' has a posture like a cobra and has his hand out for ten dollars at lunch. Our three heroes decide to form their own agency. What are their expenses and their risks? Well, they will have to rent an office and hire a couple of people, but since their plan is to take the Cosmo account with them, those expenses will be covered. Otherwise, no machinery, no inventory, no problems except how to get the accounts. In two years our heroes will have ten other accounts, the firm will have nice profits, and they can go public. Their own shares in the firm—sold at twenty times earnings—are worth a couple million apiece, and that beats $60,000 a year. (They will take that anyway, just as soon as they get that stock well distributed.)

When you buy the stock of Winken, Blinken and Nod, the new ad agency, or of Digital Datawhack Computers, you may have a chance at a very nice percentage gain. But the marvel of market capitalization, of public ownership, has already given the principals sixty times their money. Entrepreneurs, of course, are not always rewarded so lavishly, and there is always the chance that you can't sell your computers or that they blow out the light bulbs or that Cosmo will go back to the old agency.

But if a room full of people called a sales organization can go public (and many have), and another office of people called an ad agency can go public, there is really no limit to the concept. A number of brokerage firms are hungrily waiting for the day when *they* can go public, i.e., not only sell everybody else's stocks but their own, too. (Before they do, you will hear that the tremendous capital needs of Wall Street can only be met by outside financing, that the present commission rates simply do not cover the expansion that has to be made, and that half the members of the New York Stock Exchange are going broke. Then one rather offbeat firm will go public, followed by a stampede, so that the members of the New York Stock Exchange, instead of having one or two million dollars' worth of other people's companies and a share in their own, can have one or two million dollars' worth of other people's companies and twenty million dollars' worth of their own. As Lincoln Steffens said, "I have seen the future, and it works.")

Eventually there is no reason why doctors and lawyers should not go public too; it may take longer, but at some point a smart lawyer is going to see that if Bardell, Pickwick, Motley and Slick were a corporation instead of just a bunch of lawyers, they could sell the stock at twenty times earnings and that, in fact, a hungry underwriter has already suggested this. (In good markets, there is always a hungry underwriter. In bad markets, everybody is hungry and all the energies go into demanding that commissions be raised.)

Once the lawyers make it safely public, you can look forward to Brain Surgeons, Incorporated, which will be sold by brokers as "the most direct way of participating in the broadening growth of medical care, of Federal aid programs, of the increased attention to the nation's health, and of the growing trend to schizophrenia."

I am not making any value judgments. This is the way things are, and the Game has been so successful that, like everything, it will get more and more successful until it stops being successful. One of our learned economists has described our economic system as "state socialism for the rich." If socialism is the public ownership of the major institutions and industries of the nation, maybe we are just taking a unique way of getting there.

9. MR. SMITH
ADMITS HIS BIASES

Now that I have shown you the path to the really big money, you may no longer be interested in the market as a tool. If you are, I have, in all honesty, to confess my own limitations and biases. What you can then do is to correct these biases—and they will run not only through this chapter but through all of them—and by correcting them, you may get a clearer vision of the elusive *Australopithecus*. I cannot supply that vision for you. All I can do is to note my own astigmatism. There are all kinds of ways to make money in the market, and we are all creatures of some sort of behavior patterns. If we have been rewarded by pushing the red button when the bell rings, we are going to look with particular favor on the red button until pushing it gives us a nasty shock. What follows, after a slight detour, is simply my own red button. When the red doesn't work, you have to retire to a safe eminence, or find the people who are good at the yellows and the blues.

One of my biases is so strong that I have to mention it immediately, because it runs counter to an idea that is very common, i.e., that if you buy good stocks and put them away, in the long run you can't go wrong. Well, as Keynes once remarked, "In the long run we are all dead," and, as the line in the ballad says, everything is born to die. The best anti-testimonial to buying good stocks and locking them away was published by the heirs of one Timothy Bancroft. Mr. Bancroft was shrewd enough to ride out the Panic of 1857, which he diagnosed thus: "I blame the Dred Scott fiasco, the easy money policies of the past few years, and the far, far too overconfident speculation in the railroads and farm lands of the Western states." What one should do, counseled Mr. Bancroft, is to "buy good securities, put them away, and forget them." These good securities, of course, should be companies "dealing in essential commodities that the Union and the World will always need in great quantities." Sounds reasonable enough. Mr. Bancroft died leaving an estate of $1,355,250, and if you remember that those are untaxed mid-nineteenth-century dollars, and that a full eight-course meal at Delmonico's cost less than a dollar at the time, that is quite a fortune. Where Mr. Bancroft erred was in the locking up and putting away, for by the time his descendants managed to get their fingers on the portfolio, Mr. Bancroft's Southern Zinc, Gold Belt Mining, Carrell Company of New Hampshire, and American Alarm Clock Company were all worth 0, and in fact, so was the estate, an event which prompted one of the descendants to take to print as a warning to his fellow heirs.

Nothing works all the time and in all kinds of markets. This is what is wrong with systems and the books that tell you *You Can Make a Million Dollars*. What is important to realize is that the Game is seductive. If playing it has been fun, it may be difficult to stop playing, even when that button of yours is burning your finger. Repeated shocks will give you anxiety, and anxiety is the enemy of identity, and without identity there is no serenity. (This is the lyric from the song that will end the first act in the musical made from this chapter.) If you really love playing the Game, any action is better than inaction, and sometimes inaction is the proper course, if it has been taken after measuring all the measurable options.

If a decision is made not to make a decision, that is just as much a decision as a decision which initiates action. I got this out of a book called *The Functions of the Executive* by Chester Barnard, who was many years ago the president of the New Jersey Bell Telephone Company. It has been a long time since I have read the book, and the sections on deciding not to decide are all I can remember of it, but it has served me through all sorts of delightful procrastination.

Let us look first at some of the non-red buttons.

Some people can make money in the market by anticipating the business cycle. The great mature American companies do not increase their profits every year. When business is good, they make a lot of money, and when it is not so good, they make less. How well this game is played depends on perspicacity in evaluating economic intelligence. Let us say that we have had two disappointing automobile years. By determining the scrappage rates, the average age of cars on the road, the disposable personal income, the number of new buyers coming into certain age brackets, the average length of credit paper outstanding on existing cars, and a few other factors, we can have a pretty good guess that next year may be better for automobiles if the ecenomy turns up or holds up. Once—from our learned economists—we have made a guess at the economy, we are ready to make one of three choices, for that is all there are. (Other factors are involved in American Motors.) General Motors dominates the industry and the conservatives will take the safe way there. Chrysler is the most leveraged and hence the riskiest and hence the most dependent on subfactors within the major factor, i.e., whether or not its specific models will be well accepted. It is also the most profitable play if everything goes for it. Ford is the middle way.

There is a variation on this approach called the Rising Base of Cyclical Earnings. General Motors' earnings are cyclical, it is admitted; that is, they go up and down from year to year according to how good business is. Then some smart analyst will—as smart analysts did in the early 1960s—point out that while General Motors' earnings do fluctuate, both the tops and the bottoms are higher over a five-year average than the previous five-year average. In other words, the mean line drawn through all the fluctuations is rising, because the overall market is expanding, General Motors holds its share of the market, and its profit margins remain the same or improve. Therefore, it is argued, General Motors should not sell at the washed-out multiple of eight or nine times earnings like a copper company, but at something closer to the Dow Jones multiple, say fourteen or fifteen times earnings.

When General Motors goes up 30 or 40 percent, the rise adds more paper value to the total of all market values than all the whingding computer companies put together. General Motors has 286 million shares outstanding, and hence a thirty-point rise is additional wealth of nearly $9 billion. Itek, Solitron, Flying Tiger, Emery Air Freight,

Northwest Airlines, and all the favorites of this decade together do not come to $9 billion.

However, you are starting a bit late with General Motors. What you should do with General Motors is inherit it. That $9 billion of additional wealth benefits the existing holders, but if you buy General Motors shrewdly before one of its major moves, you will do well to make 40 or 50 percent on your money, and that will never get you very rich, however satisfying it may be to be in the company of all that inherited wealth.

Another non-red button. Some people can make money by anticipating the swings in interest rates. There is a whole group of stocks which are sensitive to fluctuations in the bond markets and to the course taken by the Federal Reserve, in which you anticipate whether money is getting cheaper or dearer. Nice profits can be made in bank stocks, finance company stocks, savings and loans, and utilities by those whose fingertips are sensitive to this sort of thing. The swings in these stocks are frequently greater than those in the base companies which are so thoroughly a part of the business cycle, but you do have to know not only the anticipated action of interest rates but the degree to which these moves have been discounted.

Still other investors can do well in securities which are basically commodity plays, that is, the investors can determine, let us say, that the demand for copper is going to exceed the supply for several years, that copper production will not increase proportionately, and that the therefore inevitable rise in the price of copper will flow through as profits to certain copper companies, and that this future increase has not yet been discounted.

One of the most riskless forms of investment is the Turnaround, that is, a company whose fortunes have soured and consequently the market has sold it and sold it and sold it. Finally all the sellers who react to the souring fortunes have sold, and the stock finds a level and quietly goes to sleep. Then a new management comes in, and Does Something; it sells off the unprofitable divisions, it acquires new ones, it changes the programs and the point of view. If you buy the Turnaround after a long sleep, there is little risk to it, and if whatever it is that is changing works, you can do well. But somebody does have to do the work of finding this animal and working through enough to make sure that the story is valid. And, of course, that bottom to which the sea sludge has floated has to be a real one and not just a ledge somewhere halfway down. One example of a successful turnaround in this decade is Sperry Rand, whose management pulled a splayed company into control and then got the floundering Univac division going in the right direction. One example of a turnaround that didn't quite work is Massey-Ferguson, whose management seemed to have everything lined up right for a while. Sperry did very well, but with Massey something was always faltering every six months, and after the grace period of forgiveness ebbed away, Massey lost the interest of the Turnaround buyers.

For all I know, money may be made in the future, even in the near future, by investors who are 100 percent in gold stocks and are betting on monetary chaos, or by the investors who will buy the 12 percent government bonds and leverage them well if indeed that chaos arrives.

All of these examples—and they are by no means complete—do involve a certain amount of economic intelligence and security analysis by someone, somewhere along the line. When I see this job of intelligence and analysis well done, I have a kind of intellectual appreciation for it, and if the yellow- or blue-button proponent has an authentic ring to his conviction, I can follow him. But the approaches themselves do not sing to me. They are not part of my own history, and my heart does not beat faster when I glimpse them across a crowded room.

I happened, in the fifties, to be associated with a Wall Street partner who was one of the pioneers of a concept we can call The Rate of Compounding Earnings. This is, I suppose, "growth," although that word has been used to describe almost everything in the world at some point. My friend believed in growing earnings and he went out with a missionary zeal and preached this idea in the wilderness of mutual and pension funds, and at his untimely death he had a great following among them and a sizable fortune for himself. And since we had some fun and made a little money, when I see Earnings Compounding nicely I get that warm feeling that the Old Princeton Tigers get when they hear the glee club sing "Back to Nassau Hall."

When you open your handy stock guide and see the following line under earnings, you know something is going on:

	1964	1965	1966	1967	1968
Solitron	.16	.33	.66	.88	.99

Here is a company whose profits grow every year, and at a staggering clip. The company must be doing something right. (The example given happens to be that of Solitron Devices, which sold as low as 1¼ in 1962 and as high as 275 in 1967. In 1962 the entire market value of Solitron was less than $1 million, and in 1967 the market value was more than $200 million. Solitron's earnings increased more than tenfold, but the market's opinion of that earnings increase made the stock appreciate 250-fold. Anyone who bought the stock in 1962 and still has it is happy, and anyone who put $10,000 into it in the dark moments of 1962 and kept it until 1967 could have taken his $10,000 back and still have had about $2.5 million. That is the way the market creates wealth.

Here are the compounding earnings of three of the great Senior Sisters of Growth—IBM, Polaroid, and Xerox:

	1964	1965	1966	1967	1968
IBM	4.10	4.52	4.83	5.81	7.71
Polaroid	.58	.93	1.51	1.81	1.86
Xerox	1.91	2.78	3.75	4.48	5.18

With a little bit of arithmetic, you can figure the *rate* at which earnings growth is compounding. The higher the rate, the more the market will pay for it in terms of a price; that is, the *multiplier* placed by the market on the earnings increases not only with the earnings growth but with the *rate* of earnings growth. Given a number of other assumptions—which we won't go into at the moment—the market will pay more for earnings growing at a 30-percent rate than at a 15-percent rate, and more for a 50-percent rate than a 30-percent rate. When the market finds a 100-

percent rate of growth, it flips, and the rules go out the window.

Now let us try a little bit of elemental Programed Instruction. Fill in the missing words:

To get rich, you find a stock whose ———— have been compounding at a very fat ———— and then the stock zooms and there you are.

If you filled in "earnings" and "rate" you may have a great future at taking Programed Instruction, but actually you are in trouble because it is a catch question and what you should have done was to mark the whole question *False*. Now, in twenty-five words or less, write an essay on why the statement was false. Write here:

If you wrote "because records show the past, and the market cares about the future," or something similar, you get to come back in the class.

Here is another example.*

	1954	1955	1956	1957	1958	1959	1960	1961
Brunswick	.11	.25	.68	.79	1.19	1.83	2.20	2.56

Look pretty good? But look what would happen if you kept going.

	1962	1963	1964	1965
Brunswick	1.36	.27	.03	d4.21

The stepladder is upside down; that little "d" is for deficit. Brunswick did have a pretty good lock on the pinspotter business, but the bowling boom contained within it the seeds of its own destruction, like all booms. Bowling alleys proliferated like gerbils, and a location that can support one bowling alley supports none when a second one moves in and they divide the business. Brunswick's pin-

* Source: Standard & Poor

spotters had been sold on credit, and when many of their customers failed, Brunswick had a lot of slightly used pinspotters, an enormous loss, and *that* compounded growth rate was at an end; Brunswick managed to make it from 74 to 8 in one of the steepest dives of recorded history. You can look through and find other examples of companies which seemed to be unique, and seemed to have found the golden path of stepladder earnings, only to falter. Semiconductor stocks in the early sixties looked just like that.

So you may or may not want, say, Solitron after its record of compounding earnings is already established. What you want is the company which is about to do that over the *next* couple of years. And to do that, you not only have to know that the company is doing something right, but what it is doing right, and why these earnings are compounding. Earnings do not grow automatically, even when business is good and markets are increasing. The copying business has been growing frenetically for most of this decade, and yet one could have been severely mauled in a number of copying stocks. Sometimes earnings can grow for a couple of years because business is so good that none of the competitors have gotten around to cutting prices, stealing salesmen, and in general creating the competitive fester that is good for the consumers but bad for the profit margins.

Any company whose earnings are growing consistently —or more important, are likely to grow consistently—has something unique about it. The competition can read these earnings records too, and fat earnings records are an invitation to come in and sample the cream. So a company that has something unique about it has something the competition cannot latch on to right away. Whatever it is that is unique is a glass wall around those profit margins.

Take a look at those three Senior Sisters of Growth: Xerox, Polaroid, and IBM. A lot of people make copiers but only Xerox makes copiers that copy on any kind of paper. Xerography has a ring of 500-odd patents woven around it, and there are plenty of executives with a Bruning or a Dennison copier who hand something to a secretary and say, "Here, xerox this." Xerox has become a verb, and it dominates the field. When other people can xerox as well as Xerox, Xerox had better be ready to pull the next wonder from its laboratories.

A number of companies make cameras, and a number of others make film, but only one company—Polaroid—makes a film that produces a print for you in ten seconds, and once again there is a ring of patents all around the process. IBM dominates the computer field, which itself has had a spectacular growth. It was not the first company to make a computer by a long shot, nor is each computer necessarily the best technically in its area. What is unique about IBM is the breadth of its marketing competence. Customers do not want a particular piece of machinery, they want their inventories tallied or their problems solved, or what have you; and IBM's salesmen have a vast and sophisticated array of goods to tailor to problems, and its servicemen are right around the corner.

What is unique about a company is not patents or products. Polaroid's original patents have expired, and anybody who wants to turn out a 1948-type Polaroid picture, brown and fading, can do so. What is unique is always the same thing: it is people, the brains and talents of people. Sometimes these people produce patents, sometimes they produce a reputation for service; but always they produce something that cannot be easily duplicated by anyone else. In Avon Products, for example, what cannot be easily duplicated is its army of women selling Avon's cosmetics door to door.

There is a paragraph in the prospectus of any new issue that will tell you that the company's edge is fragile. A prospectus is a legal document written by Wall Street lawyers, and its purpose is to cry so poor that no investor can claim at some time in the future that he was misled. The paragraph of this truism will say—translated from the legalese —something like this:

"The Company has obtained 244 patents on its Digital Datawhack equipment. However, the Company has Competitors which are far larger and have far greater financial resources than the Company. The Company's abilities to maintain its profits and to stay in business depend on the ability of its people to stay ahead of these Greedy Giants, to create new goods and services, and the Company isn't at all sure that it can do this in the future, but it will sure as hell try."

Obviously, the day IBM comes out with a cheaper, faster machine than the Digital Datawhack 600, and one that fits into the IBM line, that day Digital Datawhack can just sit there counting its patents; unless it has something else to innovate, its compounding earnings have had it.

Even if, by some magic, you knew the future growth rate of the little darling you just discovered, you do not really know how the market will capitalize that growth. Sometimes the market will pay twenty times earnings for a company growing at an annual compounded rate of 30 percent; sometimes it will pay sixty times earnings for the same company. Sometimes the market goes on a growth binge, especially when bonds and the more traditional securities do not seem to offer intriguing alternatives. At other times the alternatives are enticing enough to draw away some of the money that goes into pursuing growth. It all depends on the psychological climate of the time. Obviously you are safer buying compounded earnings cheap than dear, because if you have a stock at eighteen or fourteen or eleven times earnings, and it takes a very damp climate indeed to suppress a record at those ratios. But since you will never be first on the scene, there will always be something to make your little darling seem expensive: Competition is lurking imminently, the stock has already run up, or the market is going to hell in a handbasket.

If IBM, Xerox, and Polaroid have that required Something Unique, could we not just buy them and lock them away? Certainly, in the past, one would have prospered by buying them either in times of general market disenchantment or in times when there are so many alternatives to growth that the market is indifferent to it—in short, at the low end of the price-earnings pendulum. But Brunswick, our example above, had something unique or fairly unique: a mechanical pinspotter. However marvelous the product is, no company is immune to mistakes by its management. A corporation by legal definition may be bloodless and immortal, but everything is born to die even in spite of legal definitions. Companies which have had something unique do not always run head-on into disaster; more frequently they are simply debutantes who had a rosy glow of beauty for a time and have become respectable middle-aged matrons much like the matrons who were never belles at all. For a time, the market will continue to keep them at a premium; the memory of beauty will still be so strong that the gentlemen who were struck first by the beauty cannot see the lines and sags creeping in. As new gentlemen come in, though, there are new beauties to greet *them*, and memory is not enough to keep the matrons popular. Then they are vulnerable, because the multiples will come down. Chemicals, for example, sold at growth premiums to the market in the 1950s. Currently not only has their premium vanished but they actually sell at a discount to the Dow-Jones average.

There is one footnote to this business of looking at past and current success, and it is an arithmetic one. Again, our Senior Sisters may serve as illustration. The point of the footnote is that the more you grow, the harder it is to keep the *percentage* of growth constant or increasing, because the base gets so big. A company with $10 million of sales and something unique can double its profits in a year; a company with $1 billion in sales is simply too big to double its profits in a year; it takes time and energy and capital for each incremental increase, and none of these factors is infinite, ever. IBM has 56 million shares outstanding and its market value at this writing is more than $30 billion—thirty *billion* dollars. For IBM to double its market value—and hence for your own IBM to double —would take a national and international enthusiasm on the part of both professional and nonprofessional investors alike, because it takes a lot of buying power to move something up $30 billion. On the other hand, one or two or a handful of professional investors with institutional buying power can move a company which has less than a million shares and a market value of only $15 or $30 million. So I confess to a weakness for smaller companies. When a company has a million shares outstanding or less, its market is thinner and the stock is more volatile, but this gives me only slight pause. The excitement of volatility is enough to make up for the risks. A nice safe Turnaround in a big company may offer satisfactory gains, but recognition may be slow and you can get bored meanwhile. Then you must have another Game, or at least something else going on at the same time. A thin market can be treacherous in selling squalls, so one doesn't want to be in the thin-market stocks at all in some markets. You do have to know what time of market it is. Markets go in cycles like all the other rhythms of life.

If you are going to go the red-button route, which is the only one that comforts me, there is one other rule you ought to keep in mind, and that is to *concentrate*, and not only in the Zen sense. Sweet are the uses of diversity, but only if you want to end up in the middle of an average. By concentrate I mean in a few issues only. There are, at any one moment, only a few stocks that have a maximum potential, and I, for one, am not smart enough to be able to follow more than a handful of stocks at a time. (Sometimes, when the whole thinly traded side of the market is moving, you end up with more simply because little stocks can run away in thin markets and you can't buy enough of any one of them. The last few years have been just one of these periods. The popular stocks have been very thin, quite risky, and hard to trade.) The University of Rochester, which has one of the most brilliant records of any endowment fund, had only twenty-seven stocks in its $400 million fund the last time I looked, and if you counted the utilities as a utility package it had only twenty stocks.

The most famous proponent of concentration is Gerald Loeb, a partner of E.F. Hutton, who wrote *The Battle for Investment Survival*. While Loeb's book was written many years ago as a series of newspaper articles, it still contains some of the best-articulated observations on what the market *is* rather than what it should be. "The greatest safety," Loeb says, "lies in putting all your eggs in one basket and watching the basket." Loeb did not mean literally one basket, but merely close to it. Winthrop Knowlton, the former White, Weld partner who wrote *Growth Opportunities in Common Stocks*, suggests five or six issues up to $100,000, and ten to twelve stocks for counts up to $1 million. This may be even a bit high for a red-button approach. If you are concentrated in only a few stocks, you are forced to measure each of them in terms of potential against each new idea that comes along, and this in turn makes you bump the bottom stocks off—the worst-performing ones—to take aboard something more promising. Sometimes you may be in only one stock. Not for widows and orphans, this red-button approach, I suppose, but this is a recital of a bias, not a handbook, and I am neither widow nor orphan. (I am going to add a special amendment here for this paperback edition. There is nothing wrong at all with the theory you have just been reading. But one thing that can blitz a really nice game procedure is to have everybody pile into it, and that is just what has happened in the case here. These simple ideas seemed innocuous enough when I typed them out. Now we have four hundred fifty-two hungry hedge funds, the top eighty professional gunslingers, and about three million amateur gunslingers all chasing small thin stocks with supposedly rapidly growing earnings.

It doesn't take long to figure out what happens under this kind of pressure. First, it gets very hard to buy the nubile stock at any kind of price that doesn't discount 1999 earnings. If it's a new issue, it comes out at an inflated price. If it's an old issue, the minute it starts to move it's picked up by all the computers that track these moves and the top guns are all in it within 24 hours without knowing why. So it gets hard to collect more than 200 shares without attracting a crowd, and remember the nature of crowds. Finally, since the pattern of growing earnings is such an inflammatory device, why, everybody's earnings grow, even if they don't. If your profits aren't growing, you have to sell the kitchen sink, put that in operating earnings, and hope that either the accountants won't make you asterisk the kitchen sink or that nobody can read the small type that says—in as obfuscating language as you can manage—that the earnings aren't really growing but everybody wants them to, so we threw in the kitchen sink. In short, the *quality* of earnings deteriorates. The accountants are all disturbed about this. High time.

Anyway, let's assume that somehow, someday, reported earnings will be true again, and that you are smart enough to figure out what earnings really are. That makes the theory pretty again; elegant, as we say in mathematics. Now go on with the story.)

All right, you are ravenous for another Solitron. You are going to go for broke. You have stepped outside yourself and you know who you are; that face in the mirror is the face of a riverboat gambler, cool, tough, continuously measuring all the measurable options. How in the world do you go about finding the candidates? You want the next Solitron, the next Xerox, the company that is going to compound profits away consistently, so that the market falls madly in love with it. Where does such a creature dwell, and by what dragons is it guarded?

I can't tell you. I can give you a lot of guidelines, but they aren't original. You can find them in *Growth Opportunities in Common Stocks* and in Philip Fisher's *Common Stocks and Uncommon Profits*. You know that a candidate must have something unique about it, something that makes it hard for anybody else to do the same thing. Its markets are growing, it innovates, it creates its own markets by this innovation. It has talented people—financially talented as well as scientifically or design-talented—so the financing is adequate and it has been accomplished well. There is depth to its management, so that the absence of one or two key people does not harm the company. It may get older as a company, but it stays young because of its innovations; a steady or increasing percentage of sales come from products, processes, or ideas that are recent. And it is small enough to be nubile.

That description could be called Have I Got a Girl for You. She's absolutely beautiful, she has a staggering figure, she's warm, she's friendly, she's bright without being aggressive, she's intelligent, she's charming, she's enthusiastic, she likes all the same things you like, and she's already told me she's heard a lot about you.

You know what you're looking for, but you still don't know where to find it. Let us listen to Phil Fisher for a moment. He is an investment counselor in San Francisco, and he limits himself to a dozen clients or so, and he won't take you. Phil Fisher has an outstanding reputation for having found the handful of companies that came into a new area and grew from little companies into big ones.

For years, Phil Fisher espoused what he called "scuttlebutt" as the way to zero in on a new investment. You know a company; you talk to their competitors. You talk to the people who sell them things and to the people who buy things from them. An engineer, for example, might

be enthusiastic about a new oscilloscope he was using, and
that would lead you to the oscilloscope maker. People like
to talk about their work. If you go to visit the plant of,
say, the maker of peripheral computer equipment, it has
been my experience that the people there will not only
tell you all about peripheral computer equipment; they
will tell you all the gossip about the major computer makers. And not only that, they will tell you about the components within the computers because their friends, the
computer engineers, have told them which components are
exciting and every last one of these birds is in the stock
market and looking for sexy stocks just like you are. That
fellow who has just taken you through the plant will tell
you, in the company cafeteria, that he has just exercised
his options, hocked his stock in his own company, and
loaded up with Pazoomis Computer Machine Tool.

You have only one problem, and that is, if you spend
all of your time gossiping with computer engineers, when
are you going to do whatever it is that you do? (You would
have another problem if you did have the time to pursue
all this scuttlebutt, and that is that engineers can be just
as fanciful as stockbrokers, and a beautiful piece of equipment does not necessarily come from the most profitable
company. And Pazoomis Computer Machine Tool may
be just about to get swamped by Kearney and Trecker,
and Giddings and Lewis, their competitors.)

Well, Phil Fisher is an honest man, and one day he sat
down and made a study of where his successful ideas had
come from. After many, many years in the business of
scouting and evaluating ideas, and after building up an
incredible network of acquaintances and contacts through-
out a variety of industries, he found that only one sixth of
the good ideas had come from the scuttlebutt network.
And the other five sixths? "Across the nation I had gradu-
ally come to know and respect a small number of men
whom I had do outstanding work of their own in selecting
common stocks for growth. . . . since they were trained
investment men, I could usually get rather quickly their
opinion upon the key matters. . . . I always try to find the
time to listen once to any investment man. . . ."

In other words, he found some smart people. That is
one of the most important of the Irregular Rules, *find*

smart people, because if you can do that, you can forget a lot of the other rules.

My own experience is by many quanta nowhere near as vast as that of Phil Fisher, but tiny as it is, it supports this point. There was a time when I was not only a seeker of scuttlebutt but a conveyor of it. The phone would ring and a voice would say, "I hear Fairchild is having trouble with the yields on its planar interfaced integrated mini-chip that was going into the IBM 360/72; they just called up Alloys Unlimited and told them to hold up on shipping the sandwich material." Then I would get on the phone and call three people and ask them, "What's all this about the low yields on the planar interfaced integrated . . . ?" and so on, and it is true that both Fairchild and Alloys would have a sinking spell for at least three hours while these phone calls multiplied geometrically.

But the good ideas? Well, the good ideas came from smart people. It is a tribute to and probably a test of good ideas that I always greeted them with one of the two words of skepticism: either *Here?* or *That?*. *Here?* meant "I recognize the validity of the concept, but good God, man, the stock has just run up twenty-five points." And *That?* meant "We turned that old dog over five years ago, how come you're just getting around to it?" Obviously there has to be something in the story that makes the answer "yes" to *Here?* or *That?* And as long as enough people are saying *Here?* or *That?* there is skepticism enough to make the story worth listening to. When there is no skepticism, there is almost no one left to sell to.

Professional investment managers may, in the course of their careers, come to know by heart five hundred companies, what their histories have been, what their problems are, who makes up their managements, what their prospects are. But no one can cover everything, and no one can know everything. So most professionals depend on the people—their own analysts, other people's analysts, other managers, their friends—whom they have come to respect as acute intelligences and as talents at whatever course —red, blue, or yellow—they happen to be talented at. There are really no more brilliant investment men than there are brilliant lawyers or top-flight surgeons.

Finding smart people in this field is no different from

finding the best tax lawyer or the best architect. Of course, the reputation that will lead you to the smart people in the first place means that there are heavy demands on their time, and there will also be a lot of people competing for this time who have—unless you are very rich indeed—more to spend in terms of fees and commissions than you have.

If you do manage to find some smart people, and they agree to take on your account, they are not going to want them to waste their time chatting with you about the market, and then you will have to find another Game to play, and another set of psychic satisfactions.

Women have an advantage. The smart people are likely to be men, and sometimes men can be intrigued with more than fees and commissions. The Game women play is Men, and perhaps that leaves them free to be less involved in this one.

Now mind you, it may sound like I have been preaching some system for making money in the market. If I really had a system for making money in the market and it worked all the time, first of all, I wouldn't tell anybody and second of all, I would soon have just about all the money there is. What I have told you is a set of biases so you can make your own judgments. That seems only fair. I happen to have a low threshold of boredom, and I like young managements because they wear button-down shirts and know people I know; the managements who don't wear button-down shirts are already too rich to care. (Note for this paperback edition: Button-down shirts *used* to mean young managements. Now it means middle-aged managements; the young ones are wearing flashy color shirts with French cuffs. The pace of change accelerates and fashions change in clothes, just as they do in stocks.) Go find your own biases and your own colored button. In peace, of course, and work out your salvation with diligence, as the Gautama told his disciples.

II

IT: SYSTEMS

10. CAN FOOTPRINTS
PREDICT
THE FUTURE?

This has been a great decade for Research on Wall Street. Every firm, or nearly every firm, has a Research Department. (I say nearly every firm because in some firms the Research Department is one seventeen-year-old wearing gym shoes who has dropped out of not only Cardinal Hayes High School but out of everything the Office of Economic Opportunity could think up. The duties of this gum-chewing apprentice of capitalism are to go for sandwiches, to deliver stock certificates, and to stamp "Research Department, Donner, Blitzen and Company, Members New York Stock Exchange" on reports that come in from Argus Research and Equity Research Associates and the other independent purveyors of Research. Donner, Blitzen and Company sends these out with a little note saying, "We thought you would be interested in our latest check on the Chemical Industry, which our Team of Analysts has just examined thoroughly.")

Research is all to the good, but the tide of it has now become so high that no one anywhere can escape knowing that the output of the Trucial Sheikdom of Amrah increased in the second quarter to 11,674,322 barrels per day, while at the same time manufacturers' inventories of medium-priced television sets were down 5.3 percent from the year before but up .6 percent from the preceding quarter.

Unfortunately, as we have seen, the playing of the Game is not entirely a rational affair. If it were, the most impeccable fact-finding would soon dominate the market, and many of the players would be bored to death and would invent some other Game. Since part of the Game is the anticipation of how the other players will behave, it is not surprising that Systems have grown up devoted to answering the question: *What is everybody else doing?* In its most primitive form, *What is everybody else doing?* makes up part of the daily volume of the Telephone Company. Wall Street, as you already know, is part of Mar-

109

shall McLuhan's vision of the world in the Electric Age, that is, a global village dependent on oral-aural communication.

To some extent, the global villagers in their tribal rites do pick up the telephone and say, "Our oil analysts have just returned from the Trucial Sheikdom of Amrah, and production in the second quarter increased to 11,674,322 barrels per day, except the part siphoned off to the Russians, and we aren't sure how big that part is because the Minister of the Interior, Fawzi el Schnurr, wants something put into his account at the Union Bank of Switzerland before he tells us." To some extent this is the content. But more often than not, that kind of communication is limited to print, and the oral-aural communication is more on the lines of the following:

Global Villager #1: "Say, our oil analysts have just come back from the Trucial Sheikdom of Amrah . . ."

Global Villager #2: "Hot as hell there, isn't it? We sent an oil analyst there once but he came back with some weird gut disease. Poor guy. We had to put him in the Back Room."

Global Villager #1: "Gee, our oil analysts have been complaining of gut trouble ever since they got back."

Global Villager #2: "Say, did you see where Fawzi Oil closed yesterday? Thirty-one, up one and one half. Pretty good volume, too. You got any idea why?"

Global Villager #1: "Well, I just had lunch with a guy who said the boys on the coast at Continental Growth are buying it."

Global Villager #2: "Continental Growth is buying? You sure?"

Global Villager #1: "That's what he said."

The trouble with the telephone as an attempt to find out *What is everybody else doing?* is that the amount of information processed is limited by the time available.

This may help to explain some of the popularity of charts. Charts are a tangible, visible way of finding out, if not *What is everybody else doing?*, at least *What has everybody else done?*

Historically speaking, Charting actually preceded Research, for Charting was rampant when Research consisted of eavesdropping on Daniel Drew and Jay Gould. This may come as a surprise to recent arrivals, since Charting has taken on an air of sophistication.

"There is an incredibly large number of traders," wrote Thomas Gibson in *The Pitfalls of Speculation*, "who pin their faith to the so-called 'chart system' of speculation which recommends the study of past movements and prices, and bases operations thereon. So popular is this plan that concerns which make a business of preparing and issuing such charts do a thriving business."

Mr. Gibson's book was published in 1906 by Moody's. *Plus ça change, plus c'est la même chose.* If you stop to think that Mr. Gibson's book was published only a few years after the specialist in Northern Pacific literally had the shirt torn off his back on the Exchange floor by frantic short sellers, and a year before J.P. Morgan personally bailed out the Treasury of the United States, and that a dozen oysters cost eight cents at Oscars, you can see that in our vast, myriad, and changing world, some things are constant. Mr. Gibson, not an impartial observer, went on to say, "There are various offshoots and modifications of the system, but the basic plan is founded wholly on repetition, regardless of actual conditions. The idea is untrustworthy, absolutely fatuous, and highly dangerous." That, as you can see, is some years before Moody's went into the chart business.

What is the whole thing about? Well, without going into collateral lines, such as the charting of the sun and moon, we can determine from anthropologists and spelunkers that about the time of *Australopithecus,* a caveman made a wall drawing thus:

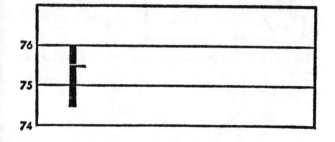

You can see that the vertical bar represents the range of the stock for that day, and the little lateral line is where it closed for the day. The next day the caveman did the same thing. After a couple of weeks, the cave wall looked like this:

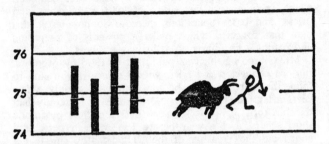

Thus was born the first "bar" chart, named after the vertical lines.* However, this first chart was trendless, which is to say nobody could make anything of it.

Then one week the cave wall looked like this:

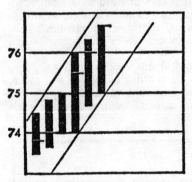

* The figures on the right include a prehistoric buffalo, and are not related.

The caveman drew a line connecting the tops and bottoms, thus creating a Channel, and the first Trend was born. In the future would come such scientific advances as line bottoms, saucer bottoms, head and shoulders tops, head and shoulders failures, true Vs, inverted extended Vs, measured moves, triangles, wedges, flags, diamonds, gaps, reversals, islands, boxes, spinners, flankers, cornerback fakes, running guards, lonely ends, and tackles eligible.

But in order to put it all into a Conceptual Scheme, Isaac Newton had first to be born. Isaac Newton was not actually a Chartist, though they claim him as their own. One day after the apple incident, Isaac Newton said, "A body in motion tends to stay in motion, and a body at rest tends to stay at rest." Or so the Chartists say.

Without Isaac Newton, the pictures on the cave wall would have been simply that: pictures. After Isaac Newton, the idea that these patterns could represent motion became acceptable. Once it is accepted that the patterns can represent motion, it follows that a Trend is a Trend is a Trend until it stops being a Trend. In other words, if something is going like this:

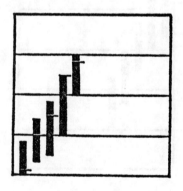

it will keep going like that until it goes like this:

unless it goes like this:

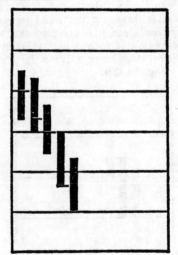

The worst problem arrives when it goes like this:

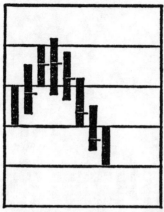

which would seem to indicate that it was about to go:

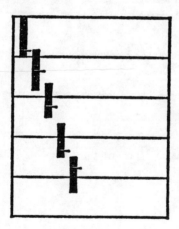

but then it turns around and goes:

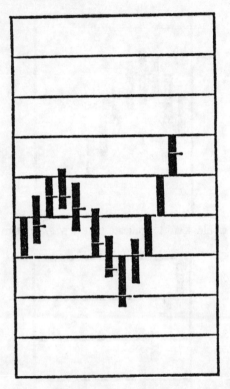

This is called a Trap, or the Exception That Proves the Rule.

You can even put the volume of shares traded along the bottom of the chart, like this:

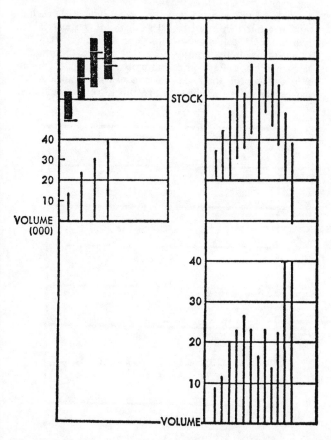

and thus you can see whether this price movement was accompanied by a lot of trading or whether it happened to be a thin stock moved by two bored backgammon players who just felt an impulse to trade.

Now you have learned some of the basic rudiments of charting. So far, there is little dispute. A chart can be a handy way of looking at what has happened; it can tell you what the price range has been, and what the volume has been.

These "bars" showed you the range, but by the definition of a bar they must be all straight-line vertical. There is a variation called point-and-figure, which is not a Regency dance but a complete map of all the footprints a stock has made. Each price movement is delineated by an *x* in a square on the logarithm paper. Thus a stock which has barely moved might look like this after three months:

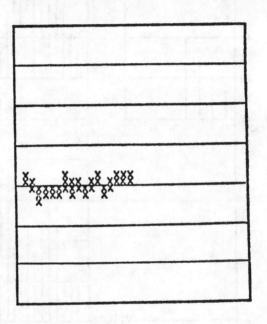

And one which has been swinging wildly could look like this after only a week or so:

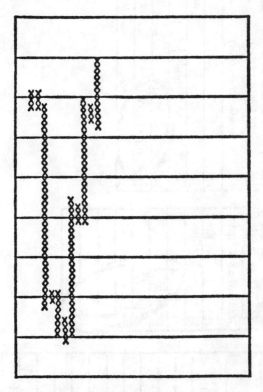

It is an informal thesis of charting that there are roughly four stages of stock movement. These four are:

1) Accumulation. To make a perfect case, let us say the stock has been asleep for a long time, inactively traded.

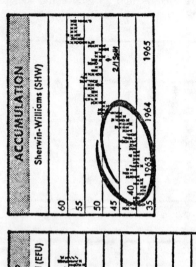

ACCUMULATION
Sherwin-Williams (SHW)

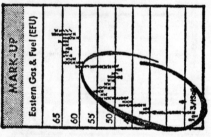

MARK-UP
Eastern Gas & Fuel (EFU)

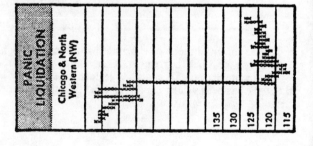

PANIC
LIQUIDATION
Chicago & North
Western (NW)

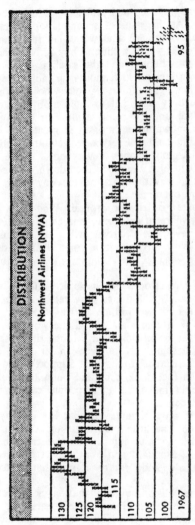

Then the volume picks up and probably so does the price.

2) Mark-up. At the stage of accumulation, there were still enough sellers around who were glad to unload the old dog finally to any fool willing to buy it. Now the supply may be a bit thinner, and the stock is more avidly pursued by more buyers, so it moves up more steeply.

3) Distribution. The Smart People who bought the stock early are busy selling it to the Dumb People who are buying it late, and the result is more or less a stand-off, depending on whose enthusiasm is greater.

4) Panic Liquidation. Everybody gets the hell out, Smart People, Dumb People, "everybody." Since there is "no one" left to buy, the stock goes down. (Of course, "someone" has to buy the stock on the way down, or it would go to zero overnight.)

Now we come to trickier ground. When the stock doesn't get anywhere after a rise, but churns around at the same price level, the Chartists call it an Area of Resistance. When a stock drops to a point where it doesn't drop any more, and churns around, they call this an Area of Support.

If one could depend on these charts, it would be a very neat world indeed. But if things were really this cut and dried, all the twenty-two million active investors would simply load up with charts and the Game would be over. Stocks have a way of blitzing right through the Resistance or the Support, pausing only long enough for chart followers to sell (at Resistance) or buy (at Support). And while the Chartists can then look back and point this out as a Trap, that doesn't make the poor people caught in the Trap feel much better.

If charts were only pictures of what has already happened, there would be little excitement about them. They would simply be used as adjuncts to statistical manuals like Moody's and Standard and Poor's. It is the idea that charts can indicate some *future* course that is so controversial.

The Fundamentalists maintain that stock prices will follow the course of business: sales, earnings, profit margins, and what have you. The Chartists maintain that all these factors have been discounted; they already exist in the price of the stock. What has not been discounted will show up in the movement of the stock.

Take another look at the idea of support and resistance. The chart will show, let us say, that Digital Datawhack churned around between 19 and 21 for a while. Then, in a marvelous spree, it zipped up to 36–38 and churned around there, and then retreated. The Chartists would say that there was support at 20. Presumably they would be willing to buy more if it got back there. Or there are people who were watching the stock, and it "got away from them"; they were unwilling to chase it to higher prices but they will buy it if it comes back to the point at which they were interested. Conversely, there are people who sold it at 38. Now the stock has backed off; presumably they will be willing to sell more at 38, or those who missed selling the first time will be willing to sell at 38.

If Digital Datawhack retreats and then goes barreling through 38, the old resistance level becomes the new support level, and the whole process is repeated.

You can see that there is an underlying assumption in charting, and that is that what was true yesterday will also be true tomorrow. Time as a factor is ignored, except time past. If there are new factors which must be reflected in time future, they will appear when Digital Datawhack breaks through either the resistance or the support, and then, the theory goes, you will know that something else is going on.

Chartists have, over the years, probably had more pressure on them than Fundamentalists. The Fundamentalist is able to report to you the news of the company, together with generalizations that provide an adequate cop-out. The Fundamentalist can say something like this:

> Recent weakness in the stock of Zilch Consolidated has prompted inquiries from investors. Production difficulties in the packaging of the new Zilchpaw Dog Food resulted in higher-than-budgeted expenses. While sales increased 4 percent, margins dropped 7 percent, and the net of this division is likely to drop 10 percent. Sales of other Zilch divisions have reflected the slowdown in the economy, and consequently net is

likely to be only slightly better than last year. While short-term considerations may determine near-term price action, we continue to feel that Zilch Consolidated offers long-term value for the patient investor.

Thus the analyst has reported what was going on, after the stock has already been bombed, but if you are patient long term, you may do all right. That phrase "long term" is the key phrase. It is used probably for 80 percent of all stocks that are not headed for bankruptcy at any given moment. Never mind that the long term is a series of short terms, or that in the long run we are all dead. The phrases "patient investor" and "long-term appreciation" ring with the virtues of capitalist ethos. The assumption of most Wall Street report writers is that their audience consists of millionaires with their own railroad cars who move from Saratoga to Palm Springs amid the muffled sounds of silent servants and distantly ticking clocks. What they really want is to be in the company of other millionaires: They are the true, patient, long-term investors, and, in short, they have so much money they don't want to be bothered with any more. The Research Departments, of course, don't really assume that their audience is railroad-car millionaires, if you get them at home on a quiet night. But the language they choose and the conclusions they reach would lead you to think that; such is the ambiguity of the cop-out. It is much easier to say, "While the near term is uncertain, long-term holdings need not be disturbed," than to say, "Dump this one."

The Chartist has less material to report, and furthermore he does not have the Free Zone of the Long Term to escape into. His thesis is that past patterns tell future patterns; therefore he must say whether the market (a set of Averages) or a particular stock is going to go up or down, and it is very easy to check up on his prediction. So he must say something like this:

We expect no furious advance unless the market is able to break through the overhanging resistance at the 920 level. Recent weakness in oils and strength in aerospace issues indicates leadership is rotating. Support exists at the 885 level, and unless that is pierced on some volume, we would expect it to hold near term. A trading range is indicated.

In short, the market will not go up unless it goes up, nor will it go down unless it goes down, and it will stay the same unless it does either.

This may not be quite so useless as it seems. The mystery and incantation do get to be rather funny sometimes, especially when Chartists are publishing opposite conclusions from the same chart. But a chart can show you what has been going on, and if this differs from what you think *ought* to be going on, maybe you ought to think again, even if the future is not there in the tea leaves. The assumption of the chart is that you ought to pay attention to it because the people who have already acted, and therefore created the chart, are smarter than you, or know something you don't know. You may reject the assumption, but it's a good check.

Can the footprints of price movements really predict the future?

If truly and universally they could, they soon would not. When everyone knows something, then no one knows anything; the market would soon become too "efficient"; that is, the gap between present and future value would quickly be closed by the predicting device. Yet a Chartist must, like the oracle of Delphi, be constantly on call with predictive aphorisms, which does produce cult and cant.

Does this mean that charts can be ignored? Perhaps charts can be a useful tool even without inherent predictive qualities. A chart can give you an instant portrait of the character of a stock, whether it follows a minuet, a waltz, a twist, or the latest rock gyration. The chart can also sometimes tell you whether the character of the dancer seems to have changed. There is even some mathematical support developing for the thesis that trends persist; a recently published Ph.D. thesis, *The Relative Strength Concept of Common Stock Price Forecasting* by Robert Levy, explores this. The first sixty pages of this book are perhaps the clearest exposition anywhere of what "technical" market work is. The rest of the book is a controversial and provocative examination of sequences in stock prices, but since the examination makes considerable use of computer-based statistics and higher mathematics, it will do little for the ink-stained Chartists whose work it would sometimes seem to support.

Finally, even though charts may not do what the Chartists and chart sellers claim, the action of accumulation and distribution which they attempt to describe—not very accurately—is part of the vocabulary of the Street, and this vocabulary is widespread enough so that it is even applied to other things. I can remember one lunch when, in a discussion of human relationships, one gentleman said, "A spike formation is basically a bad thing in a marriage," and someone else said, "There are always bound to be islands and reversals," and no one was particularly self-conscious about these descriptions. In a chart vocabulary, one of the exciting moments is when a stock takes a sudden, strong move after a long base at the same price level. One day a friend and I were having lunch when we saw a colleague across the room who was flushed, beaming, and happy. "No, it's not the market," my friend said. "He has a new girl, and yesterday they both said I love you to each other for the first time. Remember that wonderful feeling when you're coming off the base?"

Totems may be superstition, but if superstition is part of the scene and the exercise is to anticipate the actions of the crowd, then knowing the totems must become part of the anticipation.

There is one thesis that runs through all of charting which we can isolate and examine. Past patterns help determine future patterns; momentum can be shown on the charts. All Chartists, to extrapolate and visibly to determine motion, must draw some sort of a line between the prices at various times. It may be a mean line, it may be a line connecting the tops or the bottoms or both. Then the thesis is that the stock (or group) *is more likely than not* to continue along that line. Never mind whether that "more likely" is 51 percent or 99 percent; that is the point at which the enemy attacks. And the enemy is dead serious. There are all kinds of charts, and so far, we have only flipped through the Primer. Let us, for a moment, watch the enemy attack.

11. WHAT THE HELL IS A RANDOM WALK?

Charting is as old as papyrus; the "random-walk" thesis has ancient origins but, properly worked out, is as new as computers. Charting seeks to find some order in what has happened; the random-walk thesis maintains there is no order. If the random-walk people are right, the Chartists are out of business and all the security analysts are in trouble.

The random-walk people are university professors in business schools and economics departments. They have had a lot of advanced mathematics and they delight in using it, and in fact, most random-walk papers by these academics must be arcane and filled with symbols so that their colleagues will be impressed. If you want to read some of these, try a journal called *Kyklos;* it has published a number of them. The material in our glimpse at the attack is covered there; also in *The Random Character of Stock Market Prices* published by the Massachusetts Institute of Technology, edited by Professor Paul Cootner; and in paper number 16 of the Selected Papers of the Graduate School of Business of the University of Chicago, "Random Walks in Stock Market Prices," by Professor Eugene Fama.

What is a random walk? I can't understand half the papers on the subject, since my fluency in Boolean algebra is limited and in stochastic series is nil. But after a number of conversations with random-walk lads, it occured to me that the whole thing could be defined in one sentence, and Professor Cootner later told a friend of mine this was an okay definition, so without any equations, Σs, or $\triangle$s, here it is:

Prices have no memory, and yesterday has nothing to do with tomorrow. Every day starts out fifty-fifty. Yesterday's price discounted everything yesterday. To quote Professor Fama, "the past history of the series (of stock price changes) cannot be used to predict the future in any meaningful way. The future path of the price level or a security is no more predictable than the path of a series of cumulated random numbers."

Randomness as a way of beating the market is not limited to academics, of course. Senator Thomas J. McIntyre, Democrat of New Hampshire and a member of the powerful Senate Banking Committee, brought his dart board in one day. Senator McIntyre had tacked the stock market page onto his dart board and thrown darts at it, and the portfolio picked by his darts outperformed almost all the mutual funds. (Senator McIntyre's darts thus supported the random-walk testimony of Professors Paul Samuelson of MIT and Henry Wallich of Yale, given when the Senate was considering mutual-fund legislation.)

If big guns like Professors Samuelson and Wallich and the Senate Banking Committee are taking the random walk seriously, everybody had better gird up, because if the random walk is indeed Truth, then all charts and most investment advice have the value of zero, and that is going to affect the rules of the Game.

The first premise of the random walk is that the market—say the New York Stock Exchange—is an "efficient" market, that is, a market where numbers of rational, profit-maximizing investors are competing, with roughly equal access to information, in trying to predict the future course of prices.

The second premise is that stocks do have an intrinsic value, an equilibrium price in economists' language, and that at any point in time the price of a stock will be a good estimate of its intrinsic value, the intrinsic value depending on the earning power of the stock. But since no one is exactly sure what the intrinsic value is, "the actions of the many competing participants should cause the actual price of a security *to wander randomly about its intrinsic value*." (Fama speaking.)

The random-walk fellows have gone about testing their theory on "empirical evidence," and the purpose of this research is to show mathematically that successive price changes are independent. Here is a sample test, just to

scare you. This one is by William Steiger of MIT, from
The Random Character of Stock Market Prices.

> The test is based on a sampling distribution of a
> statistic pertinent to pure random walks which I have
> derived in another place. Letting t be the ratio (a ran-
> dom variable) of the range of deviations from the
> line joining the first and last observations of a seg-
> ment of a continuous random walk to the sample
> standard deviation of the increments, the distribution
> denotes the probability, P_t, that t is less than or equal
> to any t.
>
> Consider the following continuous stochastic process.
> Let

$$S(t) \qquad (m \leq t \leq n)$$

> describe a pure random walk in the segment from m
> to n where m, integers and t vary continuously in m
> $\leq t \leq$ n. Let

$$S_n = S(t)_{t=n} \tag{1}$$

> We transform a realization of S(t) in the segment
> from m to n to one which has a mean increment of
> zero as follows. Put

$$S^*(t) = S(t) - \frac{S_m(n-t) + S_n(t-m)}{n-m} \qquad (m \leq t \leq n) \tag{2}$$

> the deviations from the line joining (m, S_m to (n, S_n)
> and

$$R_m(t) = \max_{m \leq u \leq t} S^*(u) - \min_{m \leq u \leq t} S^*(u) \tag{3}$$

> let the range of deviations of the segment (m, n) at
> time t.
>
> Putting the increments

$$d_i = S_i^* - S_{i-1}^* \qquad (i \text{ integral}; m+1 \leq i \leq n) \qquad (4)$$

we define

$$s_{m,n} = \sqrt{\frac{1}{n-m} \sum_{j=m+1}^{n} (d_j)^2} \qquad (5)$$

the standard deviation of the increments, at integral times, in the segment.

Finally letting the random variable

$$t_m(n) = \frac{R_m(n)}{s_{m,n}}$$

we have the sampling distribution function for $t_m(n)$*

$$H(t) = P_r(t_{m,n} \leq t) = 2\sum_{j=1}^{\infty} \frac{1 - \left(\frac{N-2}{N^2}\right)4J^2t^2}{\left(\frac{1+4J^2t^2}{N^2}\right)^{\frac{n+1}{2}}} + \frac{\left(\frac{N-2}{N^2}\right)4J^2V^2 - 1}{\left(\frac{1+4J^2V^2}{N^2}\right)^{\frac{n+1}{2}}}$$

where

$$N = n - m \leq 2$$

and

$$V = \begin{cases} 1 & (N \text{ even}) \\ \sqrt{\dfrac{N}{N-1}} & (N \text{ odd}) \end{cases}$$

Equation (7) has two interpretations in sampling segments of random walks. Since one can only sample S_i^*, i integral, for the segment of the continuous random walk $S(t)$ in $\leq t \leq n$, one is not able to sample $R_m(t)$ in (3), but instead can only sample

$$R_{m, i} = \max_{m \leq j \leq i}(S_j^*) - \min_{m \leq j \leq i}(S_j^*) \qquad (8)$$

and thus sample only

$$t_{m, n} = \frac{R_{m, n}}{s_{m, n}}$$

In some cases R_m, i may equal R_m (i) and then and only then is (7) interpreted as an exact sampling distribution function for $t_m(n)$.

In general R_m, i $\leq R_m(i)$ and it is shown elsewhere that equality is attained with probability 1, for i $\rightarrow$ oo, m fixed.

These are, in case you didn't know, serial correlation coefficients, and they give me the same feeling they give you. Another approach is to test different mechanical trading rules to see whether they provide gains better than simply buying and holding. Professor Sidney Alexander of MIT, for example, tested all kinds of filters, inferring from the results what would happen if other mechanical trading rules were followed.

(A filter of 5 percent would work this way: If the stock moves up 5 percent on any day, buy it and hold it until the price moves down 5 percent from a subsequent high, at which time sell it and go short. Maintain the short until the daily closing price rises at least 5 percent over the low, at which time cover and buy.)

You can see that the filter is indeed related to trend analysis or the measurement of price moves. Professor Alexander reported on tests of filters from one to 50 percent ("Price Movements in Speculative Markets: Trends or Random Walks") and buying and holding consistently beat the filter.

Hence the random-walk people would say to the premise that a stock in a trend will *more likely than not* follow the trend, that that is nonsense, the chances of the stock following the trend are fifty-fifty.

You could say the same thing about flipping nickels. If you flip a nickel five times in a row and it comes up heads, what are the chances of its coming up heads the sixth time? If you flip a nickel a hundred times in a row and it comes up heads a hundred times, what are the chances of heads coming up the 101st time? Fifty-fifty either way.

"If the random-walk model is a valid description of reality," says Professor Fama, "the work of the chartist, like that of the astrologer, is of no real value."

The random-walk fellows seem particularly out to get the Chartists. As I said, one random-walk professor choked on his dessert at my house at the very suggestion that charts could be taken seriously. (We now have a rule at my house that all random-walk professors must finish their desserts before the subject of charts is brought up.) Another random-walk professor of my acquaintance had his graduate students flip nickels, assigning a plus to heads and a minus to tails, and they filled an x in the chart up for heads and down for tails, and sure enough, it made a beautiful point-and-figure chart, complete with line formations, heads and shoulders, reversals, double tops, and the whole thing.

But the random-walk fellows are not stopping with the Chartists. They are also going to bring the security analysts up on their toes. And that reasoning runs this way:

There are discrepancies between the actual price and the true intrinsic value of a stock. The analyst gathers all his information, applies his training and insight, and plumps for a purchase or sale accordingly. His action helps to close the gap between the price and the intrinsic value. The better the analysts are, the more sophisticated analysts there are, the more they become self-neutralizing, i.e., the more "efficient" the market becomes. An "efficient" market closely conforms to the random-walk model, in which the price reflects the true discount of intrinsic value.

Now obviously an analyst who is one step ahead is going to beat the average of analysts in an efficient market, but of course all analysts think they are better than average. An analyst's insights must be consistently better than a randomly chosen portfolio of the same general flavor, because every analyst has a 50 percent chance of doing better than a random selection, even if he is a complete idiot or uses darts and a dartboard instead of a slide rule.

It is a cold, austere world, the world of the random walk, and a negative one. The random walkers do believe in the intrinsic value of a stock, but they have not much help for us on that because a stock only sells for its intrinsic value—whatever that is—whenever the market rushes past it either optimistically or pessimistically, so that intrinsic value is right like a stopped clock is right twice a day.

There are, as we know, *sixteen thousand* security analysts, and there are certainly thousands of Chartists. The Chartists will not believe in the random walk, because that would make what they were doing meaningless, and no one wants to feel that a dartboard selection will do as well as one with effort. As for the analysts, they will feel the random walk is irrelevant because their insights and information put them ahead. None of them will really follow the mathematical proofs of randomness. If they did, and believed them, they might take a salary cut and switch to teaching at a business school, and no exodus has yet been spotted.

In support of the skeptics we can only look again at the premise, that the market is reasonably "efficient," that it is a market where numbers of rational, profit-maximizing investors are competing. It may just be that investors— even cold, austere, professional money managers—are not rational, or are not 100 percent rational. It may be that they would rather have *some* profit and a feeling of company than a maximum profit and a feeling of anxiety. The investor in the random-walk model is suspiciously *Homo economicus,* and we did wander among some thought that *Homo* is not *economicus.* "There is nothing so disastrous," said Lord Keynes, "as a rational investment policy in an irrational world."

No one has yet learned how to put emotions into serial correlation coefficients and analyses of runs. It is absolutely true that statistically the price of a stock has no relation tomorrow to what it was yesterday. But people— the Crowd—do have a memory that extends from day to day. You do notice one thing about the random-walk world and the chart world: There are no people in them. The prices are there, the coefficients are there, the past is there (or not there, depending on whether you are charting or random walking). Bishop Berkeley's tree has fallen in the forest, and it has made an awesome noise even though no one has heard it fall.

If the market is truly a Game, it would be possible to have the Game without any intrinsic values at all. If part of the Game is that Bishop Berkeley's tree is down when everyone decides it is down, then there need not even be a tree. If the printers will print stock certificates, the New York Stock Exchange will stay open, and the banks will print out occasional dividends, we can have the whole Game even though all the steel plants and warehouses and railroads have mysteriously disappeared, as long as no one knows they have disappeared.

The random-walk people are taking to their computers for more complex proof of their thesis, and they are going to have a big influence. The Technicians are also taking to their computers, and they are running samples and filters and runs not only of price changes but of advances and declines, moving averages, upticks and downticks, and any other serial relationship they can think of. People program computers; the computers do not reason by themselves. So the same computers will come up with varying proofs. The first challenge in mathematical language to the random walkers was in Robert Levy's *Relative Strength Concept;* an answer, in the same language, is probably simmering somewhere even now.

The influence of the random walkers must by definition be good because it will make everyone test results and performance instead of accepting myth and generalities. Meanwhile—not that it means anything—there are few rich random walkers, and few rich Chartists. But there are some quite successful investors around who have no particular system. Perhaps they are the lucky holders of serial runs, perhaps they are more rational or have better access to information, and perhaps—something not taken into account in the austere statistical worlds—they are better students of psychology.

Random walkers do not unanimously insist that the market is a random walk. It is not a random walk, some of them admit, only because the market strays from the "perfect" or the "efficient"; in short, there are people in it. "My model," says Professor Cootner, "is perfectly compatible with much of what I interpret Wall Street chart reading to be all about. Like the Indian folk doctors who discovered tranquilizers, the Wall Street witch doctors, without benefit of the scientific method, have produced something with their magic, even if they can't tell you what it is or how it works." Professor Alexander concludes a paper with this statement: "In speculative markets price changes appear to follow a random walk over *time,* but a move, once initiated, tends to persist."

You could make a chart out of a move tending to persist. ("The statisticians' findings of a random walk over the time dimension is quite consistent with nonrandom trends in the move dimension," says Professor Alexander.)

To be honest, you must apply the biases recited in the Confessions of Bias in this book to both charts and the random walk. Charts we have only glimpsed, and technical work can cover factors other than price changes (volume, advances and declines, and so on), which charts demonstrate most readily. The bias confessed in the love for those happily compounding earnings comes under the old Fundamentalist concept called The Discounted Present Value of Future Earnings, only one step removed from classic Fundamentalism, The Present Value of Future Dividends. Admittedly, there is the idea of Intrinsic Value woven into these accelerating earnings, but it can all be played as a Game even if there is Intrinsic Value there. And if the market is a Game, then the statisticians' destruction of charting may not be as important as it sounds. Enough Chartists acting together become a market force themselves. Perhaps the Chartists simply belong to the irrational, as yet unmeasured, *Australopithecus* side of the market.

There is still one other bias extant toward the academics, which should be recorded, and that is the lecture in the language which the listener does not speak, i.e., quadratic equations. "There is a special paradox in the relationship between mathematics and investment attitudes on common stocks," wrote Benjamin Graham, the dean of all security analysts, in *The Intelligent Investor:*

> Mathematics is ordinarily considered as producing precise and dependable results; but in the stock market the more elaborate and abstruse the mathematics the

more uncertain and speculative are the conclusions we draw therefrom. In 44 years of Wall Street experience and study I have never seen dependable calculations made about common stock values, or related investment policies, that went beyond simple arithmetic or the most elementary algebra. Whenever calculus is brought in, or higher algebra, you could take it as a warning signal that the operator was trying to substitute theory for experience.

As you would expect from my own confession of bias, I find it hard not to agree with the dean of analysts. I suspect that even if the random walkers announced a perfect mathematic proof of randomness, I would go on believing that in the long run future earnings influence present value, and that in the short run the dominant factor is the elusive *Australopithecus*, the temper of the crowd.

CAN INTUITION BE PROGRAMED?

In 1881 G. W. Carleton & Company published *How to Win in Wall Street* by a Successful Operator. The Successful Operator's adventures in the Erie and in streetcar companies need not concern us. There is the ring of authenticity about Successful Operator's story, but Successful as he was, Operator was far outdone by the great trader Keane. After he spent some time watching the great Keane in his brilliant maneuvers, Successful Operator approached Keane and asked if he had any rules about buying or selling. "Sir," said the great Keane, "I do not. I buy or sell much as a woman would, by intuition."

Intuition is still with us, even though it cannot be programed into a computer. Almost everything else can be programed, and my friend Albert the *chartmeister* is one of the leading computer handlers. Albert had never heard of a random walk until I told him about it, so you see a computer can be used on both sides.

Albert called me one day, excited as a nine-year-old boy who has just been given a 320 cc Black Madonna Beauty Queen cycle, just like the Hell's Angels ride. "Come and see the new computer," he said.

Albert is what the downtown folks call a Technician. Technicians believe the only thing you have to know about the market is supply and demand; never mind earnings, dividends, business outlook—that is all for the Fundamentalists. Supply and demand show up in price and volume and other statistics which the Technicians marshal onto pieces of paper, the charts. Just as the natural enemy of the baboon is the leopard, the Technicians have a natural enemy—not the Fundamentalists, who can always be tolerated, but the Anti-Technicians, the random walkers we have just met. But as you know, no random-walk theoretician has managed to write a complete paper in English yet, and most Wall Streeters cannot read those little Greek symbols lying on their sides inside the square-root symbols.

Anyway, Albert was so excited that I zipped over to see the new computer. Albert works for an Institution, a large fund of hungry money. When Albert first went to work there, he sat in a little cubbyhole drawing his charts and nobody paid much attention. I knew the Institution was paying more attention to Albert when they gave him a whole room. The Policy People who make the dignified noises at the top of the Institution still pay little attention to Albert, but now Albert's War Room, as it is called, is becoming a popular place for the salesmen and the analysts to drop in with their mid-morning coffee.

I have been to Albert's War Room before, and it always reminds me of a battalion headquarters. There are charts all over the walls, and there are charts on stands in the middle of the room. You expect a light colonel to come out with a pointer and say, "Gentlemen, Intelligence says Charlie is *here* [tap tap] in Zone E, so we will mount a helicopter assault *here* [tap tap], and cut him off before he gets to the Laotian border. Ginsberg, O'Reilly, and Alberghetti will take their companies *here* . . ." and so on.

Usually when I want to find out what the Technicians think of the market I go over and Albert walks me through the whole market. "Here we see," he says, as we walk, "that the odd-lotters are still selling. Good. And here we see they are still selling short. Good. Now, on the south wall, the two-hundred-day and twenty-one-day moving averages, we see line A is still above line B. Good. Now"—and we stroll along, like art collectors in a gallery, walking by the portrait of the advance-decline ratios, and the portrait of Lowry's differentials, and all the other portraits in Albert's gallery.

Albert is one man I know who is really happy in his work. I think when he was a small boy he classified and half memorized all the batting averages in both major leagues, and then rated them against errors and putouts and what have you. When he got out of business school—not *The* Business School, which is Harvard—he was working as an accountant, not chartered yet, at a ball-bearing factory. A vice-president of the ball-bearing company was playing the commodity market and kept charts, and pretty soon Albert was keeping the commodity charts. The vice-president did so well that he got Albert off to one side in the plant and Albert studied charting on his own. For a year he read everything that had been published and he experimented with every kind of chart. Charting is still a kind of eighteenth-century science, all empirical, and it isn't really taught. It is learned by apprenticeship and trial and error. Albert was the first man at the plant in the morning and the last to leave at night, and he was happy, and the vice-president was happy, and the commodity broker was happy.

Meanwhile, the ball-bearing sales were going to hell, as you would expect when the vice-president is worrying about May Wheat and October Mercury; but by the time they booted the vice-president—and Albert in the process —Albert had a pretty good grip on his charts. The vice-president had made so much money that he bought a thousand-acre lime grove in Florida. He shook Albert's hand warmly and wished him well, and Albert went out to look for a job as a Chartist, having found his life's work.

Anyway, Albert's Institution is still not really among the most technically oriented, because the top-level people aren't. But there is an Underground of younger people, analysts and what have you, and Albert's reputation as a *chartmeister* is such that they always check in with him. And, of course, Albert is now plotting his new computer statistics on charts.

There were two analysts in with him when I arrived. One was looking at a chart with Albert and the other one was pacing back and forth in front of Lowry's differential, waiting his turn.

"I have just been to see this company," says the analyst, "and the profit margins are expanding, sales will be up twenty percent. . . ."

Albert holds up his hand. "Don't tell me these things," he says. "I don't want to know them." Albert stares intently at the chart, the analyst waiting with bated breath for the wizard to make something out of the eye of newt and toe of frog.

"Is that a head and shoulders?" asks the analyst, nervously pointing to a formation on the chart. Albert looks at him contemptuously. Albert is very nice and very modest, but it annoys him when laymen attempt to breathe life into a chart. It isn't the chart, it's the man who reads the chart, Albert says, and I have to believe it, since if you take two Chartists and show them the same chart they will give-you opposite opinions half the time.

"It's got another leg to go," Albert says finally, "maybe seventeen, eighteen points."

"But when the earnings come out . . ." protests the analyst.

"Discounted," says Albert, and the next analyst is stepping up. This analyst has found a real mid-sixties company called Alphanumeric with a new printing device. Profits are some way away but the stock has gone from 7 to 200. Consequently the Alphanumeric chart is one inch long at the bottom and then goes straight up for three feet. In fact, they have had to glue two more pieces of chart paper together to let it go straight up for three feet. The analyst is very optimistic but he wants to know the risks. He points to a little area around 170 on the chart and wants to know if Albert thinks buying will come in there if the stock goes down.

"No," Albert says. Albert does not waste words.

"Where would you say there is solid support?" asks the analyst.

Albert points to the one-inch line at the bottom. "I'd say at seven, but you never can tell," he says, because he is not really taking the Alphanumeric seriously. It is way out there in the blue, on its own, and practically unchartable. Now visiting hours are over and the patients leave, and I have the *chartmeister* to myself.

"Look," Albert says. On a table in the middle of the War Room is something that looks like a television set. This is the display device. In front of the display device are keys, like typewriter or calculator keys.

I can't see what all the fuss is about. Albert and computers are not strangers to each other; he has been using one in a time-sharing program before, and I have sat with him while he circles in red little numbers on the green-and-white computer print-out sheet.

"On line, real time," Albert says. On line is just what it sounds like, the information is all there on the same system. Real time is practically instantaneous. This means the system works like one of those airline computers which scans all the seats on all the planes and tells you if there is a seat on flight number 1 on Christmas Eve. Maybe the analogy is not right, and I think even Albert was wrong, and in order for this computer to know what is going on, the trade actually has to happen and be printed and recorded. Anyway, let's just say this is a smart young computer; Albert worked on the program himself. Albert seats himself at the keyboard like Van Cliburn or Glenn Gould —more like Glenn Gould, wrists at the ready, shirt cuffs out.

"Momentum by groups!" Albert cries, and goes tappety-tappety-tap. The display device lights up.

1 AIRLINES
2 ELECTRONICS
3 AEROSPACE

says the computer. This is what is moving. Motion is what the random-walk people deny.

"Which airlines?" I ask. Albert goes tappety-tappety-tap.

TRUNKLINES

says the smart computer.

"Thanks a lot," I say. "I could have figured that myself."

"Airlines, trunklines, weighted," Albert says, tappety-tappety-tap.

```
1  E A L
2  T W A
3  N W A
```

The computer says Eastern is moving well.

"Now watch," Albert says. "Eastern relative to the group. Eastern relative to the market."

```
     E A L
1 :4  17 :5  4 x 1 x 3
```

"It just lost me," I say. "What are those other numbers?"

"That's my own system," Albert says. "These are parameters. Don't worry about it."

Just my luck. I don't know anything about computers, and when I am around them all they say is stupid things like 01001100100101101.

"Now here is Eastern, relative to previous days and weeks, weighted on a current basis," Albert says, and tappety-tappety-tap, the screen lights up with

```
   E A L
  99 :97
3 x 4 x 1
```

"More buyers than sellers at the moment," Albert says.

I lean over and press the symbol of another airline, and then the same keys Albert has pressed.

E R R O R

"This machine is a one-man dog," I said. "It's no use unless you personally are sitting at it. It knows its master's hands."

Albert grins. We sit there for another quarter of an hour, playing tappety-tappety-tap. You can see the final fulfillment of a boyhood dream, all the batting averages of all the players, ranked by height of player, weight of player, number of years in the majors, whether he does better against right- or left-handed pitchers, whether he does better to right or left field, on cloudy days or on clear days.

"I can see that this gizmo processes a great deal of information," I say. "But on any given day, the whole thing could turn around."

"The whole thing could," Albert says, "but the mix of odds would show up."

"Great," say I. "Now all you have to tell me is why, with all the sophisticated tools, the Chartists were bullish in July and bearish in September at the bottom."

"Somebody has to make the first move," Albert says. "Not us."

"The new toy is pretty, but it doesn't do anything you weren't really already doing," I say. "I grant you, you can scan more stocks faster. You can rank everything that happened up to an hour ago. But it's the same game: What Is Everybody Else Doing?"

Albert grins. "That's the name of the game," he says. He jerks his thumb skyward. "*They* are impressed," he says. *They* are the people up on the floor where everybody has carpeting, where the policies are made.

Now suddenly I see what the whole game is about. To anyone who has grown up under the Stern Calvinist Dictum of the Prudent Man, securities are Quality or Not, and Quality means in business a long time, and generally big. To these people, the Chartist was an odd little fellow with carbon on his fingers, sitting on a three-legged stool at a drawing board. But now he is a Technician with a Computer, and here is mystery indeed, for who will thumb his nose at the Computer? Does it not calculate the payroll ever so fast? So I see why Albert is so happy. It isn't just a bright new toy, although there is a lot of fun in that, especially when you make a simulated stock market and play with the model. What makes Albert happy is a new status. *The computer is going to sanctify charting.* The Chartists are on their way.

Of course, we have had Chartists for years, and there are very few rich Chartists, so there is no need to be terrified. In the end, a pair of human eyes has to read the numbers, and the brain behind them will either be smart or not, and that spectrum will be no different. Meanwhile, let us be happy for Albert.

You do see the possibilities. All we have to do to make money in the market is to find out what the Computer-sanctified Charts would like to do. There is already a crude version of this afoot, not so different from some of the beautiful pictures painted on the tape in the 1920s, when there were some very artistic tape-painters around.

The crude version I will call Fourth and One, Let's Go for It. This means the stock is on its own forty-five-yard line, fourth and one to go, and it has been moving well. If it crosses the Upside Breakout line on the charts, it gets a first and ten. Let us say, for laughs, that we have Brunswick at 12.

We are sitting at our computer, and all the Theys are sitting at theirs. The name of the game is: What Is Everybody Else Doing? The computer has shortened the time span and improved communication. The telephone need not be used at all. Everyone can see immediately that if Brunswick crosses 12½, Upside Breakout on all the published charts, it gets a first and ten.

You can almost hear the crowd begin to roar. There is a feeling in the air, Fourth and One, Let's Go for It. The ball is snapped: 12, 12⅛, 12¼, 12½, 12⅝! First and ten! No need even to bring out the measuring chains. No need to worry about a sudden retreat back to 7. The old Breakout line is now a defense line, a little consolidation, a quiet off-tackle play, and we are ready for the Bomb, the crowd-winning touchdown pass.

I can see where this is all going to lead. Somebody will not be content with a good thing. Here we are with a very comfortable maxim, *a stock is going up as long as it's going up,* a very serene way to be in the market. And since we are all watching each other, it is very comfy. This is called a Trend. And if we all stay with the Trend, then we have only to worry about how we will all get out when the Trend reverses, but maybe we can get the public enlisted for that.

But one night a maintenance man is going to walk into Albert's office. I visualize him wearing a cap like Railroad Bill, and carrying an oil can with a long spout. In his pockets are screwdrivers and little wrenches and what have you, so nobody questions him if they run across him. They assume he is there to stop the fluorescent light from flickering in the hallway. Railroad Bill looks around, and steps quickly into Albert's War Room.

Aha, you are ahead of me: You know he is not Railroad Bill at all. Anyway, he goes up to the computer. A few quick turns of a screwdriver and some panels come out. From an inside pocket appear some odd swatches of tape. Railroad Bill works swiftly as a safe-cracker. A few more taps, the pocket flashlight goes off. Footsteps in the hallway. Railroad Bill steals out, then strokes his chin, looking at the flickering light.

The next morning Albert comes to work. He confers with an analyst; they hold up a chart, like surgeons looking at an x-ray. Then Albert sits down to play, the cuffs shoot out, the first crashing chords of the cadenza echo forth.

"Greatest momentum of all stocks," Albert asks this current-day Jeep. (Everyone has forgotten that before the Jeep was a car it was a little animal that could only tell the truth.) And the latter-day Jeep lights up and says:

MURGATROYD BONBON

"Murgatroyd Bonbon?" questions Albert. "Never heard of it."

The analysts race for their manuals. There it is, a tiny little company that would interest no one.

"Oh, well," Albert will say. "A fluke." Then Albert will ask for the leader in percentage strength.

MURGATROYD BONBON

The crowd around Albert is growing. "Ask it the resistance level," cry the voices. "Ask it how far it can go." The crowd senses history, fortune in the making.

Tappety-tappety-tap, goes Albert, asking what stock of all stocks is going to go up most.

MURGATROYD BONBON

"I'd say we have to buy a little, just on the technical action," one wise man will say. And a progressive, forward-looking fund manager will take a little plunge, just enough to get his toes wet.

Meanwhile, in a small furnished room on the other side of town, Railroad Bill will be waiting for nightfall, polishing his tools, checking his list.

And that night, and that night . . .

12. COMPUTERS AND COMPUTEERS

You may think I am putting you on about Albert and his computer, and about Railroad Bill. The strange thing is, the Railroad Bill sort of thing is actually happening. Railroad Bill is, of course, not Railroad Bill at all; he is a computer. In order for you to see how Railroad Bill the Computer works, let us take a sidelong glance at the whole computer phenomenon.

When computers first came in, a lot of people on Wall Street and in investment management palaces signed up for them. Computers were new, scientific, and the wave of the future. The reason everybody signed up for a computer was that everybody else was signing up for a computer. Gustave Le Bon in the Electric Age. The first thing everybody did with their computers was to give the machine the straight-line back-room stuff to do, i.e., the payroll, figuring out margin accounts, and so on. This was on the noninvestment side.

The computers got bigger and faster and pretty soon the computer could do this stuff and still take the afternoon off for a ball game. So the Computer People were hired. The Computer People soon affected the whole scene. "Facts" went out; "bits" came in. A bit is one little zot of information and a computer can not only remember millions of bits, it can remember where each bit is, rearrange the bits in any specified order, add them, subtract them, divide them, play with ratios of them—and still take the afternoon off for the ball game. (All this spare computer time is expensive, which gives rise to "time-sharing," in which the same computer can be used by different people for different purposes.) Security analysts used to walk around with a slide rule poking from one pocket. Now using a slide rule is like starting a fire with a flint, so the analysts have taken to using computer words like "input."

The next step for the computers was called *screening.* Screening is just what it sounds like; you just saw Albert do a little bit of it. Having ingested all these bits, the computer could be called upon to arrange them in any order it was asked. When interrogative systems, like Albert's, arrived, the analyst could simply sit down and say, "Computer, give me the fifty lowest price–earnings ratios of any stocks," and the computer would print out, carefully ranked, the price–earnings ratios, or it would display them on its television-like display screen. Then the analyst could say, "Computer, of the stocks you have given me, which ten have the greatest return on invested capital?" And the computer could give them. Then the analyst could play with these ad infinitum. He could say, "Computer, adjust the current price–earnings ratios of these ten stocks to moving three-year averages of their earnings," and the computer would do that.

All of the computer's calculations were what good analysts were doing anyway, but no analyst could take the time to perform thousands of calculations. What the computer did was to screen millions of bits of information and create different patterns from them, something no analyst would have the time, physically, to do.

So today anybody can subscribe to a service that will give profiles of a stock over ten years, rank companies within industries by various characteristics, or rank the industries themselves against other industries.

Meanwhile the analysts and programmers have gone on to other adventures. One of these is *projection,* which is also just what it sounds like. A model of an industry is created, and then the profits of the industry are tried out against differing sets of circumstances. This is the adaptation of input-output analysis. The computer can even adjust bits for seasonal variations.

Finally, the analyst can just sit there playing with the toy, trying moving averages, exponential smoothing, and all kinds of different sets of series and ratios, just to see if any one of them will fit a hypothesis he has thought up. (This is why Wall Street bookstores can rack up big sales of books with titles like *Smoothing, Forecasting and Pre-*

diction of Discrete Time Series.) The analyst may just try for a "feel" of the statistics, or he may try correlating various measures of price–earnings ratio, say, with the growth rates of sales and earnings and the deviations from these sales and earnings, isolating through this multiple-regression analysis—for that is what they call it—the variables that *seem* to affect the price–earnings ratio. Again, this is what analysts have always done, but they have done it by sight, feel, and slide rule, and hence only approximately and not for very many stocks. Not only can the computer print out all these things, but if it is really equipped it can change this linear information to graphics and draw you a chart.

(If you get a chance sometime, try playing with a computer equipped for graphics. You can take your light pencil (like a pocket flashlight), draw a circle in light on the screen, and the computer will correct it to a perfect circle. This is old stuff to aerospace engineers, but for amateurs it is the most fun since Mother put you in the attic with a tracing board that rainy afternoon.)

All of this kind of computer work deals with Fundamentals and factors related to Fundamentals: the business, sales, profits, profit margins, and so on. The real fun comes when the computer is used for Technical Analysis, i.e., what is everybody else doing? You saw a bit of this when Albert asked the computer to rank the momentum of stocks—to come up with the stocks that had just moved a greater percentage in price than all the other stocks.

I have a friend called Irwin the Professor at one of our nation's leading universities who must rank as one of the top architects of computer-based technical analysis. Irwin is the professor of technology, mid-sixties style *par excellence,* which is to say that he is busy doing sixteen other things besides teaching the youth of the nation, and his university salary is only about a third of his earnings. Two thirds comes from consulting and various commercial ventures Irwin gets into, and of course he has all these bodies chained to the oars, the graduate students who are writing theses for him. I went by to see Irwin not so long ago. When you go by to see Irwin you do not have to come within three miles of the university. Irwin has a snazzy set of offices in a nearby office building, complete with Jens

Risom furniture and a receptionist. This is where three of his companies are based. I can't tell you the names of the companies, but they all have words in them like "computer," "decision," "application," "technology," and so on. Vice-presidents at big companies who are faced with some decision hire Irwin at a fat fee. Irwin and his computer models then tell the vice-president, after some complicated model building and computer work, that the new licorice toothpaste will not work because it is black, Americans do not want to have black teeth, and the people who do want black teeth are already chewing betel nuts and comprise only 4.6623 percent of the potential toothpaste market.

Irwin's computer system was bankrolled by a couple of interested institutions and it is on line, real time, and all that. It is hooked up to the tickers of the New York and American stock exchanges, and it doesn't even have to read the tapes optically; it picks up the original electrical impulse which drives the stock tickers and whisks it right into the memory. To Irwin's computer, screening, projecting, and multiple-regression analysis are like Fish in the Ocean to a champion bridge player. I wanted to know how Irwin's computer worked on the Technical side of the market.

"The first thing it does is to monitor every stock transaction, the price, the volume, and the percentage move," Irwin said. "We have a Behavior Pattern for every stock. When a stock is behaving out of its pattern, the monitor flashes on. It says, 'Hey, look at this.' "

(Like many computer people, Irwin tends to think of his computer as a large, faithful talking dog, and the objects to be scanned as sheep which are always getting out of line.)

Irwin pressed a couple of keys, but the large display screen on his table stayed dark.

"Nothing on the air at the moment," Irwin said. "Let's play for a while."

We were happy playing some multiple-regression analysis game—I think it was whether if you bought every morning before eleven and sold every afternoon before two-thirty you could make money by outflanking the specialist—when Irwin's computer flashed a monitor signal.

MONITOR

it said. We held our breath.

DIGITAL DATAWHACK
EXCEEDED LIMIT
38-½   2:14   500
58/56   54/52   12/12/12   47/47   42/56

"Digital Datawhack is out of its pattern on the upside," Irwin said. "This happened sixty seconds ago, at two-fourteen, on five hundred shares."

"What's all the rest of that stuff?" I wanted to know.

"Parameters," Irwin said. "Don't worry about it. Let's see the trades in Digital Datawhack today."

DIGITAL	DATAWHACK,	said Irwin's computer.
200	10:12	36-¾
100	10:15	36-⅝
600	10:27	37
200	11:38	36-¾
500	1:51	37-¼
1100	1:59	37-¾
3000	2:05	38
1000	2:07	38-¼
500	2:14	38-½

"That's every trade today in Datawhack and what time it happened and on what volume," Irwin said.

"This sounds to me just like charting," I said. "Upside breakout and all that."

"Most of the patterns Chartists use are sheer myth," Irwin said. "The principle of monitoring the stock movement is the same, except of course the computer can monitor thousands of stocks simultaneously and our patterns are statistically tested."

Then Irwin sat bolt upright. The display screen was still flashing away cheerily about Digital Datawhack.

"Hey!" Irwin said. "There's another computer on the air! There's another computer on the air!"

As if sirens had gone off and a loudspeaker had barked

"Battle Stations!" two graduate students rushed in from the next room. Irwin did not actually mean "on the air" like a broadcast, but discernible as if it were.

DIGITAL DATAWHACK
54/52   52/52/52   61/65   99/99/99

said Irwin's computer.

One of the graduate students was busy toting in bulky computer print-outs from the library shelves.

"I bet it's that IBM 360/50 in Minneapolis that bought those blocks of Boeing the other day," said the graduate student.

"That's unscientific speculation," Irwin said. "Call up the big computer."

"The big computer?" I said.

"Our computer can't store everything," Irwin said. "When it gets a problem it can't handle, it calls up an IBM 7094 we share. We gave it an open phone line to the 7094. The 7094 has all the patterns there are."

"You mean computers are buying and selling?" I asked.

"Most buying and selling is still done by individuals and institutions," Irwin said, "just as it was in the old days." (The old days to Irwin are 1962 or so, when computers were still doing only clerical chores.)

"But," Irwin went on, "there are a couple of sophisticated funds that have computers like ours on the air. Then it really gets to be fun. Our computer scans the pattern of the other computer on the air, what its buying and selling programs seem to be. Once we get its pattern, we can have all kinds of fun. We can chase the stock away from it. Or even better, we can determine where the other computer wants to buy. Let's say this computer is just getting its feet wet at thirty-eight and a half on Datawhack, but it will really open up and buy at forty-two. Maybe we can buy enough at forty and forty-one to bump the other computer into its major buy pattern at forty-two, and its buying will run Datawhack right up to forty-six. Then we've got a hell of a trade."

"Just like Fourth and One, let's go for it, on the charts," I said.

"Same principle," Irwin said, "only the game will be over by the time the Chartists get around to making their little marks. The Chartist has to sit down with his quill pen and.let the ink dry and stare at it for a while, and besides, the Chartist's pattern is probably wrong. It's not scientific."

"Is the other computer looking for your computer?" I asked.

"It might be," Irwin said. "We haven't really gotten into defensive strategy yet, because there aren't enough computers on the air. But there will be soon. Unfortunately, not everybody believes in computers yet. Even our own subscribers drag their heels a lot of the time. They insist on following their own judgments, their intuitions, all their old ideas from the archaic pre-computer days. That means our computer doesn't have a fair chance, because it's not used consistently."

"But your computer does buy and sell," I said.

"Unfortunately, a *person* still has to give the order," Irwin said, "because the stock exchange won't accept orders from a computer, although the computer could certainly give the order directly. But the answer is, yes, our computer is running one portfolio."

"How is it doing?" I asked.

"When we first put the computer on the air, we asked it what it wanted to buy and we couldn't wait to see what it reached for. It said, 'Treasury bills. Cash.' We couldn't get it to buy anything. So we checked out the program again, and while we were checking out the program, the market went down. Then we asked it again. The computer insisted on staying in cash. The market went down some more. We begged it to buy something. 'There must be *one* stock somewhere that's a buy,' we said. You see, even computer people are victims of these old atavistic instincts from the pre-computer days. The computer just folded its arms. It wouldn't buy anything. Then, just when we were worried that it never would buy anything, right at the bottom it stepped in and started buying. The market started going up, and the computer kept on buying. Pretty soon the computer was fully invested and the market was still going up."

"What did it do then?" I asked.

"The market was still going up," Irwin said, "and then one day it came *and asked us for margin.* It wanted to keep buying. So we gave it some margin. After the market went up some more it sold out a bit and came back to being fully invested. Right now it's got buying power."

"Irwin," I said, "tell the truth now. If all these computers go on the air, as you say, does an individual investor have any chance?"

"There's always luck," Irwin said. "Luck—which is to say a serial run of random numbers—can happen any time. And the computer is out for really aggressive performance. An individual with a longer time horizon might be able to do passably. But on the whole, and over any given period of time, the computer will always win. It has to. The investing world will be divided feudally into fiefdoms, with the peasant investors all grouped around various computer castles."

I was a little disturbed by some of the implications of the future as seen by Irwin the Professor, so I dropped by one of the investing institutions, not Irwin's, which I knew had a computer-picked robot portfolio, and talked to an analyst I knew.

"All the robot portfolios do well at first," the analyst said. "Then they begin to go a little bit off, as soon as people find out how they work."

"Why do they go off? I would think they would get better."

"Well, here we run a portfolio picked by the analysts against the robot portfolio, and of course the analysts get to use the computer for Fundamentals, screening and so on."

"But if the computer uses screening too, why doesn't it beat you?"

"Because the computer has to be updated all the time with fresh analysts' opinions, new information, and so on."

"So?"

"Well, we have twenty-one analysts working here, and the analysts supply the computer with fresh information. And every one of those twenty-one analysts knows that if that robot portfolio wins consistently, there will be twenty-one analysts out on the sidewalk."

"You mean the analysts *are subtly sabotaging the computer,* just a little bit at a time?"

"You said it, not me. Sabotage is too strong a word. Just believe me, the robot is going to lose. Not by much. But when the final score is tallied, flesh and blood is going to beat that damn monster."

13. BUT WHAT DO THE NUMBERS MEAN?

You can see that there are a lot of numbers floating around Wall Street, that the Game is played with numbers, and that with computers more people can play with more numbers in more combinations than anyone would have dreamed possible in the old, archaic pre-computer days BC in 1960. But what are the base numbers? They are the figures reported by the subject companies as sales and earnings, and earnings, in anybody's systems, are one of the most important factors.

But what are earnings?

It really ought to be easy. You pick up the paper, and Zilch Consolidated says its net profit for the year just ended was $1 million or $1 a share. When Zilch Consolidated puts out its annual report, the report will say the company earned $1 million or $1 a share. The report will be signed by an accounting firm, which says that it has examined the records of Zilch and "in our opinion, the accompanying balance sheet and statement of income and retained earnings present fairly the financial position of Zilch. Our examination of these statements was made in accordance with generally accepted accounting principles."

The last four words are the key. The translation of "generally accepted accounting principles" is "Zilch could have earned anywhere from fifty cents a share to $1.25 a share. If you will look at our notes 1 through 16 in the back, you will see that Zilch's earnings can be played like a guitar, depending on what we count or don't count. We picked $1. That is consistent with what other accountants are doing this year. We'll let next year take care of itself."

Numbers imply precision, so it is a bit hard to get used to the idea that a company's net profit could vary by 100 percent depending on which bunch of accountants you call in, especially when the market is going to take that earnings number and create trends, growth rates, and little flashing lights in computers from it. And all this without any kind of skulduggery you could get sent to jail for.

How can this be?

Let's say you are an airline, and you buy a brand-new, freshly painted Boeing 727. Let's say the airplane costs you $5 million. At some point in the future the airplane is going to be worth 0, because its useful life will be over. So you must charge your income each year with a fraction of the cost of your airplane. What is the life of your airplane? You say the useful life of the airplane is ten years, so on a straight-line basis you will charge your income $500,000, or 10 percent of the cost, this year. If your net income from ferrying passengers and cargo is $1 million, it will drop by half when you apply this depreciation charge. Obviously the year you buy the airplane your earnings are going to look worse than they are next year, when you have the full use of the airplane and it is shuttling back and forth all the time. Your profits will certainly look better if you are still running that airplane in eleven years, because that year there will be no charge at all for depreciation; it will have been written off.

But that is only the beginning of the complications. Right next door at the airport is another airline. It has also bought a brand-new, freshly painted Boeing 727. So you and your competitor can be compared side by side when you both report your earnings on the same day. Right?

Hardly. The airline next door says it can run an airplane twelve years. So it is depreciating its airplane over twelve years, and its depreciation charge this year is $\frac{1}{12}$, not $\frac{1}{10}$, so it has only penalized its earnings $416,666 instead of $500,000, and for this year on that basis it has made more money than you have.

Don't the accountants make everybody charge the same thing for the same airplane? No, they don't. It just makes another little bit of work for the security analysts, who have to adjust the varying depreciation rates to constants. Accountants are not some kind of super-authority, they are professionals employed by clients. If you say the life of your airplane is twelve years, you must know your busi-

ness; the life is twelve years. Delta Airlines depreciates a
727 in ten years; United in sixteen.

The airplane example is, of course, a very simple one.
But what about two second-generation computers, say a
Honeywell H200 and something in the IBM 1400 series?
Do they have the same life? They may, as far as usage is
concerned, but if you are going to sell or trade up it may
be easier on the IBM. Then there is an investment credit
available on new equipment, a tax assist passed to encourage capital expenditures. Is the investment credit "flowed
through," as the jargon says, right to the earnings the first
year? Or is the investment credit spread through the whole
life of the equipment?

If everybody used the same depreciation method but
with different periods of use, life would be tough enough.
But equipment is not always depreciated straight-line, an
equal percentage for each year. Some companies use heavy
charges at the beginning, say 150 percent declining. Some
use a method with the charming appellation "sum-of-the-
years-digits." If you really want to go into details, call up
your accountant and ask *him* for definitions.

This is only the beginning. Look at inventories: Some
companies value their inventories last-in, first-out. Some
companies charge their research costs as they incur them,
some amortize them over several years. Some companies
amortize their unfunded pension costs; some do not amortize them at all. Some companies make provisions for the
taxes on the profits of subsidiaries as these profits are
earned; some make no provision until the subsidiary re-
mits a dividend to the parent.

When companies purchase other companies, the accounting gets even more arcane. The acquisition can be a
purchase, a pooling of interests, or a combination of the
two. Good will can be amortized or not amortized. The
base of depreciation can vary wildly.

In short, there is not a company anywhere whose income statement and profits cannot be changed, by the
management and the accountants, by counting things one
way instead of another. Not too long ago Price Waterhouse
did a study captioned with the rhetorical question, "Is Generally Accepted Accounting for Income Taxes Possibly
Misleading Investors?"

Generally—but not always—a real sleuth of an analyst who doesn't have to spend time answering his own phone, talking to customers, selling stock to pension funds, and attending meetings, can crack an income statement and balance sheet in a couple of days. This means real donkey work, digging out notes, making comparisons, finding the tunnels, and in general unpainting the carefully painted picture. But most analysts do have to answer their own phones, sell stocks, attend meetings—and still cover all the developments in their areas. So there are not many who can do the job. Even if every analyst could do this job, there are ten times as many brokers as analysts, and 200 times as many eager customers as brokers, so you can see the odds against Truth at any given instant, when your phone rings and a voice says, "Zilch is earning one dollar and selling at only twelve times earnings." On the other hand, as we have learned, Truth will not make Zilch go up, but the Crowd's general feeling about Zilch just might.

Most accountants are honorable men, trying to do a job. But they are hired by corporations, not by investors. Not only are they professionals hired by the corporations, but they are frequently further involved in company affairs as tax and management consultants.

For years, Wall Street accepted with religious faith an accountant's certification as the Good Housekeeping Seal of Approval, especially those of the great national accounting firms, Price Waterhouse, Haskins & Sells, Arthur Andersen, and so on. Then came a couple of cases in which corporations reported profits, had their reports audited and certified, only to come back several years later and say that the original certified reports were, for one reason or another, off by a very wide mark. In the famous and well-publicized instance of Yale Express, the corporation reported profits for the years it was sliding into bankruptcy. (It is now being reorganized under Chapter X of the bankruptcy laws.) The angry stockholders took to the courts, suing not only Yale Express, but Peat, Marwick, the Certified Public Accountants who had put their seal on Yale Express' reports. The air is now full of litigation, and it is not our purpose here to get into it. Suffice to say that with lawyers and the SEC in full cry, the accountants have begun to try to thread some consistencies, but there is genuine confusion among these accountants as to what earnings really are. Corporations, they say, are not all the same, and there has to be some flexibility just to reflect the differences in businesses.

The accountants have my sympathy. But not much of it. I have a lingering skepticism about reported numbers, because I have lost money accepting the reports of accountants, and there is nothing like losing money to burn in a lesson. A leading Wall Street publication says the letters CPA do not stand for Certified Public Accountant but Certified Public Assassin. I will tell you the origins of my own anti-accountant bias in a minute. It may serve you to listen well.

If the profit numbers on income statements are treated with such reverence, it was obviously only a question of time before some smart fellows would start building companies not around the logical progression of a business but around what would beef up the numbers.

Such a corporation is called a "conglomerate" or a "free-form" company, very popular when the market gets to tulip-time. A conglomerate is a company that grows by acquiring other companies, and the other companies can be in wildly different businesses. Conglomerate managers are supposed to be a new breed of brilliant wheeler-dealers, and the idea of the whole game is to take an ice-cream freezer company and merge it with a valve company and merge that with a flour mill. The valves and the flour and the ice cream never get together except on a balance sheet and an income statement, but Wall Street does look for growing earnings, and with the right accountant this whole process can make the earnings grow like crazy. Capitalism enters a new stage.

I happened to be in on the birth of a brand-new conglomerate, so you can see just how it is all done. The whole thing started with a lunch at the Colony.

I am well aware that Messrs. Batten and Durstine and Osborne did not invite outsiders that historic day at the oyster bar in Grand Central when they decided to go into advertising, and there is no record of kibitzers when Mr. Ash and Mr. Thornton were hatching the senior conglom-

erate of them all, Litton Industries, but this fellow called
Sidney phoned up and wanted me to come uptown to the
Colony for lunch.

Lunch at the Colony beats lunch at the places in the
vicinity of Wall Street because of the girls in spring Pucci
prints who swivel past your table, right up to the tables
against the east wall. There, waiting for them, are grand-
fatherly gentlemen of obvious means who hold their hands.
It gives one hope for the future. I spent this historic lunch
listening to Sidney outline the new conglomerate, but I
confess that while I was listening I was watching the prosperous grandfathers nibble the fingertips of the sweet young
things. The sweet things weren't nibbling, they were wolf-
ing down lunch like it was never going to come again, and
I even interrupted Sidney once or twice to ask what happened *after* lunch with the well-valeted seniors there, and
Sidney said not much, but not for lack of trying. Anyway, out of this lunch I did get a new ambition for my
autumnal years: I am going to sit against the east wall
of the Colony with some porcelain-skinned thing who
smells good and has a laugh like a brook, and let the young
tigers in the middle tables spend their energies planning
capers.

Before this lunch, I had only met Sidney once. Sidney
is a broker, a customer's man, at a firm that does a lot of
retail business. He wears Bernard Weatherill suits and
Countess Mara ties, and the corners of his handkerchief
are always pointed properly in his breast pocket. He is
considered a bright fellow by one and all, especially his
Uncle Harry. He has done very well with Uncle Harry's
account, Uncle Harry having made the original stake in
Wide-Stretch Flexi-Boost, or some such, a brassiere company.

Sidney has been around a lot of action and his interest
in conglomerates stems from an inability to see any kind
of opportunity pass by without reaching for it. The Colony
was not Sidney's choice but Uncle Harry's, and I have to
report that Wide-Stretch Flexi-Boost picked up the tab.
Uncle Harry also brought two eager but considerably less
prosperous associates.

I didn't quite know what Sidney was up to, but as he
began to talk it was obvious that he had his very own con-

glomerate in mind. He had seen it done a couple of times, and now why not try it himself? Sidney began warming up with the contemporary okay words like "input" and "synergy." "Input" comes from talking to the computer people and is just what it sounds like—a friend has called you with a tip. The computer calls this a "bit." "Synergy" is when the sum of the parts adds up to more than the whole, and is a word greatly favored by Harvard Business School graduates.

Uncle Harry likes Sidney, and is convinced of his abilities in the market, but it slowly dawned on him that what Sidney had in mind was using Wide-Stretch Flexi-Boost as the basis for his new free-form company. To Uncle Harry, of course, free form could be the name of a new bra.

"Sell the company? You're crazy," said Uncle Harry.

"Not sell it, not sell it," said Sidney. "Go public. Create a vehicle."

"Vehicle," snorted Uncle Harry. "Wall Street doesn't like the rag business."

"I am talking," said Sidney, "about a conglomerate, a growth company, with sophisticated management, using sophisticated financial techniques. I'm talking about a market value of one hundred million dollars."

Uncle Harry started listening, because Wide-Stretch would never make it public by itself, and this was the nephew who got him into Delta Airlines before it went up ten times.

"It's not important what our company *makes*," Sidney said. "What is important is the image, the management, and the concepts. Wall Street loves all three."

"The management in my company is me and I'm not sophisticated," said Uncle Harry. "I've done very well without it."

"Each division will run itself without interference, unless, of course, it needs help. The sophisticated management I'm talking about is on the overall corporate level, making the mergers, talking to Wall Street."

"Finagling the piece of paper," said Uncle Harry, listening well.

"I have a very bright manager already lined up, he's graduating from Wharton this June," Sidney said, "and I have a very, very sharp P.R. man ready to deliver concepts. As soon as we get the name changed and the stock public, we go after other companies. Maybe we could get somebody who used to work at Litton."

"I know a business you could buy," piped up Uncle Harry's unprosperous Number One associate. We gave him our attention. "Maybe it's not big enough," he demurred. We coaxed him. "It belongs to my sister's niece's husband," said unprosperous associate. "It's a diaper service in Queens."

Uncle Harry snorted and I thought Sidney would too, but he didn't. I could see the wheels turning.

"That's not a bad idea," he said. "I can see a new division. Demographic Research—no, no—I've got it! Population Explosion, Inc.!"

"Does the diaper service make money?" Uncle Harry wanted to know.

"There are problems—"

"Management cures problems," said Sidney. "We can juice up the accounting. He's probably depreciating the diaper trucks too fast. Population Explosion, Inc.! It's got a real ring to it. And the other part of the division will be devoted to research and products in the fantastic field of population—birth-control pills . . . who sells birth-control pills?"

"My cousin Carl sells birth-control pills," said unprosperous Number Two associate. "He's a druggist in the Bronx. Maybe he'll sell you the drugstore."

Sidney was now in a state of high excitement, but Uncle Harry wanted to know what Sidney was going to use for money. "We swap stock, we create a convertible debenture, we create preferreds," said Sidney.

All of these, of course, are perfectly respectable instruments. But Mr. Meshulam Riklis, one of the champion conglomerateers, gave a seminar recently on how to build a conglomerate, and he called these instruments "Castro pesos" and "Russian rubles," which does give one the feeling that they are not being used in quite the same old way.

"Computers," Sidney was saying. "Computers are hot. Look at Control Data, SDS, SEL, the computer programing companies. We need a computer division."

"I don't know about computers," said Uncle Harry's

Number Two unprosperous associate, "but my cousin Carl has a brother-in-law who reconditions adding machines. Sells adding machines, rents adding machines, also desk lamps, filing cabinets, anything you like. Very reasonable."

"Where is the store?" asked Uncle Harry.

"Lower Lexington Avenue," said the Number Two friend.

"Lexington!" shouted Sidney, rising from his chair. "That's great! Lexington Computer Sciences! That one can go public by itself!"

By now you have realized that in my usual manner I have changed the names and numbers of the players, and I may have even exaggerated a bit. But not much, not much. There is really no reason why Uncle Harry's bra company cannot be known as Space Age Materials. We *are* in the space age and it *does* use materials. Teledyne has a Materials Technology Group that used to be Vasco Metals, and before that Vanadium-Alloys Steel, but those are low price–earnings names these days and the object of the game is to get the market to chase the stock. That is why the annual reports of conglomerates are so slick and so beautiful with art work and P.R. men's fingerprints that Albert Skira is going to bring out a $25 coffee-table edition.

In Beverly Hills, in the colonial mansion on Little Santa Monica formerly inhabited by MCA, sits the senior conglomerate, Litton Industries, and Litton has been so successful that conglomeration is respectable and the scoffers have retired to lick their wounds. Litton has collected boats and adding machines and books and made it all seem like the most contemporary of economic philosophies. They have even invented their own form of securities so that everybody is pleased when Litton buys something. Litton also has crew-cut squads from business schools that race off to shape up the kitchen-sink company when the kitchen-sink business goes down the drain.

So I suppose there is a right way to do everything, but I was once bitten by an accounting firm. As you know, the price of the stock depends to some degree on numbers, such as the numbers describing the profits. If you are only in the sealing-wax business, there is only so much leeway about what is a profit and what isn't, short of actually fudging, which is frowned upon. But if you are busy buying and selling companies, every time they pass through your accounting firm you get the chance to try to describe artistically some of the assets as earnings, to capitalize costs that have previously been expensed, and in general to create what Wall Street is looking for, which is a neat pattern of constantly growing earnings.

If you really want to know all the accounting tricks, ask your accountant, or if he is loyal to his brethren you can call up Bart Biggs, who runs a hedge fund in Connecticut and is good at spotting tricks. I don't know Bart Biggs, but he sounded off recently in a way that makes me think he was also once bitten by an accountant. So I will not go into the pooling-of-interests technique of buying a company when a price is over the book value, and a purchase-of-assets method when the price is below book value, but let us just say that accounting is supposed to be uniform and consistent and it isn't, but the accounting associations are working on this.

Just so that you don't believe everything I say, I will tell you why I am biased. A number of years ago I was running a tiny tadpole of a fund, all tail and motion and no body, and one day a salesman walked into my office, an institutional stock salesman. This is a man sent by brokers to call on institutions—mutual funds, pension funds, insurance companies, and so on—and since we had "Fund" on our door, salesmen came calling, even though the total assets of the Tadpole Fund were about what the Prudential spends on stamps.

Now I know full well that this salesman was dressed in a nice Brooks Brothers suit with a vest, but such is the power of memory and experience that when I think of him now I see him as Professor Harold Hill, the Music Man, dressed in a striped blazer and a straw hat and white spats. If you are sitting behind the desk, you do not ask the salesman, "Well, what are you hawking today?" You say, "What is the Concept?" and you make a little teepee with your fingers to show you are not easily impressed. If you really want to make the salesman uneasy you keep

making your big toe go in a square while he talks. But
Harold Hill was undaunted.

"You say you want ideas?" he said. "You say you want
a Concept? Tell you what I'm gonna do. I'm gonna give
you a Concept/That'll put roses in your cheeks/And spring
in your step/It'll put such life in your portfolio/Your
chairman will think you're a genius/And your wife will
think she's on another honeymoon, yessirree Bob."

I sent my big toe into the square, but it was faltering.

"Now I can tell by your intelligent face that I have a
welcome reception here," said Harold Hill, "a reception
for one of the most unique ideas of this bull market, a
stock that's going to double and maybe double again, yessirree Bob, and I have the report right here in this brief-
case, and if you'll give me the order I'll tell you the name.
A tiny order, say five thousand shares, and your success
in life is assured, I guarantee it, yessirree Bob."

So I bought too much Certain-Teed Products. There was
a caper going on in shell homes, sort of "We'll give you
four walls and you finish the house on Sunday with your
cousin the plumber." And Certain-Teed, which had been
an unglamorous producer of shingles and asphalt roofing,
created a division to build shell homes which gave it a
glamour multiple in the market. The new division was
called the Institute for Essential Housing. It had a nice
ring to it, like the Institute for Advanced Study at Princeton.

"It's not just another division," said Harold Hill. "It's not
just a new product. It's a social revolution! You're buying
in on a social revolution!"

If memory serves me, you paid something like $4.95
down on one of these houses and you got E-Z terms to
pay off the rest of the $50,000, say, $25 a month. Certain-
Teed reported as income the sale price of the whole
house, even though the buyer had actually paid in cash
only $4.95, and Certain-Teed's reported earnings there-
fore went rocketing up.

Then Certain-Teed, which was selling about 60, tipped
on one wing and started spiraling down, belching black
smoke and developing the whine that indicates our boys
have knocked off another Messerschmitt. A friend of mine
called and said that the buyers of these houses were get-

ting restive, they weren't having their cousin the plumber finish up the house at all, they were just abandoning their $4.95 down payment. I called a vice-president of Certain-Teed, who had made a nice large, round earnings estimate, to ask him if he was sticking to it. Certainly, he said. In fact, I called the Certain-Teed management so much, as the stock collapsed, that the vice-president would have saved time if he would just have let me live at his house.

I continued to fret about the difference between $4.95, abandoned, and the whole price of the house, and finally I had a bright idea. I would go to see the accounting firm which certified Certain-Teed's statements, one of the great world-wide accounting firms. The paneling was rich, the carpeting was thick, the portraits of the senior partners glowered from the walls. And, feeling like Oliver Twist, I was ushered in to one of the great senior partners, who naturally had mutton-chop whiskers and a scowl, just as Harold Hill wore a striped blazer. Timidly I asked whether everything was absolutely okay with reporting as income a whole house when all you had received so far was $4.95. And the great senior partner drew himself up to his full nine foot three and indicated in stentorian tones that the great world-wide accounting firm of —— would never sign anything that wasn't true.

Two years later they had a little footnote to the financial statements. They said there were "certain readjustments," recognizing in effect that a lot of the houses were still standing there. This whacked the earnings back retroactively to the price the market seemed to have recognized much earlier. "Sorry about that," said the footnote. But of course the stock had gone from 62 to 11, so the little footnote was two years too late. I managed to bail out about halfway down, but it made a parenthesis on the portfolio sheet, indicating a loss, and parentheses are Very Bad. The president of the fund was very nice to me. He took me over to the window, his arm around me in a fatherly way, and we looked at the beautiful view from our thirty-third floor.

"Everyone makes mistakes, my boy," he said. "It's nothing to worry about. It's all a part of learning, part of the great panoramic parade of life."

Then he tried to push me out of the window.

So perhaps I am just not a qualified observer, and perhaps the conglomerates are indeed a new way of life. If the Federal Reserve is printing money like a banana republic, why shouldn't some private citizens try it? Where there is a market there are those who fill the need, and right now Wall Street firms are busy poking through the quiet, slumbering portfolios of great banks and insurance companies, demonstrating there has been no "performance" or price action, and the Wall Street firms need earnings records and Concepts to help dynamite loose the long-slumbering ancient blue chips. When the dynamite goes off, the Wall Streeters gather buy-and-sell commissions to their bosoms. The Antitrust people have helped to justify conglomerates because obviously if you're buying an unrelated business there can't be anything antitrust about it. The conglomerate managers are bright and much more fun than the sealing-wax people, and any kind of action is better than inaction, as Our Lord Keynes once said.

14. WHY ARE THE LITTLE PEOPLE ALWAYS WRONG?

If all the numbers, accounting variations, computer systems, and infinite possibilities are beginning to bewilder you, there is one indicator that professionals still use that is simple. That is to find out what the average investor, or the little investor, is doing. Then you do just the opposite. The sophisticates never feel comfortable unless they can be reassured that relatively uninformed investors are going the other way with some conviction. It all has to do with Accumulation and Distribution. When the sophisticates are Accumulating, they have to be Accumulating from someone, and when they are Distributing, somebody has to be there to buy.

There is nothing really new about this. A Successful Operator, the one who wrote *How to Win in Wall Street* in 1881, asked the question rhetorically thus:

> Who is it that supports every one of the ruddy-faced and round-bellied brokers, furnishes their brownstone houses in velvet and ebony, their tables with wine and silver, their wives and daughters—aye, and mistresses too—in silks and diamonds and laces? It is the lamb, the meek-eyed confiding and innocent little lamb.

Some things have changed since 1881. The ruddy-faced and round-bellied brokers are trying to get that round belly down with exercise and Metrecal, which they didn't bother with in 1881, but otherwise—well, otherwise, a lot of things haven't really changed at all. (Nobody uses the word "mistress" much any more, and the girls who might qualify under that category of Successful Operator are more interested in a couple hundred shares of a very hot new issue, and a stake in the Caribbean pad, than in silks and laces. Progress is progress.) But the sophisticates still have those yellow wolf-eyes peeled for the lambs.

Two friends of mine, for example, run a very zippy fund. Whenever they get a bit nervous about the market, they go up to the order room of Merrill Lynch, Pierce, Fenner & Smith, where all the teletypes print all the orders from the myriad branches of Merrill Lynch all over the world. Merrill Lynch, as you know, is the A & P of the investment world, known as "We the People" for serving small investors.

"We walked around the room," said one of my friends, after a particular visit, "and orders were pouring in from all over the country, and all the orders we saw said sell, sell, sell. So we knew the market was still all right." In other words, the Little People were selling, so the market was still all right, because the Little People are always wrong, at least that is the way the mythology goes.

The Little People are not actually short of stature, they are small accounts who buy stocks in less than hundred-share lots because that's all the money they have. You can keep track of them by the Odd-Lot statistics in the papers, and there are also various savants who ponder these statistics and tell you whether you can truly continue doing the opposite of what the Little People are doing, or whether there is some sort of False Move involved. False Move is the cop-out phrase savants use, like that legal paragraph on the bottom of brokerage house reports that says in legalese, Nothing Contained Herein May Be True, and We May Be Selling This Stuff We're Recommending, but Our Lawyer Has Read This Report and We're Covered.

Shortly after my friends' trip to the order room a genuine Odd-Lotter of my acquaintance dropped by, and we had a heartrending lunch in which I was able to take my own soundings to see, on the Do the Opposite theory, what is likely to happen next.

It is a little hard for me to adjust to talking to a genuine Odd-Lotter, just as a matter of scale, because I hear so much gossip from professional money managers and their numbers are so much bigger. They say things like, "The Justice Department cost me twenty-two million dollars in my American Broadcasting when they stopped the ITT merger," and they are, of course, telling the truth, but it isn't their money, it's their job. Or I sit with someone contentedly watching the tape, and a block of Sperry Rand goes by, and they say, "Oh, look, Gerry is selling his Sperry for the third time this year." Wise inside things like that; in other words, Gerry, whom they had breakfast with on Tuesday, has been buying and selling Sperry Rand and has managed to make $50 million go in a circle, at some profit.

Anyway, I geared up for this lunch because I had just read a market letter about the Little People. This particular letter writer thinks the actions of small investors are an exercise in mass masochism, that they keep losing because it feels so good when it hurts. Says he: ". . . the odd-lotters continue their selling-on-balance, replete with a puerile confidence that the 'bad' economic news they read in the papers will shortly be 'understood' by the market. Not until the market begins Top Formation will these individuals realize that they are beginning to 'understand' what the market has seen all along." The Odd-Lotters, it is said, sold all the way up in the 1962–66 market rise, and then they bought all the way down as it fell, and now they have been selling again as it goes up. Somebody has to be on the other side.

"First of all, I may be a small investor, but I am not your average small investor," said Odd-Lot Robert, my lunch companion. "I'm a speculator and I admit it. Second, my information is much better than the average small investor's. I get a lot of inside information."

Inside information has been the undoing of many a wise man, so I asked him where he got it.

"I have a terrific broker," he said. "He really knows ahead of time when things are going to happen. He tells me when stocks are going to split."

"Splits are usually discounted and the two pieces of paper are worth the same as the old one," I said, feeling avuncular.

"There was a split in February and I made three points on it," said Robert. "Then, I get even more information from this guy in my office. His sister works for a guy at City Hall, and those people in the government really know when things are going to happen."

I began to get a certain glimmer of Robert's world: They, with a capital T, are always about to do something. To me, They are sitting around at Oscar's at five o'clock and you can talk to Them any time, for one round of drinks; the trick is to know when They are telling you the truth and when They are faking you out.

"Both my broker and this guy's sister have done very, very well," said Robert. "Very, very well indeed."

"I'm glad to hear it," I said. "What are you doing in the market now?"

"I'm selling," Robert said. "That is, I've already finished my selling."

"You feel the economy is heading for trouble," I suggested.

"That's what it says in the paper," Robert said. "So I'm taking profits. I have some particularly good issues I'm going to get back into as soon as they go down."

"Do you really have the courage to buy when the market is going down?" I asked Robert.

"Absolutely, I'm very courageous. I told you, I have steel nerves, I'm a speculator."

I have to admire Robert, because if you know any of the real gunslinging speculators, especially the ones managing pressure performance funds, you know they have no fingernails and are always chewing Gelusil and complaining about how they don't sleep. But then, they don't have steel nerves.

"You have to consider what's open to someone like me," Robert said. "I used to have war bonds. Then I woke up to the fact that you lose money on war bonds. You buy the bond, you get the interest, and by the time you cash it in, haircuts have doubled, and suits have doubled, and doctor bills have doubled and you've got the war bond and the interest, you're way behind. A lot of people don't see through that, but I do."

"The depreciation of currency is a major world problem," I said, avuncular again. "Every major world power is running the printing presses."

"Right," Robert said. "The same goes for life insurance. The bucks you get out aren't the ones you put in."

"Very shrewd," I said. "Good thinking."

"So you have to buy something that will keep pace,"

Robert said. "I have eleven Kennedy half-dollars that have already gone up a lot, but of course that's just a handful. And I have a number of rolls of 1937 Denver nickels, and they have practically doubled."

"I didn't know you were a coin collector," I said.

"I dabble in a lot of things," Robert said.

"How did you do in the market break last year?" I asked.

"I did beautifully, beautifully," Robert said. "I had a little bad luck at the end, though. Back last spring, I figured color TV was going to be very big. I still believe it. Everyone's going to have a color TV set. So I bought some Motorola."

"What price?"

"I bought the first Motorola at two hundred and four dollars," Robert said. "Then it got hit in the break, and I bought some more. That reduced my average cost sharply. My second batch of Motorola only cost me one hundred and fifty-six."

"But Motorola's down around par, around one hundred dollars," I said. "You have a loss."

"A tax loss, I took it last year," Robert said. "I sold it at ninety-eight dollars, so you see it hasn't gone up since I've sold it."

"That's true," I said.

"I sold it to switch into Polaroid, I knew that little Swinger camera was going to be a hit, and a friend of mine who is a buyer for a very, very big chain said they just couldn't keep them in stock."

"That was brilliant," I said. "If you switched into Polaroid when Motorola was selling at that price, you've made eighty percent on your money and made up your loss."

"I would have," Robert said, "only I didn't actually buy the Polaroid. You see, just at that time my wife and I went away for the weekend and on the Merritt Parkway on the way back the car developed this clunking sound, and the garage man said it needed a complete reconditioning, so we traded it in and bought a new car."

"So you were out of the market."

"Except for my short sales."

"You sold short in the big break?"

"I was short Douglas Aircraft at thirty-eight dollars. I read this story in a business magazine how they were losing six hundred thousand on every airplane they produced and were practically bankrupt, and I figured the market in general was going down because we were heading into a recession."

"You made a few points there—Douglas got down to around thirty dollars."

"It did, but I was out of town that day and couldn't call my broker, and when I got back there were all those rumors about McDonnell taking it over. So I covered it in the low forties. I'm very quick to take a loss when things are going against me, unless I plan to hold the stock as a long-term investment."

"What does your wife think of your market activity?" I asked.

"She's trying to make me get out," Robert said. "But what do women know, anyway? I was out for a while last fall, and you know what? I missed it, every day I wasn't in it. I enjoy talking to an intelligent broker, exchanging views. The truth is, *I can't stand to stay out of the action.* I love the market."

"Tell me something," I said. "I know it's hard to keep track, because you've taken money out for a new car, and so on, but have you ever added up what your record is?"

"Sure," Robert said. "I started with nine thousand dollars, that I got when my uncle died. And I took some out, for the car and so on, and I've learned a lot, and I know what I've been doing wrong, and I'm very confident about the future."

"And what is the nine thousand now?"

"I still have twenty-one hundred left," Robert said.

I have to confess that Robert can almost make me a believer in a theory that has been quite erratic, and I hope to keep in touch. Actually, Robert is part of a bigger picture; all individuals have been consistent sellers for years now, no matter what the size of their accounts, round lots as well as odd lots, because the pension funds have been the big buyers and there does have to be a seller for each buyer. The volume has been enormous, but part of that has been because some of the institutions forgot how big they had grown and were trying to get out of stocks and into cash and then back into stocks like elephants in a ballet. I leave to you Robert's endeavors in the market. Right now I am trying to corral some rolls of 1937D nickels, because I have a hot tip from someone with real inside information that they are really about to move.

III

THEY: THE PROS

15. THE CULT
OF PERFORMANCE

If you listen either to Successful Operator, eaves-dropping on the great Keane, or to Odd-Lot Robert, eaves-dropping on the sister's friend from City Hall, you will notice one attitude in common: There is a They out there in the market. They, says Successful Operator in 1881, are about to pull another Bear Raid on the Erie; They, says Odd-Lot Robert, are about to split the stock.

Who are They? Well, They are the people who move stocks. They get the information first, maybe They even create the information, and They are about to put the stock up or down. They are mysterious, anonymous, powerful, and They know everything. Nothing fazes Them. They are the powers of the marketplace.

Is there really a They? Only a few years ago, such a question would have been greeted with hoots of laughter. Sure, the answer would have been, there was a They in the days of the great Keane, when you had to stay out of the way of J.P. Morgan and James J. Hill, because when the elephants fought, the grass was trampled. Sure, there was a They in the twenties, when if you didn't know what Joe Kennedy and Mike Meehan were up to, you had better stay away from Radio lest they move the Pool right over you. But now we have full disclosure, the Securities and Exchange Commission, the Justice Department, the Internal Revenue Service, regulations, examinations of books by Peat Marwick and Haskins & Sells, Investigate Before You Invest, Merrill Lynch offices on every street corner, and twenty-six million investors. Reforms have reformed. *They* have gone away.

Have They? Well, They, in the sense of Joe Kennedy and Mike Meehan and James J. Hill, have indeed gone away; the market is too broad. Even Charley Allen is not what J.P. Morgan was in 1907. So there is no They, it is all a myth?

No, Virginia, there is still a They, which may come as a surprise. They do get information first, They do have the ability to move stocks, and it helps a lot if you know what They are doing.

There is a difference. There are few tycoons these days; most corporations are run by managers for thousands of shareholders, the managerial revolution, the New Industrial State, all that. The same thing has happened in the investment business. The tycoons have been replaced by managers, the managers of what are called Institutions: mutual funds, pension funds, insurance companies.

For years, it didn't really matter that the managers had taken over. The portfolio was not yet an Instrument of Personality. The Portfolio Manager was instructed to leave speculation to the speculators; he was participating in the Long-Term Growth of the American Economy. His portfolio had two hundred stocks, and they were the two hundred biggest companies in America. The two hundred stocks were only two thirds of the portfolio; the other third was bonds. The portfolio manager's charter came from an ancient case, Amory *vs.* Harvard College, 1831, which ruled that a fiduciary act "as would any Prudent Man." To be a Prudent Man, one preserved capital, one was conservative, one ate breakfast, lunched at the Club, and died with an estate that won the admiration of the lawyers for its order and efficiency. The Prudent Man managing securities did his business with his classmates who happened to be brokers, and in a radical move he might reduce Steels from 3.3 percent to 2.9 percent of the portfolio, and buy a little more Telephone.

Then a couple of things happened. One was that a new group of managers came along. You remember—there is a Missing Generation on Wall Street because nobody went there from 1929 to 1947. The generation that came in during the twenties is now in its sixties and seventies; the next generation is in its thirties or early forties. The difference in the attitudes of the generations is even greater than the usual fracas between fathers and sons. To the elder generation, the Depression of the thirties was a profound, traumatic experience. Stocks crashed in 1929, but that was not the worst. They rallied in 1930, and then started a steady erosion that scarred for life anyone who experienced it. United States Steel, which sold at 262 on September 3, 1929, drifted down to 22. General Motors slipped to 8 from 73. Montgomery Ward went from 138 to 4. It was even worse for the investment trusts. United Founders dropped from seventy dollars to fifty cents. American Founders made it to fifty cents from $117.

It is a sobering experience to read through—as once I did—all the *Wall Street Journals* and *Barron's* from 1929 to 1933. Quarterly, reports came out saying, "the outlook is favorable," "a sustained recovery is on its way," and so on. But nobody was listening. Those on margin had been sold out in 1929 and 1930. But from 1930 to 1933, a real blight of the spirit took place. The Prudent Men, not on margin, believing in the Long-Term Growth of the American Economy, saw their unmargined holdings in the bluest of American blue chips drop by 80 to 90 percent. Professor Irving Fisher of Yale, who had immortalized himself by stating, on October 17, 1929, that "Stocks have reached what looks like a permanently high plateau," had to move the plateau down 90 percent and join the ranks of Gustave Le Bon. "It was the psychology of panic," he explained. "It was mob psychology, and it was not, primarily, that the price level of the market was unsoundly high. . . . the fall in the market was very largely due to the psychology by which it went down because it went down."

The senior generation—those who hung on—lived not only to see better days but to see real prosperity. But for most of them, the shadow of Deflation hung always over one shoulder; there was always a chance that it might happen again; and this feeling, even unconscious, took a lot of conscious effort to overcome.

To the next generation the Depression was only a dim memory, and Inflation was much more visible: The haircuts that once cost fifty cents cost seventy-five cents and then one dollar and then two. The next generation also arrived at positions of responsibility without the thirty-year apprenticeship that can bank the fires of the most ambitious. So there was the new generation, itching to shake things up because the old boys had been in the wrong game for twenty years.

Simultaneously, discretionary income—what is left after the essentials for food, clothing, and shelter are taken out of the paycheck—began to burgeon. Middle-class savings turned into a torrent of money. Investments in mutual funds went from $1.3 billion in 1946 to $35 billion in 1967. Pension funds increased in size to $150 billion.

And then one day there was a pool of money $400 billion strong accounting for half the business done on the New York Stock Exchange, and run by a group of tigers who knew they were right just because the old boys had been so wrong. The stage was all set for "performance."

"Performance" is just what it sounds like. It means your fund has performed better than all the other funds. Its net asset value went up a greater percentage. In other words, all the stocks of your fund went up more.

Now, as we have seen previously, the great mature American companies do not consistently offer the greatest possibilities for capital gains. So the "performance" fund managers moved out of the two hundred biggest companies into, quite simply, stocks that would go up. They bought the growth stocks, the senior sisters like IBM, Polaroid, and Xerox, though they were not so senior in those days because they had not yet gone up the last 1000 percent.

Not only did the "performance" fund managers buy the growth stocks—they traded them. Trading was not for the Prudent Man; the short-term fluctuations in the market were not for him. The "performance" fund managers figured the safest way to preserve capital was to double it.

Up until a very few years ago, you were safe as a fund manager if you bought the great blue chips, Alcoa and Union Carbide, Telephone and Texaco. You couldn't be criticized even if they performed badly, because that would be like criticizing the United States of America. If you bought Polaroid at sixty times earnings, however, you could very well be criticized unless Polaroid went up from there. And if you bought it at 40 and sold it at 70 and bought it back at 55 to sell it at 90, trying to catch the swings, you had really better be right.

A couple of funds and a couple of managers turned out to be very right. Then the salesmen of mutual funds noticed that when they spread the literature from all the funds before prospective customers, a lot of the customers weren't interested in nice, balanced, diversified funds any more. They wanted the funds that had gone up the most, on the idea that those were the funds that would keep going up the most. So the assets of the Dreyfus Fund and Fidelity Capital and Fidelity Trend grew by the hundreds of millions of dollars, and all the salesmen everywhere called up the mutual-fund management companies and said, "give us more of these funds that perform like Fidelity." Thus was performance born, out of distrust for fixed income, out of suspicion of the erosion of the dollar, out of the capital gains available from the companies that had some sort of lock on something, technological or otherwise.

You can almost see the point in time when "performance" surfaced. In February, 1966, Gerry Tsai, born in Shanghai and tutored at Fidelity, came to New York. He had been running Fidelity Capital. He had a reputation as a shrewd trader, and he was doing well, but, as he told Mister Johnson, "I want to have a little fund of my own." Gerry thought maybe he could raise $25 million, and so did the underwriters, Bache & Co. But the spirit was abroad in the land. The orders went over $50 million to $100 million, finally to $274 million on the first day, and within a year to more than $400 million. Gerry Tsai was not the first "performance" manager; Mister Johnson and Jack Dreyfus had pioneered that well. But he was the first real "star." Joe Namath may not have been the best quarterback in a decade, but the idea that Sonny Werblen had paid $400,000 for a quarterback gave a new dimension to a pro football league because nobody had ever paid that much for a quarterback. So Gerry Tsai became a part of They, and men could sound wise by watching the tape and saying, "Ah, Gerry is buying again."

Once the tide of "performance" started, there was no stopping. More fund managements started aggressive, capital-gains-oriented funds. The officials responsible for pension funds thought they could use a little growth in those funds, instead of sticking to bonds all the time. The

University of Rochester and Wesleyan University turned small investments into sizable endowments by aggressive investing, and pretty soon the trustees of other universities were coming into the great trust companies which handled their endowments and saying, "Rochester has come from nowhere to the fifth-richest university, and Wesleyan is building new buildings all over the place, and they did it with Xerox, find us another Xerox." McGeorge Bundy, head of the Ford Foundation, said, in a blast that is still echoing:

> It is far from clear that trustees have reason to be proud of their performance in making money for their colleges. We recognize the risks of unconventional investing, but the true test of performance in the handling of money is the record of achievement, not the opinion of the respectable. We have the preliminary impression that over the long run caution has cost our colleges and universities much more than imprudence or excessive risk-taking.

That shook everyone up so much that they forgot McGeorge Bundy's foundation had one of the doggier records around.

What is it "performance" fund managers do? No one ever schooled "performance," so there are no tenets, only what has grown up pragmatically. The characteristics of performance are *concentration* and *turnover*. By concentration, as I said before, I mean limiting the number of issues. Limiting the number of issues means that attention is focused sharply on them, and the ones that do not perform well virtually beg to be dropped off. If you have two hundred stocks, no one of them can make a real difference to you, but if you have only six stocks, you are really going to be watching all six. Furthermore, you are going to be scouting for the best six ideas, because if you find a really good one it may bump one of your other ones off the list. Turnover means how long you hold the stocks. If you buy stocks and put them away, your turnover is 0. If on December 31 you have replaced all the stocks you had the previous January with other stocks, your turnover is 100 percent. It used to be that a bank trust department would have a turnover of 2 percent or so and a mutual fund might turn over at 10 percent. Now the bank trust departments are turning over at 10 percent and the aggressive funds are turning over at more than 100 percent. All that turnover has doubled the volume in the last couple of years, and the brokers are getting very rich.

You can see that if the "performance" fund managers like a stock, and it is not a great, broadly traded stock, that stock is going to go up. And if they own it and something turns sour, there can be a stampede for the exits. There were some remarkable examples of this in 1966, when Fairchild camera, up from 28 to 220 in a year, dropped 100 points in six weeks. With all that concentration, the time horizon shortens considerably. If the report for the next quarter is going to be disappointing, you are going to try to beat the other managers out of the stock, perhaps to buy back in some other day.

So there derives a great hunger for short-term information. Add to this the "technical" and computer work of Albert and Irwin, which flags every movement, and you can get a very volatile and nervous group of stocks, if not an entire stock market. It all began to bug William McChesney Martin, the head of the Federal Reserve, last year. He made some headlines with this statement:

> Increasingly, managers of mutual funds, and portfolio and pension fund administrators, are measuring their success in terms of relatively short-term market performance. In effect, they set a target on a growth stock, attain that target, unload, and then seek other opportunities. Given the large buying power of their institutions, there is an obvious risk that speculative in-and-out trading of this type may virtually corner the market in individual stocks. . . . however laudable the intent may be, it seems to me that practices of this nature contain poisonous qualities reminiscent in some respects of the old pool operations of the 1920s.

All you have to do is say "the 1920s" and people get nervous, because everybody can remember what happened after that, or at least they have read some stirring stories about it. But when Mr. Martin said the managers "set a target . . . attain that target, unload, and then seek other opportunities," the managers replied, "What does he want us to do, ride the stock back down again?"

There is obviously one genuine threat in "performance," and that is the threat to liquidity. All the funds simply can't get through the exit door at the same time.

On the floor of the Stock Exchange stand, at various posts, gentlemen called specialists. They are supposed to make sure the market is orderly and smooth. When a broker arrives with a stock to sell, they buy it from him; if he arrives with cash to buy, they sell stock to him. Perhaps they sell the stock to him out of their own inventory, and when they buy, they use their own capital. Thus they cushion the swings in the market. It all works pretty well for 100- and 500-share orders, although I (and everybody else) have been witness to specialists who do not exactly hold their ground when the first shot is fired. This is not the place for a discussion of the Role of the Specialist, but that Role is the subject of some professional discussion.

When three funds, each with 100,000 shares to sell, arrive at the opening on the same morning, the specialist simply cannot handle it. He calls a Governor of the Stock Exchange and asks for time to round up buyers. They "shut the stock down" it simply ceases trading. If you arrive five minutes later with fifty shares to sell, you are out of luck. You might as well sell them to your brother-in-law. The stock may reopen that day, or the next day, or the day after. For that moment; liquidity has come to a halt and liquidity, you remember, is the cornerstone of the market. (When the stock does reopen, it is likely to be a good 20 points lower, and if you haven't heard the same news the fund managers have, you will begin to get the true feeling of They.)

If this makes you nervous as an individual investor, think how mousetrapped a fund manager can get. He hears the news that trading has been stopped in Zilch Consolidated, he quickly finds out the Story, and there's nothing he can do about it. If a couple of funds have already sold, the market is going to be lower. But if he still shows the stock in his portfolio at the end of the quarter, when results are published, that caved-in, bombed-out stock fires off yellow smoke flares from the printed page and says "Our portfolio manager got sandbagged."

That is how gunslingers are made, not born.

All this is new only in degree. Our good Lord Keynes had it all spotted in 1935, in one of the most acute passages ever written:

> It might have been supposed that competition between expert professionals, possessing judgment and knowledge beyond that of the average private investor, would correct the vagaries of the ignorant individual left to himself. It happens, however, that the energies and skill of the professional investor and speculator are mainly occupied otherwise. For most of these persons are, in fact, largely occupied, not with making superior long-term forecasts of the probable yield of an investment over its whole life, but with foreseeing changes in the conventional basis of valuation a short time ahead of the general public. They are concerned, not with what an investment is really worth to a man who buys it "for keeps," but with what the market will value it at, under the influence of mass psychology, three months or a year hence. Moreover, this behavior is not the outcome of a wrong-headed propensity. For it is not sensible to pay 25 for an investment of which you believe the prospective yield to justify a value of 30, if you also believe that the market will value it at 20 three months hence.
>
> Thus the professional investor is forced to concern himself with the anticipation of impending changes, in the news or in the atmosphere, of the kind by which experience shows that the mass psychology of the market is most influenced . . . (thus) there is no such thing as liquidity of investment for the community as a whole. The social object of skilled investment should be to defeat the dark forces of time and ignorance which envelop our future. The actual, private object of the most skilled investment today is "to beat the gun," as the Americans so well express it, to outwit the crowd, and to

pass the bad, or depreciating, half-crown to the other fellow.

This battle of wits to anticipate the basis of conventional valuation a few months hence, rather than the prospective yield of an investment over a long term of years, does not even require gulls amongst the public to feed the maws of the professional; it can be played by the professionals amongst themselves. Nor is it necessary that anyone should keep his simple faith in the conventional basis of valuation having any genuine long-term validity. For it is, so to speak, a game of Snap, of Old Maid, of Musical Chairs—a pastime in which he is victor who says *Snap* neither too soon nor too late, who passes the Old Maid to his neighbour before the game is over, who secures a chair for himself when the music stops. These games can be played with zest and enjoyment, though all the players know that it is the Old Maid which is circulating, or that when the music stops some of the players will find themselves unseated.

That is the way it is, and no one has ever said it better. Nothing, for the foreseeable future, is going to hinder the impulse to volatility. If all the fund managers have been piling into airlines, and if (as they did recently) the funds own more than 40 percent of Northwest Airlines, and if a number of funds want to get out of Northwest Airlines at the same time, it may be hard to find buyers, and Northwest Airlines is going to have some wide swings.

There is, of course, yet another danger, one spoken of only in hushed tones. A mutual fund, an "open-end" mutual fund, is by definition a fund which will redeem the shareholder's shares for cash any business day he desires. If a bunch of shareholders all redeem together and the mutual fund doesn't have enough cash, it has to sell some stocks to carry out the redemption.

Recently the thirst for performance got to the point where a number of funds were buying stock in companies that had no public markets, hoping for a nice gain on the day hence when the companies would go public. If the fickle redeemers gang up, those funds will have to find buyers in a market that can make the market for 1956 De Sotos look like a marvel of liquidity. Other funds have bought restricted stock, called "investment letter stock," which they cannot legally sell for a certain period of time. That's a procedure which can provide a manager with nice discounts from the market, or with a block of stock that would be hard to accumulate. But it also, needless to say, cuts down on liquidity.

For a while, in 1968, the fund leading the performance derby was called the Mates Fund, after its president Fred Mates. The young fund made its short record in some volatile stocks that turned out to have less than total liquidity. Before the year was over, the Mates Fund had to cease redemptions because of a couple of stocks it held that were, for various reasons, illiquid. So if you were a Mates fundholder as of the day redemptions ceased, you were locked in until the day they started again, unless you could get your brother-in-law to take the shares off your hands.

Obviously, if the fickle redeemers all gang up one day and present their shares for cash and the cash is not there and the stocks are illiquid, that will not be a very good day. In fact, it might just make the vest-wearing Prudent Man an object of affection, and the swinging, sideburned performance manager an object of tar and feathers. But let's not think about that.

There are some corrective forces at work. For one thing, at the rate they are now being consumed, there may not be enough Gelusil and tranquilizers to serve all the fund managers with their triggers filed hair-thin. More reasonably, some fund managers are going to bring in the factor of the other fund managers, and expand their intended holding periods back again to a more manageable distance. The legal beagles may even make some rules, though if history is any guide, they will be rules that treat the situation as it was when people began thinking of rules, and not with the situation as it will develop to be.

You should make one note of my own bias in this account. From the previous list of biases you can see that anything other than "performance" is, to use the words of the Master, "intolerably boring and overexacting." The name of the game is making money, not sitting on it.

I happen to know a number of fund managers, and

they belie the old stereotype of Wall Street. To most Vassar juniors—and to many other people—a money manager has to be a dull fellow. He wears a vest and is boring, pretentious, and pompous. "Performance" managers can be very good company, just as diplomats or foreign correspondents or any group that represents a cross of disciplines can be. They have to be alert, they must keep constantly scanning for changes in the environment and for new ideas, because literally anything that happens can have an effect on all that money. They have to be good brain pickers, and a good brain picker is usually alive enough to be a good dinner companion.

Of course, the "performance" funds still represent only a tiny fraction of all the managed money. The influence of the trend extends far beyond the actual amounts of money involved. There are still a lot of vests around, and a lot of bankers who disapprove of everything that swings. It may all go too far, and they may be right. At the moment "performance" seems like the logical reaction to a worldwide inflation, an inflation that reflects the aspirations of much of society running ahead of society's ability to pay for these aspirations on a current basis, or at least the discipline of paying for aspirations in the traditional way.

16. LUNCH AT
SCARSDALE FATS'

With all that money in so relatively few hands, it was inevitable that someone would get the hands together on an informal basis, just as a pleasant, tension-relieving gesture. The gentleman who is the Madame de Staël of the institutional investment business is called Scarsdale Fats, and he really does exist. He exists, he gives lunches, and everybody comes. Lunch on Wall Street is working time, and what started at Scarsdale's informally has developed to such a point that the lunch guests bone up beforehand and take notes.

On any given day, the lunch guests at Scarsdale's are likely to represent a couple of billion dollars in managed money. Now, when you handle this kind of money, you are, believe me, welcome almost everywhere. You could eat at any place on Wall Street, free, in private dining rooms where the paneling has been flown over from busted merchant banks in the City of London, where the silver is hallmarked with the house mark, the house being Lehman Brothers or Eastman Dillon or Loeb Rhoades or even the places that fly their own flags over the Street. Over in the other private dining rooms the waiters move on cat feet and dishes never clatter and the cigars are pre-Castro Uppmanns out of the firm humidor, and through the pleasant masculine Havana haze after lunch you can feel, as the voices murmur about pieces of empire, $100 million here, $200 million there, that all's right with the world, if there's trouble anywhere we send a gunboat and give the beggars a good thrashing.

So why are they here at Scarsdale Fats', these guys with all the money? Here there is no French chef, no house silver, no paneling, no carpeting, no noiseless, perfectly uniformed corps of waiters. The chairs are metal folding chairs, the tables are plastic, there is a big bowl of pickles on the table, the napkins are paper, and if this is the private dining room of a New York Stock Exchange firm, Wall Street is not what it used to be. If the trend catches on, Robert Lehman will look at the empty seats in his dining room and think the chef has been putting flour in the gravy, and John Loeb will be sitting in *his* like Stella Dallas wondering if everybody somehow got the date wrong, not that either of them is going to get any poorer.

And here is Scarsdale himself. As far as I know it was a couple of the Boston institutions that hung the nickname on him, which shows that Boston institutions are not as stuffy as they used to be. In the old days they wouldn't talk to anybody who didn't have a Groton nasal drip, and now they'll talk to just about anybody they think will make them some money. Anyway, here is Scarsdale, pressing the hors d'oeuvres on his guests with mother love, eat, eat. He has already wolfed down about a third of the deviled eggs himself, so the guests better be quick on the draw. Obviously he stepped over, not on, the scale his partners keep beside his desk to save his life. One of his enthusiasts describes him as "glob-shaped." Minnesota Fats is an ectomorph and Sydney Greenstreet would blow away in the Scarsdale Fats ratio! All Scarsdale will say is that he is comfortably over two hundred pounds. Let's say he is pyknic. Look it up.

Scarsdale introduces the guests. There is a guy who handles the trust accounts from a Very Big Bank. And a second Very Big Bank. And two guys from Very Big Funds. A young gunslinger type from a performance fund. A hedge fund-er and a man from one of the statistical reporting services. The effort of introducing everybody makes Scarsdale so nudgy he washes down the hors d'oeuvres with a roll and butter.

And why are they here? Because Scarsdale asked them. Let him tell: "I had to do it to compete. What have I got? Nothing. Those hot young research analysts at Donaldson Lufkin can write hundred-page reports. Bache can field a thousand salesmen. The white-shoe firms can fly the Old St. Wasp flags. So I thought: Who has money? The funds. Be nice. Ask them to lunch." To corned-beef sandwiches, to meatballs? "Everywhere else these guys go, somebody is trying to promote them, to sell them something. Not me. I have no opinions."

So what Scarsdale did was to call, say, Wellington, and say that Keystone and the Chemical were coming to lunch, and then he called, say, Keystone and said the others were coming, and then he called, perhaps, the Chemical and pretty soon there he was, Perle Mesta. Two more things helped. One was the rules: Everything is off the record, informal, no names, no sandbagging. You don't want to say what you're buying, fine, but don't say you're selling what you're buying or Scarsdale will come and lean on you himself and then no more meatballs forever.

The other thing is Scarsdale himself, the way he runs the lunch with no nonsense, as if he were Lawrence Spivak and there were only thirty minutes minus commercials to extract the truth.

Now look at it another way. You are thirty-two years old and you are a portfolio manager making $25,000 a year. All you have to do is handle $250 million and make sure it does better than anybody else handling a portfolio anywhere. You get two phone calls, lunch invitations, one from the old firm with Wedgwood plates in the private dining room and one from Scarsdale. You already know what stocks the Wedgwood-plates-dining-room people are selling. At Scarsdale's you can find out—maybe, because there is a certain poker-game aspect—what some of your compatriots are up to, and nobody will try to sell you. Certainly not Scarsdale; he prides himself on not knowing anything, even though his corned-beef sandwiches are buying the best research in the country. All you have to do is stay friends. Maybe—it's not required—you give him a little order sometime, a thousand Telephone, just to help pay for lunch. Where do you go?

"Awright, everybody siddown," Scarsdale says. He calls on the man from the Very Big Bank. What's gonna happen, and what are they buying?

The man from the Very Big Bank starts talking about the gross national product and productivity and other verbal smoke-screen items and Scarsdale cuts him down.

"You had seven hundred million in cash last week. You still got it?"

"We spent fifty million," admits the man from the Very

Big Bank. "We bought some utilities, at the bottom, before they went up last week."

"Of course before they went up," Scarsdale says. "Anything else?"

"This bear market isn't over yet," says the man from the Very Big Bank. "You fellas—you young fellas under forty—you haven't seen a real bear market. You don't know what it is."

"Did you buy anything else? Come on, come on," Scarsdale says.

"Nothing else," says the Big Bank man, but nobody is leaning forward to hear because most of the other guests are under forty and they don't know what a real bear market is. They've just seen the market go down $100 billion and their best holdings have melted and if this isn't a real bear market they don't want to know about the real one. Maybe next time the Chinese will have ICBMs.

"All right," Scarsdale Fats says. "Give the man over there some meatballs," he tells the waitress. Scarsdale Fats strikes like an adder at the meatballs as they go by and manages to spear two before the bank man falls gratefully on his portion. Then he butters up another roll to refuel. He turns on one of the fund men.

"Charley X was here for lunch Tuesday," he says, mentioning a rival fund manager. "He says this market is like it was in fifty-seven–fifty-eight. He says he bought stocks at the bottom."

"He bought at every bottom this year," says the fund man, "and every bottom was lower than the last. I'm surprised he has any chips left."

"Where is the market going?" says Scarsdale.

"We've seen the lows," the fund man says. There is a collective *ah-h-h* from the assembled guests. Candor. Commitment. The market turns around and drops through 744 on the Dow, this guy has committed himself wrong, but he's definitely committed himself.

"What three stocks do you like?" Scarsdale says.

"We nibbled at a few airlines," the fund man says.

"The airlines have had it; we're selling our airlines. Look at the strike settlement. Look at equipment delays. You can have them," says a counterpart fund manager across the table.

"So go sell your airlines," the first fund man says. The guests are warming up, and the lunch is turning into a success. "We think the growth stocks will move up thirty percent or forty percent from here, the true ones will double, and the others will drop away and disappear."

"What growth stocks? What growth stocks?" says Scarsdale. Scarsdale does not even know it, he is being such a good moderator, but at the moment he is eating all the remaining rolls in the roll dish.

"I bought some Polaroid, down around the lows, maybe at one hundred twenty-five," says the fund man. There is another collective *ah-h-h*. Nine other slide-rule brains are working away: Even if he says he bought it at 125, maybe he bought it at 135. If he bought it at 135, and the earnings go up, he's not going to turn around and sell it. Strongly held Polaroid at 135. *Ah-h-h.*

"What earnings next year for Polaroid?" says Scarsdale. "Four dollars? Four-fifty? Five?"

"What's the difference?" the fund man says.

"Good," Scarsdale says. "What else? What other stocks? What else?"

"Well-l-l," says the fund man, "I may have bought some Fairchild at the lows. I think I bought some at ninety-six."

"Fairchild never sold at ninety-six!" hollers the second bank man. "The low was ninety-seven."

"No sandbagging!" Scarsdale cries.

"Maybe it was ninety-eight," the fund man says. "I recall buying a lot at ninety-eight."

"Fairchild is falling apart," says the man from the hedge fund. With a hedge fund, you can go short. "Fairchild has lost control of its inventories. The Street doesn't know it yet, but Fairchild's fourth quarter is going to be disappointing."

"I don't care," says the fund man.

"Next year could be *extremely* disappointing," the hedge fund man says.

"I don't care," says the fund man.

Now the lunch has really warmed up. Maybe the hedge fund is short the Fairchild the other fund is long. Gunfight at the Broad Street Corral. Or maybe the hedge fund man isn't short the Fairchild—he hasn't said he was—maybe he is just making growling noises to make people *think* he is short the Fairchild. When the Rothschilds got the word about the battle of Waterloo—in the movie it was by carrier pigeon—they didn't rush down and buy British consols, the government bonds. They rushed in and *sold*, and then, in the panic, they bought.

"What else? What else?" cries Scarsdale.

"The market is going up," the fund man says. "I don't know for how long, and I may change my mind. Maybe next spring. But, for the moment, up."

"Good!" says Scarsdale. "Give the man some meatballs! Give him some salad! Where are all the rolls?" Scarsdale cries to the waitress.

Lunch is over and Scarsdale is back at his desk. Two of the guests didn't eat their cheese cake and the empty plates are now on Scarsdale's desk, plundered, a few crumbs stirring after the pounce. Scarsdale is on the phone keeping his other institutional managers wired in, trusting there will be orders and other profitable fallout. He has his notebook open.

"Larry X was here to lunch today and he thinks we've seen the lows and he is buying some airlines. Joe Y was here and he thinks we have another leg to go on the downside and he isn't buying. Harry thinks Joe's figures on capital spending are ten billion dollars too low. Here are the airlines Harry likes . . ."

At the next desk, Scarsdale's secretary is lining up some senators for a dinner Scarsdale is giving. The legends are already starting. Scarsdale is supposed to have introduced Neddy Johnson, the junior Johnson of Fidelity, to a senator and to have said, "This man controls two billion dollars." And the senator says, "So what, we spend that in half an hour." Senators! Next thing you know, there will be a tablecloth in Scarsdale's dining room, and the pickle bowl will be gone, the silver will have a leopard's head and the mark SF, everybody will turn stuffy again, and we'll all have to figure out somewhere else to go.

It has been a while since that lunch where the hedge fund type who was short Fairchild and the other fund which bought it met head-on. The pickle bowl is still there, and Scarsdale does not yet have SF and a leopard's head on the silver, or a house flag, like Brown Brothers, fluttering over Wall Street. When senators come to lunch —and they do, including some Presidential hopefuls— there are steak sandwiches instead of corned-beef sandwiches. Sometimes there are tablecloths, too. Some day the whole operation will get upgraded to the point at which it will be just about the same as Robert Lehman's, and nobody young goes to lunch *there*. Then some bright young fellow out of Yale will set a plastic table with corned-beef sandwiches and call up six funds, but by then Scarsdale may have replaced Lawrence Spivak or Mike Wallace as an interrogator, or he may have gotten so rich from the commissions the luncheon guests leave behind that he may not care. Because of certain changes in the Stock Exchange rules, it is harder to pay for lunches with commissions. But meanwhile, in the world of institutions, Scarsdale's lunches are one themselves.

17. LOSERS AND WINNERS: POOR GRENVILLE, CHARLEY, AND THE KIDS

The trouble with instant communications and a market that responds momentarily is that there is always somebody who doesn't get the word. I have a friend, Charley, who is a master gunslinger running a very aggressive fund. Charley's fund is so aggressive that brokers love it, because an aggressive fund can churn up commissions bigger than those of great insurance companies. Charley's turnover rate must be 500 percent. At the trading desk in Charley's fund they move so fast that the man at the wall end of the desk sometimes ends up buying what the guy at the window end has been selling. Consequently brokers offer Charley their houses in Jamaica, their boats in Maine, their golf clubs in Pebble Beach; but Charley is so cool he never takes any of this, because his hobby is staying ahead of the Word.

Consequently Charley can afford to be magnanimous to his less fortunate brethren. At one particular turn in the market he called and said, "Chester's charts are singing," in the tone of one bringing a Bull from the Pope. "The breadth is beautiful, and the angle of acceleration is the best since the Cuban missile crisis." Never mind the translation of this. You don't have to know all that flankerback-cornerback jargon to watch a football game. Suffice to say that Chester is a Chartist at a big and influential fund. The public and most of Wall Street have never heard of Chester, but if Chester's charts are singing and the angle of acceleration is coming off the floor, there is going to be action, because Chester has a good record and his fund swings. In fact, the other Chartists will be making an *extra* line of little *x*'s just from the price movement made by the stocks bought by Chester's fund after Chester gives them the word about the technical action.

We live in an age of charts and computers, and the thing about charts and computer studies is that they show what is moving, and if everybody plays this game, then what moves is what is already moving. Sort of Newtonian. This may sound simplistic, but that's the way the game is played. The trouble is that unless you have peripheral vision and extrasensory perception, you get mousetrapped very easily, and a lot of very sophisticated performance fund managers were caught in the Great Mousetrap of 1966.

In fact, as soon as the Signal was given, when the Dow-Jones broke, as they say, the "range in which it was locked," my friend Charley was back on the phone. "A roily-boily market," he said.

"So I've been hearing," I said. I am getting itchy to buy just with all this conversation about Signals and buying.

"I want you to come on a mission of mercy," Charley said. "Poor Grenville is in town. Competition is competition, but we have to help Poor Grenville."

Poor Grenville runs a fund, one of a group of funds, and he is in charge of $100 million or so. This is the first time I have heard he was a Poor Grenville, since Poor Grenville's great-grandmother had a duck farm in one of our major metropolitan centers and on top of the duck farm there are now some office buildings and busy city streets and Poor Grenville's family still has the duck farm, sans ducks, of course.

But you never know. Maybe he doesn't have any of the money; maybe it's all tied up in trusts and he really needs this job.

I asked Charley why Grenville was suddenly Poor Grenville.

"Poor Grenville," said Charley, "has gotten caught with twenty-five million in cash. It's a disaster. How would you like to have twenty-five million in cash with the Buy Signals you've just seen? Come to lunch. Poor Grenville has to lose his cash, right away."

I know it sounds a little funny that having $25 million in cash is a disaster. It sounds just as funny to me as the phrase "lose cash," when it isn't your cash in the first place and all you are doing is taking the cash—somebody else's—and buying stocks with it. But professional money managers love to say, "We lost five million in cash this afternoon," meaning they bought stocks with it. I guess it sounds professional. Just as underwriters say, "We lost two thousand shares to Hutton and four thousand to Hornblower," when what they mean is they *sold* these shares and busted a gut trying.

As to why Poor Grenville's $25 million in cash was a major disaster, that is more comprehensible. Grenville should have all $100 million fully invested if the market is coming off the floor; his fund is "performance-oriented," trying for big capital gains. If Poor Grenville has $25 million in cash he guessed dead wrong at the bottom of the market, and in one career you don't get too many chances like that. Poor Grenville had gotten himself all ready for a big drop in October and now in January the market turned around and ran away without him. He has to make it up in a hurry.

So we slide into this booth at the Lunch Club—Poor Grenville, Charley, myself and two brokers. Poor Grenville's nails are bitten down to the nubs, a clear sign that he is one of the young gunslingers in trading stocks. To the average observer, Poor Grenville, with his height and his golden locks and his Repp tie, looks like an ad for Establishment splendor. But the nails do not denote serenity; the nails are a gunslinger's nails.

"You're my friends," Poor Grenville says to Charley and one of the brokers. "What do I do?" The other broker is along to generate some commissions out of Poor Grenville's misery if he can.

"I have been thinking about your problem," starts the broker pretentiously. "I have brought along some studies done by my firm, which I think you will find . . ."

"Who is this guy?" Poor Grenville says, cutting him off.

"Cut it out," Charley says. "You'll get your commissions if we can help Poor Grenville here."

"We have some very nice aluminums this afternoon, just designed to get you out of the hole," says the first broker. "Capacity situation good, price rises sticking, stocks fairly well sold out and not too far off the bottom. A lot of funds haven't bought aluminums yet. You're safe in the middle. Alcoa, Kaiser, Harvey . . ."

"Not now," Poor Grenville says. "Earlier, or later. Right now I have to make up for lost time. If we're really in a bull market."

"It doesn't matter at this point whether it's a big rally in a bear market or a new bull market," says Charley. "If you're not in it, you're dead."

"Rubbers," says the first broker. "We have some very nice rubbers. U.S. Rubber, B.F. Goodrich, replacement demand, adequate price structure . . ."

"Not sexy enough," says Poor Grenville. "Later. In June. We have two quarters of the year coming up in which everybody will be saying business is going to turn up at the end of the year. So I don't want business-turning-up stocks. I have two quarters to play."

"Let's work backwards," Charley says helpfully. "It's March thirty-first. You have to put out your quarterly report. What big winners *must* you have bought? They won't know whether you bought them March thirtieth or January second, as long as they're in there."

"Polaroid," says Poor Grenville mournfully. "Fairchild." He coughs, he can barely get the words out, "Solitron."

I nudge Charley and ask him why Poor Grenville is coughing over these words.

"Because he just sold them all sixty days ago," Charley whispers. "And they are up fifty percent since then."

"Can I buy them?" Poor Grenville asks, meaning is the market smooth enough to put a couple million dollars to work without forcing the stock.

"In this market you can," Charley says. "When they're trading fifty thousand shares a day, you can spoon in okay."

"Okay," Poor Grenville says. "What else?"

"The garbage is moving," Charley says. "It is the best garbage market since sixty-one." By garbage Charley means the untried-and-untrue stocks, some of them over the counter, all of them with hairy "stories," wild gleams in their eyes.

"Tell me some stories," Poor Grenville says. By now both the brokers are just listening to Charley; they are really out of their league.

"Well, you know the Itek story," Charley says.

"Another Xerox, as soon as they figure out how to do

whatever it is they do cheap enough, and that could be a long time," says Poor Grenville. Charley shrugs. "You know the EGG story? Edgerton, Germeshausen and Grier? They are going to blow up atomic bombs under exhausted oil wells and bring up more oil that way."

"What's it worth without blowing up atomic bombs?" asks Poor Grenville.

"There's already fifteen points of atomic bombs in the stock," Charley says. Poor Grenville leans forward. "What about the *real* garbage?" he says. And everybody falls to, like a pack of hounds that has caught up with a rabbit. Rumors, tips, remarks from barbers, usually you get this stuff at the tail end of a bull market. It sounds like the fall of 1961 all over again: tetronics, computeronics, New Science Horizons. Charley mentions a brand-new little company on the periphery of the computer business.

"What's it going to earn?" Poor Grenville asks.

"Last week it was selling at eight, and I heard it was going to earn forty cents," Charley says. "This week it is at eleven and I hear it is going to earn seventy cents. By next week it will be selling at fifteen and you will hear they have one dollar in the bag, easy."

Logic, to an outsider, would say that you have a company selling at 10 and you go and do a lot of research on it and figure out the sales and the profits and you figure if they can earn one dollar it will sell at 20. So you buy it and wait and the story gets that they earn the one dollar and it goes to 20.

But the market does not follow logic, it follows some mysterious tides of mass psychology. Thus earnings projections get marked up and down as the prices go up and down, just because Wall Streeters hate the insecurity of anarchy. If the stock is going down, the earnings must be falling apart. If it is going up, the earnings must be better than we thought. Somebody must know something we don't know. With all the analysts and all the research and all the statistics and all the computers, it is still possible to be 51 percent wrong, and you can do better than that by flipping a coin.

Anyway, Poor Grenville got back in the market, $25 million in one big gulp. He bought a mixture of high flyers like Xerox, Polaroid, and garbage. And that was part

of the reason for the roily-boily market we had a while
ago. The cyclical stocks reflecting business were sold down
all they would go. Then along came Poor Grenville and
his gunslinger competitors selling stocks because stocks
were going down, riding with the trend instead of against
it. Some of them must have been reading the charts upside down, or their Chartists have mirror-image reading
problems and made the *x*'s go in the wrong direction. When
the gunslingers hit the volatile stocks, Fairchild and Xerox
and Polaroid and what have you, they knocked them down
so hard that the *x*'s on the chart made downtrend lines
and then the downtrend said sell, and then you just didn't
want to show a bombed-out stock in your portfolio; it
made you look dumb. So out went all the bombed-out
stocks. Somebody has to be last at this sort of game.

Then when the scramble to get back in started, there
were air pockets, vacuums over these very same stocks and
whoosh—away they went. And when stocks—even just
some stocks—made spectacular gains, the market took on
a very ruddy glow. All the Grenvilles getting in together
fired up the market, and then the marks were there on the
charts, saying "Up."

Poor Grenville made out all right. My money will always be on Charley, because he always seems to be three
hours ahead of Poor Grenville, but Poor Grenville always
scrambles back.

Sometimes, however, all the Grenvilles together can go
into a real panic. One such day was September 27, 1966. It
was a good day for a panic, coming at the end of a nice,
rumbling slide, in the market. Charley—I have to hand
it to him—stayed cool. With the benefit of hindsight old
Charley really looks pretty good. A lot of professionals
headed for the exits at the same time that afternoon. Here
is the account, the videotape replay. You Are There.

That day, September 27, 1966, is going to be one of
those days like December 7, 1941, peculiar to history, the
day Wall Street stopped believing in anything, at least
for that Bear Market, and you can mark it by minutes
on the clock, just the way it happens in the disaster books
when the water goes gurgling into the *Titanic*. September
27 was the day they red-dogged Motorola.

At the moment it was happening I was having lunch at

the Bankers Club. My friend, the very same Charley, is sitting there stirring his coffee and telling me the bearish news from all over, such as that one of the major New York City banks is busted except for its float, i.e., it is kiting money over the weekends and if they ever speed up the United States mail the bank is in trouble. "Kiting over the weekend" means writing checks on Friday on money that doesn't exist and rushing to cover the checks with new funds by Monday morning.

"They're out," Charley says. "They can't go to the Fed because the Fed will slam the window on their fingers if they look at their loans, so they have been scrambling around Europe sopping up Euro-dollars."

If you understand what Charley said, fine, and if you don't, it doesn't have much to do with Motorola except that it sets a nice, dark, ominous atmosphere. Money is tight and Wall Street doesn't like the Vietnam war at all. Then a fellow we both know comes by and says Motorola is getting red-dogged down on the floor of the Exchange. Already there is a little crowd around the Dow-Jones broad tape in the anteroom, where the carpet is worn.

Meanwhile, a couple of blocks away at 15 William Street the boys are spilling what is left of the tuna fish in order to get to the phones. All this from a speech by Mr. Robert W. Galvin from Franklin Park, Illinois. Mr. Galvin is the chairman of the board of Motorola, one of the flyers of the time, and he is addressing the sage and august New York Society of Security Analysts. Motorola, as you know, makes color TV sets, and that's growth, and semiconductors, and that's growth, and two-way radios, and that's growth. Growth, growth, growth. Six months ago all this growth is worth $234 a share. On September 27 it's worth $140. A bad gassing, but how much worse can things be? They're going to earn $8 a share. It says so in Standard & Poors. Business, Mr. Galvin says, is so good it's bad. They have all the orders they can handle, they just have trouble producing the goods—shortages here, labor problems there. They can sell all the color TVs they can make, they just can't make them fast enough. Earnings will be up—but to $5.50, $6 on the outside. Everything else is rosy.

The sage and august analysts look at each other for a

moment: $6? $6? What happened to the other $2? Then it is like the end of the White House news conference, except nobody has even said, "Thank you, Mr. President." They are all running for the phones. Except they are security analysts, not newsmen, so they use the Olympic heel-and-toe walk instead of the outright sprint. There is a question-and-answer period, but Mr. Galvin's audience has been depleted.

Back at the Bankers Club, Charley has melted into a phone booth and is giving orders to his girl. "Sell ten thousand Motorola," he is saying; that's about a million three. I can tell that the girl has the portfolio in front of her and is looking for Motorola, and I can even hear (because I am making a special attempt to do so) her saying, "But we don't *own* any Motorola." Charley is going to short the Motorola, so he hollers a bit. He'll buy it back some other time. Right now the important thing is to sell it, whether or not you own it. This is one of the pressures of a performance fund.

We stand there watching the tape, and there goes MOT, 137, 136, oof, 134. Big blocks are appearing.

"There goes Gerry Tsai's Motorola," says some wise man behind us. That's the *in* thing to say. Gerry Tsai does move in and out fast, but how anybody can tell it's the Manhattan Fund's Motorola is beyond me. Gerry might have sold it long before. It's useful, though. You can always sound wise by saying, "Gerry Tsai is buying," or "Gerry Tsai is selling." Gerry had better watch out, though, because if you're They, things have to be good. I know a Chartist who says the Dow-Jones is going to 380. If it does, I would go long apples because there will be plenty of demand from all the street-corner salesmen, and they will be looking for a scapegoat. There will be a book sponsored by the John Birch Society called *The Protocols of the Elders of Shanghai*, in which it is proved that Gerry Tsai was really Mao Tse-tung, and there will be a public ceremony in front of the Federal Reserve Bank while Gerry Tsai is exorcised of demons by a god-fearing chaplain just before they drive the water buffalos to which he is tied in opposite directions.

Now down on the floor the pressure is on the specialist. He is standing there on the floor at Post 18, his Hippocratic oath bidding him make an orderly market in Motorola, and suddenly there he is, like an adolescent fantasy, a quarterback in Yankee Stadium with the crowd roaring. Only it's the wrong dream. The crowd is roaring because all his receivers are covered, his defense has evaporated, and the red-dog is on: two tons of beef descending on him, tackles grunting and linebackers growling *Killll*. Nothing to do but buckle, eat the ball, and hope you're still alive when they stop blowing the whistle. Guys are bearing down on the specialist and he can tell that if he bends over in a reflex from the first chunk of Motorola that hits him in the stomach, they will hit him over the head with the rest. That's not an orderly market. So they blow the whistle. No more trading in Motorola.

Charley is chagrined. He needed an uptick, a sale higher than the previous sale, to get off his short; they've had that rule since the Great Crash. In the good old days without that rule the bears could all get together and short the stock right down to 0 and practically into negative territory.

"Gee, and I was going to go to Europe next week," Charley says. Now he thinks he had better stick around. I ask Charley for a prognostication.

Charley likes to sound like the oracle at Delphi, not in print, of course, because that can catch up with you, but just to his friends.

"Everything is going to par," Charley says. Par is 100, or it used to be, and everybody still calls it that, and "everything" means those high flyers so popular with the performance boys. Well, the flyers have about forty points to drop before they hit par and naturally Charley doesn't mean every one, because they aren't all selling at the same price, but that's a steep drop. "After Motorola, nobody will believe anything," Charley says. "Tomorrow they will start saying Fairchild has terrible problems. Xerox gives you cancer, handling Polaroid film makes you sterile." So everything is going to par. At that point John Jerk and his brother will figure the way to make money is to go short.

You have already met John Jerk as Odd-Lot Robert. They live in the Hinterlands, John Jerk, his brother, his cousin Odd-Lot Robert—all those folk—and their movements are watched by the yellow-eyed wolves.

Charley and I drift back to his office. "It's a terrible market for everybody but me," Charley says. "Nobody believes anything. They don't believe Johnson, they don't believe anything in Washington, they believe taxes are going to go up but not enough, they don't believe we'll ever get out of Vietnam, and after Motorola, nobody will believe any earnings. Let Peat Marwick the CPA's certify them, they still won't believe them."

This is what the French sociologist Émile Durkheim called *anomie*. In market terms it means anxiety builds up as the market drops, and then as you get all the noise about "resistance levels" and so on, and the market goes plunging through them, and you get *anomie*. It's like alien- ation, only it means "Where's the bottom? Where's the bot- tom? Where's the bottom?" Nobody knows where the bot- tom is; nobody can remember where the top was; they're all way out there in the blue, riding on anxiety and a shoe- shine. The Dow-Jones average is going to 0. Only Charley is in good shape; his fund is a hedge fund and he is short.

"At par," Charley intones, "there will be a rally, while we all chase John Jerk and his brother."

The translation of this is that Mr. J., having lost on the stocks he owned, will try to make up his losses by selling short, and then as Charley buys, the stocks go up, giving Mr. J. a loss on the short sales. Then he panics and he has to buy all the way up with Charley chasing him.

I sit in Charley's office while he cancels his European vacation. At 3:29 the specialist reopened Motorola, just as the bell rang. That's like a boxer who manages to get on one knee just as the referee counts ten. Motorola re- opened and closed at 119, down 19¼ on the day. In the marketplace it was worth $114 million less at 3:30 than it was at 10:00 A.M., and, say, $684 million less than it had been a few months before. And it was the same com- pany, more or less, and this year is better than last year and next will be better than this year.

Now you can talk about tight money and Vietnam and taxes all you want, but something happened on Septem- ber 27. It started happening before, of course, when the banks started getting all loaned up and then all the whistles and shrieks and bells and yellow smoke signals of the indicators went off late last spring. On September 27, the bell was tolling for belief.

And what now? Well, the odd-lot figures, say Mr. J. and his brother, are short a lot of stock, and Charley has the hounds ready. Our trader says the tape has to stand still for forty days and forty nights to prepare the way for the next bull market. Charley is going to Europe in November. We have come to the moment in *Peter Pan* when the play stops and Mary Martin or whoever comes to the footlights and says, "Do you believe? Do you believe?" The only two times I saw *Peter Pan*, everybody believed.

Some day, maybe not so far away, Charley will be back from Europe. Mr. J. will be in the Hinterlands, pantsless, and the first daisy will push through the soil and say, "I believe," and the game will be on again.

See how good Charley looks in retrospect? Everything happened just like he said. First, everybody stopped believing everything. Then "everything" went to par, and the little investors, Monsieur Jerk and his brother (Charley said it, not me), went short (look up the statistics), and then Charley and his cohorts chased them all the way up into a bull market. How Mr. J. ever has any pants to wear is beyond me.

It didn't take long for everybody to start believing again. "Everybody," at this writing, still doesn't believe any word that comes out of Washington, they still don't believe we'll ever get out of Vietnam, and they certainly don't believe half the earnings that are reported. But when prices go up enough, everybody believes something, even if it is only that everybody *else* is just about to believe.

One day Charley ambled by and said he couldn't understand the market any more. "I like a roily-boily market as well as the next man," he said, "but *this is madness*. It will all come to no good end."

I carefully noted the day and hour of this remark, because you have seen what a good record Charley has. "What do we do now?" I asked.

"The kids are taking everything over. It has gone from

a garbage market to a kids' garbage market. Only the kids would buy this kind of garbage. You can do two things. One is you can come to Europe with me. John Aspinwall has a new place in London, and Teddy has his boat off Nice, or we could go to Japan. It would be good for us to get away from the madness for a while. The only other thing you can do is find yourself a kid."

It so happened that I couldn't get away just then, and another friend of mine, the Great Winfield, had opted to stay and play the kid's market. Here is the videotape replay of that particular moment in history.

Everybody has some sort of infallible market indicator they use to help them in the difficult business of piling up a fortune, and I am in the process of devising one myself. It is called the Adam Smith Jericho Indicator, and I will tell you about it in a minute, just as soon as I relate another market indicator, which came up on a recent visit with the Great Winfield.

"My boy," said the Great Winfield over the phone. "Our trouble is that we are too old for this market. The best players in this kind of a market have not passed their twenty-ninth birthdays. Come on over and I will show you my solution."

The Great Winfield is a friend of mine who is a tape-reader, super-speculator, and most recently, Marlboro-commercial rancher. That is, he has rejected the Wall Street identity of vests and haircuts for that of the Marlboro man. Ordinarily all you find in the Great Winfield's country-sheriff-type office is four days' worth of ticker tape on the floor and a few refugees from Establishment firms seeking a change of pace. Now, in addition to the usual denizens, I found three new faces in the Great Winfield's office.

"My solution to the current market," the Great Winfield said. "Kids. This is a kids' market. This is Billy the Kid, Johnny the Kid, and Sheldon the Kid."

The three Kids stood up, without taking their eyes from the moving tape, shook hands, and called me "sir" respectfully.

"Aren't they cute?" the Great Winfield asked. "Aren't they fuzzy? Look at them, like teddy bears. It's their market. I have taken them on for the duration."

The Great Winfield casually flicked some straw from his Levis. I don't know where on Wall Street he gets the straw; he must bring it down in his pockets and then flick it off, piece by piece, during the day.

"I give them a little stake, they find the stocks, and we split the profits," he said. "Billy the Kid here started with five thousand dollars and has run it up over half a million in the last six months."

"Wow!" I said. I asked Billy the Kid how he did it.

"Computer leasing stocks, sir!" he said, like a cadet being quizzed by an upperclassman. "I buy the convertibles, bank them, and buy some more."

"You must be borrowing heavily," I suggested.

"Not too heavily, sir!" said Billy the Kid. "I put up at least three percent cash. When I am conservative, I put up five percent cash."

"Gee," I said, "on the New York Stock Exchange you have to put up seventy percent cash."

"We know hungry banks, sir," said Billy the Kid.

"Isn't that great? Isn't that great?" said the Great Winfield, beaming. "Brings back memories, doesn't it? Reminds you of the old days, doesn't it? Remember when we used to be in hock to the little Chicago banks?"

"I am awash in nostalgia," I said. Billy the Kid said he was in Leasco Data Processing, and Data Processing and Financial General, and Randolph Computer, and a couple of others I can't remember, except that they all have "Data Processing" or "Computer" in the title. I asked Billy the Kid why these computer leasing stocks were so good.

"The need for computers is practically infinite," said Billy the Kid. "Leasing has proved the only way to sell them, and computer companies themselves do not have the capital. Therefore, earnings will be up a hundred percent this year, will double next year, and will double again the year after. The surface has barely been scratched. The rise has scarcely begun."

"Look at the skepticism on the face of this dirty old man," said the Great Winfield, pointing at me. "Look at him, framing questions about depreciation, about how fast these computers are written off. I know what he's going to ask. He's going to ask what makes a finance company worth fifty times earnings. Right?"

"Right," I admitted.

Billy the Kid smiled tolerantly, well aware that the older generation has trouble figuring out the New Math, the New Economics, and the New Market.

"You can't make any money with questions like that," said the Great Winfield. "They show you're middle-aged, they show your generation. Show me a portfolio, I'll tell you the generation. The *really old* generation, the graybeards, they're the ones with General Motors, AT&T, Texaco, Du Pont, Union Carbide, all those stocks nobody has heard of for years. The middle-aged generation has IBM, Polaroid, and Xerox, and can listen to rock-and-roll music without getting angry. But life belongs to the swingers today. You can tell the swinger stocks because they frighten all the other generations. Tell him, Johnny. Johnny the Kid is in the science stuff."

"Sir!" Johnny the Kid said, snapping to. "My stocks are Kalvar, Mohawk Data, Recognition Equipment, Alphanumeric, and Eberline Instrument."

"Look at him, that middle-aged fogey. He's shocked," the Great Winfield said. "A portfolio selling at a hundred times earnings makes him go into a 1961 trauma. He is torn between memory and desire. Think back to the fires of youth, my boy."

It was true, I could hear the old 1961 Glee Club singing the nostalgic Alumni Song. "I loved 1961," I said. "I love stocks selling at a hundred times earnings. The only problem is that after 1961 came 1962, and everybody papered the playroom with the stock certificates."

Sheldon the Kid waved his hand for recognition.

"This one will really take you back," said the Great Winfield. "Sheldon's Western Oil Shale has gone from three to thirty."

"Sir!" said Sheldon the Kid. "The Western United States is sitting on a pool of oil five times as big as all the known reserves in the world—shale oil. Technology is coming along fast. When it comes, Equity Oil can earn seven hundred and fifty dollars a share. It's selling at twenty-four dollars. The first commercial underground nuclear test is coming up. The possibilities are so big no one can comprehend them."

"Shale oil! Shale oil!" said the Great Winfield. "Takes you *way* back, doesn't it? I bet you can barely remember it."

"The shale oil play," I said, dreaming. "My old MG TC. A blond girl, tan from the summer sun, in the Hamptons, beer on the beach, 'Unchained Melody,' the little bar in the Village . . ."

"See? See?" said the Great Winfield. "The flow of the seasons! Life begins again! It's marvelous! It's like having a son! My boys! My kids!"

The Great Winfield had made his point. Memory can get in the way of such a jolly market, that malaise that comes with the instantly gone, flickering feeling of *déjà vu:* We have all been here before.

"The strength of my kids is that they are too young to remember anything bad, and they are making so much money they feel invincible," said the Great Winfield. "Now you know and I know that one day the orchestra will stop playing and the wind will rattle through the broken window panes, and the anticipation of this freezes us. All of these kids but one will be broke, and that one will be the multi-millionaire, the Arthur Rock of the new generation. There is always one, and we will find him."

I asked how much it would cost to rent a kid. "A buck fifty an hour, room, board, no baby-sitting, only one day's lawn-mowing a week, and half the trading profits," said the Great Winfield.

I put in my application.

Now that you have gotten the feeling of a kids' market, I can go on about the Jericho Indicator. It is related to the number of walls in Wall Street office buildings that come tumbling down. As more and more walls come tumbling down, the Indicator starts flashing. The reason the walls come tumbling down is that prosperity touches Wall Street, the partners have a meeting, they figure they could make twice as much money if they had twice as many registered representatives—brokers—on the telephone. They take over another floor, they move to another building. Tumbling walls are a slightly lagging indicator, but walls never tumble in a bear market. You can count the number of tumbling walls yourself, and multiply by the number of interior decorators at work.

My final indicator is hard to explain, because it is the number of caps removed on Bufferin or aspirin bottles per night when nothing is actually removed from the bottle. Pay attention.

The swinger stocks have moved so swiftly that there are a lot of paper millionaires again, and this means there are a lot of excited fellows so stimulated by the day's events that they have trouble getting to sleep. They lie there on the pillow, mentally thumbing their portfolios like a rosary: "Let's see, Polaroid was up six today, I got a hundred and fifty Polaroid, I still got the one hundred eighty Xerox, that was up five, I got that Digital Equipment, then there's the three hundred Control Data—no, I sold fifty, that was dumb—but the Digital, let's see, at sixty-four, times three, carry the eight, my God, I'm getting *rich*, so I'm worth forty-two and sixteen is fifty-eight there and thirteen is, what did I just have, fifty-eight or fifty-six . . ."

What happens is that they start dropping digits and pretty soon it bugs them, so they get up and silently steal over to the phone table and take out a pen and a piece of paper and then they steal into the bathroom, turn on the light, and start adding up the numbers. The wife wakes up.

"Herbert, are you all right?"

"I'm all right."

"What are you doing in there? What's the matter?"

Now Herbert cannot say that he is in the bathroom adding up his portfolio in a state of high excitement, because wives do not understand the emotional power of the marketplace. So Herbert says instead that he has a headache, and he takes the cap off the aspirin bottle, rattles the aspirin, and runs the water, but no aspirin actually leave the bottle. The wife is satisfied. There is nothing new in this. Balzac had exactly the same scene, only without the aspirin. That was in another country, but emotions are universal and there is no stopping the flow of the seasons.

18. TIMING, AND
A DIVERSION:
THE COCOA GAME

The further we come along, the more apparent becomes the wisdom of the Master in describing the market as a game of musical chairs. The most brilliant and perceptive analysis you can do may sit there until someone else believes it too, for the object of the game is not to own some stock, like a faithful dog, which you have chosen, but to get to the piece of paper ahead of the crowd. Value is not only inherent in the stock; to do you any good, it has to be value that is appreciated by others. (Analysts at White, Weld walk around repeating "I have always preferred recognition to discovery" because that is an aphorism of one of the partners.)

It follows that some sort of sense of timing is necessary, and you either develop it or you don't. You could have a chapter on how to swim, but it wouldn't teach you a tenth as much as getting tossed into the water.

The best chapter written on this problem of timing was done by an unknown second-century author who wrote under the pen name of Koholeth, or the Preacher. What survives of Koholeth is not much, but it says all there is to say on this subject. (If you seem to hear a faint rock beat behind what follows, it is because Pete Seeger made a song, "Turn, Turn, Turn," out of this passage of Koholeth and the Byrds made a hit record of it.) In later versions of the Old Testament, Koholeth appears as Ecclesiastes, so you have the best chapter on timing right there on your shelf already.

To everything there is a season,
And a time to every purpose under the heaven:
A time to be born, and a time to die;
A time to plant, and a time to pluck up that which
    is planted;

A time to break down, and a time to build up;
A time to mourn, and a time to dance;
A time to cast away stones, and a time to gather
    stones together;

A time to keep, and a time to cast away;
A time to rend, and a time to sew;
A time to keep silence, and a time to speak;

and so on.

There isn't anything else to say. There are some markets that want cyclical stocks; there are some that do a fugal counterpoint to interest rates; there are some that become as stricken for romance as the plain girl behind the counter at Woolworth's; there are some that become obsessed with the future of technology; and there are some that don't believe at all.

If you are in the right thing at the wrong time, you may be right but have a long wait; at least you are better off than coming late to the party. You don't want to be on the dance floor when the music stops.

If what you are doing doesn't seem to be working, the game may not be on even, though the brokers continue to mail out recommendations, and the pundits say things are getting fatter than ever, and the customers' men are busy with smooth reassurances.

It may be all very well to say: *When there's no game, don't play,* but the Propensity is very strong among those who have been playing. I once got involved in another game because the main game was not on, and the best I can say is that it kept me out of the main game at the right time. This particular cautionary tale is slightly afield, but since it contains international intrigue, lust greed, piracy, power, valor, racism, witchcraft, and mass psychology, I am including it.

At that time the Dow-Jones average was pointing for 1,000, and all over Wall Street, the lads were so busy calling their customers with buy recommendations that their index fingers were beginning to bleed from all the dialing. I was sitting in the Great Winfield's seedy office, the same Great Winfield who hired the Kids. We were both watching the stock tape chug by, lazily, like two

Alabama sheriffs in a rowboat watching the catfish on a hot spring day.

"They ain't movin' right," said the Great Winfield, crossing one cowboy boot over the other. Years ago, as an earnest and sincere young man, I saw the Great Winfield wear suits from Paul Stuart and Tripler, back when he was trying to be a good boy on Wall Street. Then he made some money and bought a ranch and figured that if the Establishment didn't like him (and it didn't), why should he like the Establishment. So he gave away his Establishment clothes and came down to his office in corduroy coats and cowboy boots, his ranch identity, you see, coffee perkin' in an iron pot—as I said before, the whole Marlboro country commercial bit.

The Great Winfield does not bother with real facts. They only confuse things. He just watches the tape, and when he sees something moving, he hops aboard for a while, and when it stops moving, he gets off, just like a bus. This is good for about a million dollars a year.

Tape traders like the Great Winfield develop a feel for how these stock symbols "act," whether Polaroid is feeling bouncy or whether KLM wants to lie down and go to sleep for a while. The tape tells the story, they say, and they sniff and inhale the atmosphere and proceed on what their Indian-guide awareness tells them.

"No, sir, they ain't bitin', it's time to go home," said the Great Winfield. Now, with hindsight this looks pretty acute, because there was the market near its all-time peak, so a lot of people were obviously buying, and there was the Great Winfield packing up, because the tape was telling him the game was not afoot any more.

"We should all go away for a year and come back fresh, just as everybody is fatigued from riding the market down and watching it rally," said the Great Winfield. "But we can't do nothing for a whole year, so I have us something that will give us ten times our money in six months."

I began to tune in—$1,000 in January becomes $10,000 in July wins my attention any time.

"Cocoa," said the Great Winfield. "There isn't any cocoa. The world is just about out of it."

Now all I know about cocoa is that it comes in little

red cans in Gristede's, and as far as I could see there were a lot of little red cans on the shelves.

But the Great Winfield was warming up, in hypnotic tones. He does this with each little discovery, sort of hypnotizes himself. Then he can generate practically infinite enthusiasm for it.

"My boy," said the Great Winfield, "when the world is just about out of something that it wants, the price goes up. The Cocoa Exchange is unregulated. A three-cent rise in cocoa doubles your money. It's going to be wild. Come along for the party."

What the price of cocoa is depends on how much cocoa there is. The main crop is picked from October to March, so along about February or March every year, with the current crop in the bag, the speculation starts about the next year's crop. Now starts the political and international intrigue.

"My informants in Ghana tell me things are in a bad way," said the Great Winfield, sounding like M giving 007 a new assignment. My informants in Ghana, he said. Usually his informant is one company treasurer, but now suddenly he is far-reaching and international.

"The Redeemer, Mr. Kwame Nkrumah, has built himself palaces and a socialist state. The socialist state is printing forms; bureaucrats are supposed to go out and count the cocoa and fill in the forms so the Ghana Marketing Board knows what it is doing. But under the Redeemer, the bureaucrats do not go out and count the cocoa because if they fill in the wrong numbers it throws the five-year plan out of kilter and they are executed. So they find out what the numbers are supposed to be and they fill in those numbers. Consequently, no one knows how much cocoa there is. And my informants tell me there isn't any."

It is impossible to resist: international intrigue, the mockery of socialism, the chance to profit by the tides of history. "Tell me the game," I said.

"You buy a contract on the New York Cocoa Exchange," said the Great Winfield. "The seller promises to deliver to you, say next September, thirty thousand pounds of cocoa at the current price, twenty-three cents. Ten-percent margin, an unregulated market. One contract, one thousand dollars. Cocoa goes up three cents and you double your money. Cocoa goes up six cents, and you triple your money."

"Cocoa goes *down* three cents, I lose *all* my money," I said.

"How can cocoa go down?" said the great Winfield. "Cocoa is going to forty cents. *Minimum*. Six times your money. With some luck, cocoa is going to fifty cents, nine times your money. In 1954, cocoa went to seventy cents." Anyone can buy or sell cocoa in New York—just the way you can buy and sell flax, hides, silver, wheat, and just about any other commodity. Just bring money to your broker. These contracts for future delivery enable the producers and consumers to hedge their operations and they lubricate the flow of commerce.

Rapid calculation showed me a repeat of 1954 would bring $15,000 for every $1,000 contract. I went away, called a broker I knew who had never heard of the Great Winfield, just to get another pipeline open, and pretty soon for only $5,000 somebody was going to deliver me 150,000 pounds of cocoa in September.

Very heady stuff, being an international cocoa speculator. All of a sudden I was meeting guys I had never met before, fellow members of the International Cocoa Cabal. I met a tweedy consultant type whose business takes him to West Africa. We bought each other drinks.

"I do believe," said the consultant, "that our dark brothers have fabricated the figures. There is no cocoa."

Two weeks later the Redeemer, Mr. Kwame Nkrumah, was paying a social call in Peking when the Opposition took the country away from him—all but the $25 million the Redeemer has stashed somewhere—and the afternoon papers had eight-column headlines, REVOLUTION IN GHANA. My phone rang. It was the Great Winfield's assistant.

"The Great Winfield," he said, "wanted you aboard in the cocoa game because you are a Communicator and you know people. So call up somebody in West Africa and find out who took over Ghana and what does it mean for cocoa."

The Great Winfield had $3 million worth of cocoa, and by hypnotizing me into five contracts he had an intelligence service. But now I wanted to know myself, so there I was on the phone at midnight with a CBS correspondent I once met, his voice fading and burbling from Accra in distant Ghana. The situation was confused, he said. I wanted to know were the new fellows from a cocoa-producing tribe or not. The CBS man said he didn't know, but he thought some of the new cabinet was from the interior, where they produce the cocoa.

Now people I don't know were calling me out of the blue, saying, "You don't know me, but what do you hear from Ghana? Is the new government pro-cocoa or not?"

Cocoa went to twenty-five cents. Now without putting up any more money I could buy two more contracts.

There was a dinner for the cocoa industry and a man from Hershey gave a speech and said there was plenty of cocoa for everybody. The next day, faced with this vast surplus, cocoa plummeted—cocoa is an unregulated market—so fast they had to shut up the trading. At the bottom the man from Hershey steps in and buys from the panickers. This confuses me. Why should he buy if there is going to be plenty later?

Now I suddenly realized there were three lions in the middle of this ring called Hershey, Nestle, and M&M, and we were all mice trying to cast them in a net. Hershey has only to lean on the market and the mice are mouse pâté. Hershey, Nestle, and M&M have to buy the real cocoa down the road somewhere, and meantime they were hedging themselves with millions of dollars, buying and selling cocoa contracts.

The object of the game is for the mice to keep the cocoa away from the lions so that the lions have to pay up for it when it comes time to make the chocolate bars. However, if the lions catch the mice, they skin them and take their cocoa contracts away, and then they can pay the going rate for cocoa. In their pockets they have the mice's contracts.

After the Hershey speech there was a mouse panic, cocoa dropped to twenty-two cents, and I got a margin call and several rolls of Tums. Happily, cocoa bounced to twenty-four cents immediately and I was saved.

The Great Winfield was on the phone, soothing. "Hershey and M&M are trying to get cheap cocoa contracts, panicking the speculators," he said. "Well, we don't panic. *They* know there isn't any cocoa, that's why they're trying this. The farmers aren't spraying the trees. They're leaving the farms. This crop is already bad. If next year's crop is bad, we'll see cocoa at forty cents, at fifty cents, at sixty cents. The chocolate people will be screaming for cocoa, their backs to the wall."

Cocoa went to twenty-five cents, and now I was beginning to get reports from brokers saying cocoa should be going up soon. That should have warned me, but it didn't. The phone rang. It was the Great Winfield's assistant.

"I am distressed to report violence in the cocoa-producing country of Nigeria," he said, and the Great Winfield picked up the extension.

"Civil war!" he said happily. "Civil war! The Hausas are murdering the Ibos! Tragedy! I don't see how they can get the crop in, do you?"

I didn't. Of course, a little research would have shown that the trouble between the Ibos and Hausas was in the East and North and the cocoa was in the West, where the Yorubas live, but there we were, a part of every headline. Now the bulletins came thick and fast.

"I am grieved to report," said the Great Winfield's assistant, "that General Ironsi, head of Nigeria, has been murdered. Civil war. No cocoa."

Cocoa went up to twenty-seven cents.

"I am grieved to report," said the Great Winfield's assistant, "that the main rail line to the coast was blown up this morning. The Great Winfield had nothing to do with it, no matter what they are saying in London. We abhor violence. We love truth. Truth is that there is no cocoa, and that Hershey will be screaming for it at sixty cents."

"Seventy cents!" cried the Great Winfield, on the extension. "Not bad, making a couple million when the stock market is falling apart, eh?"

Now I heard a rumor from another quarter that the Great Winfield was asking his friends in the drug industry if there was any way of injecting a tree so it would catch Black Pod, a dreaded cocoa disease.

"Wait a minute," I said. "You told me there wasn't any cocoa, the trees haven't been sprayed in five years, the farmers are leaving the farms, civil war, riot, chaos, no cocoa. Now all of a sudden there's cocoa out there and we need a plague so it won't grow and the price will go up."

"Don't worry about it," said the Great Winfield. "The crop is going to be very bad. A little rain now, a little outbreak of Black Pod, and we've got 'em. You ever see cocoa trees with all their pods turning a horrible black? A terrible thing to behold, terrible. I think we'll get seventy cents for our cocoa."

I heard another rumor: A doctor walked into the Philadelphia warehouse where the cocoa comes in and discovered rats. Rats! He was shocked. He embargoed the warehouse. The doctor was a friend of the Great Winfield's and had bought five contracts. Two hours later the Hershey doctor arrived at the warehouse and un-embargoed it, and the rats were all gone. I had no way of checking the story. I was building up my own set of anxieties: We needed rain, heavy rain, to encourage the Black Pod. If only torrential rains would burst from the heavens over Ghana, we had a chance for a Black Pod epidemic and sixty-cent cocoa. It was so much on my mind that I introduced myself to a Ghanaian diplomat at a cocktail party.

"Tell me, sir," I said, *"is it raining in your country now?"*

"It always rains in August," he said.

"I know," I said, "but is it raining *hard? Torrentially?"*

The Ghanaian diplomat stared at me as if I were some kind of nut and walked away.

Meanwhile, to an old tape-trader, cocoa was not acting well. It had faltered at twenty-seven cents. The volume was huge. It was drifting down, and no one knew whether there was any cocoa or how big the crop would be. The Great Winfield decided we must send our man to West Africa to find out if it was raining and whether the Dreaded Black Pod Disease was spreading and whether indeed there was any cocoa crop at all. The Great Winfield picked Marvin from Brooklyn, a busted cocoa trader. Marvin usually bought a few cocoa contracts, pyramided them, made a lot of money, then got killed, went broke, and then hustled around for odd jobs trying to get a stake to get back in the game. At the time, Marvin was in the broke stage, so he could perform the mission. Marvin weighs 240 pounds, wears glasses, and had never been west of the Catskills or north of Hartford, and as far as I could tell, he didn't know a cocoa tree from an elderberry bush. To him cocoa was a piece of paper traded on Wall Street, but Marvin was Our Man in West Africa. I went up to Abercrombie & Fitch with him. The Great Winfield had $3 million worth of cocoa at stake, and he was paying Marvin $500 and expenses.

As Marvin got togged out in his safari suit, I was beginning to get vague feelings this was no investment but a chapter from some early Waugh.

Marvin bought a hunting knife, a compass, a kit that kept the martinis cold, a waterproof cover for the cards. We spent a serious hour talking to a salesman about a Wesley Richards .475. That is an elephant gun.

"You're not going to run into any elephants, you're going to count cocoa," I said.

"You never can tell what you need," Marvin said, taking a careful bead on the elevator of Abercrombie & Fitch, the barrels wavering uncertainly.

Then we went to a drugstore where Marvin got pills for dysentery, jaundice, snake bite, yellow fever, ragweed allergy, poison ivy, and constipation. He also got 100 Meprobamate, a tranquilizer. Then we went to Kennedy, and Marvin hefted himself and his kits into a Pan American jet. He gave a gallant wave of his hand and was gone. Only twenty-four hours later we got our first intelligence.

RAINING OFF AND ON

MARVIN

Back to our man in Ghana went a cable:

GET PRODUCTION FORECAST BASED NUMBER TREES WHAT WEATHER HOW MANY TREES DISEASED WHAT PRICE TO FARMERS

WINFIELD

Back came a cable:

BRITISHER IN HOTEL SAYS SAME NUMBER OF TREES AS
LAST YEAR AND CAPSID FLY UNDER CONTROL

"Capsid fly? Capsid fly?" I said.

"Eats cocoa trees," said the Great Winfield's assistant.

"Dammit, I didn't send him there to sit in the hotel,"
roared the Great Winfield. "Tell him to get out and check
the cocoa warehouses, the major plantations, find out
about the crop. I got three million bucks in this and cocoa
is down to twenty-six cents."

"Maybe he doesn't feel safe without that elephant gun,"
I said. Cocoa was down to 25.5 cents. Somebody knew
something we didn't know, or perhaps the lions were
frightening the mice again, no way to tell. The next cable
was not much help.

BRITISHER HERE SAYS SOME BLACK POD IN ASHANTI RE-
GION LEAVING FOR ASHANTI REGION TOMORROW STOP IT HAS
STOPPED RAINING

                                                    MARVIN

In the next two days, cocoa dropped a hundred points
to 24.5 cents. I got a margin call and they sold two of
my contracts. The Great Winfield scowled and wondered
where the hell Marvin was. I visualized Marvin, in his in-
imitable way, going up to a Ghanaian outside a warehouse, asking, "Say, boy, any cocoa in there?" And the
Ghanaian saying, "Nosuh, boss, no cocoa in deah." And
then, as Marvin trudges off, the Ghanaian, who had been
to the London School of Economics, goes back in the
warehouse, chock-full of cocoa, puts his Savile Row suit
back on, gets on the phone to the next warehouse, and
says in crisp British tones, "Marvin heading north by
northwest."

That was the last we heard from Marvin for some time.
Apparently it happened this way: Marvin rents a car and
a driver. The road turns into a mud track and the mud
track becomes impassable, so the driver goes ahead to get
some help. The driver doesn't return and Marvin sets forth
by himself, gets lost, finds himself stumbling through the
dark humid jungle, gnats and flies buzzing around his

head, the laughter of howling monkeys overhead. Leeches six inches long fasten themselves to his legs. His safari suit is soaked through.

Hours later, frantic and nearly out of his mind, Marvin stumbles to a clearing, to find himself surrounded by grinning citizens pointing spears at him. The grinning citizens seize him and strip him of his clothes. Marvin lets out a great scream.

Meanwhile on the other side of the world cocoa has plummeted another hundred points and the Great Winfield sent another cable:

NO NEWS EXYOU LONDON REPORTS CROP AT LEAST FAIR
CABLE AT ONCE

WINFIELD

The grinning citizens have now laid down their spears and are hoisting Marvin into a big vat of oil heated by a fire. Marvin is bellowing like a steer on the way to the steak house.

In New York, the panicked speculators were unloading their cocoa and the price plummeted to twenty cents. At that price the gentlemen from Hershey and M&M were at the Cocoa Exchange buying. Cocoa had gone down three cents from the original twenty-three cents and M&M got all my cocoa contracts. The Great Winfield was unavailable. Brooding, said his assistant.

It turns out the grinning citizens with the spears are friendly. They know when a visitor comes through the jungle with leeches, a bath of warm oil soothes the hurt. So they are doing Marvin a favor by stripping him and plunking him in the warm oil, and as a matter of fact, after a few more bellows Marvin stops screaming when he finds out the oil is not boiling. He is a rather delectable morsel at 240 pounds, but the citizens dry him off and feed him and trot him along to a police outpost, and eventually to a government cocoa station, where his own driver is waiting to be paid.

There were revolutions in Nigeria and Ghana and outbreaks of Black Pod, and railroads blown up, but apparently something like this happens almost every year and there is still a cocoa crop.

So there was a cocoa crop. Not big. Not small. Medium.

But the cocoa crop was less than consumption, so going into next year's crop there will be very small supplies.

I was busted and the Great Winfield's assistant was busted. The Great Winfield himself lost about half his contracts and kept half. "If you can't make it one way, you make it another," he said cavalierly, and went off to chase the shorts in KLM and Solitron Devices, and made his cocoa loss back in the chase.

Marvin has been back a while now. The warm oil really did heal his leech bites, and he is willing to go back to Ghana or Nigeria any time anyone will send him. Just give him a stake to get back in the game and he will have his safari suit packed.

Every once in a while, I glance at cocoa quotations. Nigeria has broken up into real civil war. Ghana has devalued its currency. Black Pod is everywhere. A bad crop and cocoa could be at fifty cents. Every year the world uses up more cocoa than is produced, and yet the price of cocoa seems to stay in the same range. It doesn't make sense, so I have to assume that in this game the lions are too far ahead of the mice. I know which side I am on, and the next time someone says there is nothing going on in the stock market, but an interesting situation has come up in commodities, I am going off to some mouse beach and wait in the sun until it all blows over.

(Still another note for this paperback. In 1968, the civil strife and the Black Pod finally did their work. Cocoa went straight up and hit 45¢. But Marvin was chasing hot stocks and The Great Winfield was skiing, and nobody told me about it in time. The moral remains.)

IV

VISIONS OF THE APOCALYPSE:

Can It All Come Tumbling Down?

19. MY FRIEND THE GNOME OF ZURICH SAYS A MAJOR MONEY CRISIS IS ON ITS WAY

Everybody reads about the Gnomes of Zurich, and people even sometimes talk about them when they are trying to puzzle their way through all the noise about gold problems, but I am the only man I know who really does know a genuine Gnome of Zurich. In fact, the Gnome of Zurich is staying at my house at the moment. He jets over every once in a while, plays with the kids, reaches up and pats the dog on the head, and explains gold and international money crises to me. This is very useful stuff, because if the Gnome of Zurich is right, we will get a major stock market debacle like nobody in this generation can imagine, suddenly, like a tornado out of a blue sky.

Notice I said Gnome, singular. There is only one Gnome of Zurich. That is my Gnome. "The other Gnomes," says the Gnome of Zurich, "are really Gnomes of Basle, where the Bank for International Settlements is, or Gnomes of Geneva, where you get the Arab oil money and such as that. I am the only Gnome of Zurich, fol-de-rol-de-rally-o, and the very fact that the press keeps worrying about the Gnomes of Zurich plural just shows how unhip they are."

Anyway, I have this working arrangement with the Gnome of Zurich, sort of a Distant Early Warning service, and the Gnome's job is to keep me posted on gold so I can get out of the market before the price of money goes through the roof and all the gunslingers at the go-go funds do another job like they did a while back.

Gnomes, of course, are the original gold-bugs. They are related to the original *Heinzelmaennchen,* who worked in the mines, and distantly to the *Hulduvolk,* who were really pretty evil, and all that mine work gave them a fixation about gold. Currently most Gnomes are working in Switzerland, because they like to be near the gold, and are members of *Geldarbeitsgeschrei* Number 11, which is currently, I believe, affiliated with the Teamsters.

"The crisis," said my friend the Gnome of Zurich, "will take Wall Street completely by surprise. Wall Street is only distantly related to economics and money, so it is not surprising that only seventeen people on Wall Street really understand money."

Naturally I wanted to know right away who were the seventeen people. The Gnome of Zurich reached for one of my pre-Castro Montecristo Churchills, took his time about lighting up, and blew out the match carefully. "One of them is Robert Roosa at Brown Brothers," he said, "and the other sixteen know who they are. That's all I'm going to say, fol-de-rol-de-rally-o." It is not the easiest thing in the world to deal with one of these damn Gnomes, but if we want to find Truth in the marketplace we must listen to all sides. You have to realize that my friend the Gnome of Zurich is biased, because the world looks different from three-feet-six than it does from six-three. After the Crisis, the Gnomes, according to the terms of their recent contract, will be custodians of all the gold, and will be a very rich union indeed. If you are really interested in all the technical details, maybe Robert Roosa, who used to tinker with these things at the Treasury Department, will tell you about them, but as I said, I am only interested because if the Gnome is right, you can forget about trying to outguess the market; the Crisis is one that will creep up from behind and mug you, because you don't understand it.

Even though I learn a lot, I am never really happy to see the Gnome; the world, as T. S. Eliot said, cannot bear too much reality, and the Gnome counts himself a realist. So it was rather depressing to answer the front door and find the Gnome of Zurich with his little Swissair bag slung over his shoulder, but I listened.

"One day in spring, or maybe not in spring, it will either be raining or it won't," said the Gnome of Zurich. "The market will be hubbling and bubbling, there will be peace overtures in the air, housing starts will be up, and all the customers' men will be watching the tape and dialing their customers as fast as they can. On Wednesday the market will run out of steam, and on Thursday it will weaken. Profit-taking, profit-taking, the savants will say. Do not listen. Call me.

"The only stocks to go up on Thursday will be American South Africa and Dome Mines, gold stocks, and there will be a perceptible flutter in the other golds—Western Deep Levels and such, and the South Africans with unpronounceable names like Blyvooruitzicht. On Friday the market will weaken some more, because the sixteen people I told you about will be moving; Robert Roosa will be in Washington.

"On Friday night the Treasury will make a quiet little announcement. I'll explain it all a bit later. We live in a modern age, the Treasury will say. Gold is a barbaric relic. So we are cutting gold from the dollar; they will float free. Ho ho ho," said the Gnome of Zurich, like the Jolly Green Giant commercials he watches.

"Monday morning the market will be down twenty points, and Tuesday morning, fifteen. Wednesday William McChesney Martin will say he has been wanting to resign for a long time. And when it is over—and it will be over fairly fast—the market will be down four hundred points. There will be chaos and shambles, and people will be looking for scapegoats. The scapegoat will be me. The Gnomes of Zurich did it, they will say, but by then we will have all the gold. Sticks and stones may break my bones—say anything you like."

"Help yourself," I told the Gnome of Zurich, because his fingers are creeping into the cigar box, and I wanted to know why this Crisis was coming and ways that maybe it wouldn't come so the wonderful stock market can keep going.

"Don't mind if I do," said the Gnome of Zurich.

The phrase "the Gnomes of Zurich" was coined by George Brown, the Deputy Prime Minister of Great Britain. The year was 1964, and the Labour Government had just squeaked in. The Labour people had been waiting to get in for a long time and they had a lot of plans, so it was very frustrating to get into power and find that the plans had to wait because Britain was facing a Financial Crisis. Very simply, They—whoever They are, perhaps the international branch of They—took a look at Britain's trade balances and balance sheet and decided to sell sterling. Then all the currency speculators began to sell sterling, and pretty soon nobody was buying sterling except the Bank of England, which has to, and poor Mr. Hayes from the Federal Reserve Bank of New York had to stay up all night getting the financial surgeons together and preparing a massive trans-Atlantic transfusion. George Brown lashed out at the International Conspirators who were out to make a killing by busting the pound—and England in the process. "It is the Gnomes of Zurich," he said, rolling the words out with hatred, lingering over them, pronouncing the *g* hard in Gnomes, making it a two-syllable word. Thus the Gnomes of Zurich came to stand for International Speculators, or for skeptics. But as I told you, most Gnomes are in Basle and Geneva, and the Zurich Gnome is at my house.

"Skeptics, yes," said my friend the Gnome of Zurich. "We stand for disbelief. We are basically cynical about the ability of men to manage their affairs rationally for very long. Particularly politicians. Politicians promise things to the people for which they cannot pay. So we Gnomes stand for Reality, or discipline, if you will. Without us, the printing presses of every government would simply print currency, there would be wild inflation, and in no time the world would be back to barter."

I told you the Gnome of Zurich was biased.

"Whether we have a crisis or not," said my friend the Gnome of Zurich, "depends on who wins the race between belief and disbelief. The dollar is the real international currency. Some may always wish to believe in it, because the alternative is shambles, international trade crumbling from uncertainty. So the nations of the world get together and try to set up something else, a kind of international checking account. Meanwhile the disbelief in the dollar is growing, because every year there is a balance of payments deficit."

When I hear the words "balance of payments" and "deficit" I start to get a headache. It is only the thought of Xerox dropping from 230 to 18 and General Motors from 74 to 8 that makes me pay attention.

"Let me get this right," I said. "If we fix up the balance of payments, then everybody believes in the dollar for a while longer, time enough to set up an international currency. So that's all we have to do."

"That would be a good start," said the Gnome of Zurich. "But nevva happen."

The Gnome of Zurich is a cynic, I told you. Now about this balance of payments stuff, you have probably been all through it. In trade the United States is in pretty good shape—a couple billion more coming in from sales of soybeans and wheat and aircraft than go out for the Volkswagens and Scotch and copper. But then the tourists take wing—more of them every year—and scatter dollars abroad like autumn leaves. *Zap* goes the beautiful trade balance.

"Very easy to fix," I said. "We put a big airport head tax on everybody leaving the country."

"I foresee that," said the Gnome of Zurich, "but it is politically unpalatable, interfering with the basic right of Americans to travel. And you are further along toward Judgment Day than most people know. The Treasury has suggested a thirty percent tax on foreign stocks, so already Americans are finding it tough to invest abroad. The Treasury has already renegotiated all the foreign debts, and Mr. Roosa's currency swaps are well oiled. Now you are selling off assets of the U.S. Government, called participation certificates, a very pretty bookkeeping trick. But the hourglass is running and we are getting down to the real nitty-gritty."

"How else can we fix this problem?" I asked, mentally fingering the portfolio.

"You could bring your quarter of a million troops and all their wives and PXs home from Germany," said the Gnome of Zurich. "Mr. Krupp is building plants all over the Communist countries. Fiat is going to make cars in Russia, and so is Renault. The Europeans do not seem scared of the Russians."

"But we're committed to stay," I said.

"The Germans want the troops—it's better than a quarter of a million tourists—but they don't want to pay for them," said the Gnome.

"We're committed. What else?"

"There's Vietnam," said the Gnome of Zurich. "Now, I care nothing about politics—only about money. And Vietnam is costing you a lot of gold. You know that the money you spend there goes into the Bank of Indochina, owned by the French, and then goes back to Paris, where it becomes a claim presented in New York for gold. But did you know the Chinese actually take the gold home?"

"Chinese? What Chinese? How?"

"Easy. Out of the black market in Saigon—and you know even soap distributed to villagers shows up in the black market, not to mention all the goods stolen right on the docks—out of the black market come dollars to Hanoi, sent by Charlie—the Viet Cong. They go from Hanoi to Hong Kong, where the Bank of China (Mainland) exchanges them for External Sterling. This is presented as a gold demand to the London Gold Pool, and the gold bars are shipped via Pakistan International Airlines, London to Karachi to Peking. So you lose twice there, both the means and the gold, because you are providing fifty percent of the London Gold Pool."

At this point I began to get skeptical; it all sounded a little too James Bond-y.

"Not at all, it's reported in your own papers. *The Engineering and Mining Journal*, for example. Ask anybody. Ask Franz Pick."

Franz Pick is a currency expert. All of a sudden my headache is worse.

"Well, if you know a way out of Vietnam, I'm sure President Johnson would like to hear it," I said.

"Politics are not my trade, gold is," said the Gnome of Zurich. "I could go on with specifics, but perhaps a generalization would help. You have the mightiest economy in the world. Even the Vietnam war hardly makes a dent in it; you are spending a smaller percentage of gross national product this year on arms than six years ago. But internationally, you do have problems. Your posture in the world does not match your resources. This is not 1948. You are not the benevolent father of everybody in the world. It's very difficult to reconcile your posture of saving the world with your balance of payments deficit. I suspect it is because you did save the world, and the statesmen who produced this triumph are still in power. Men tend to linger over their triumphs. So you fight in Vietnam and keep troops in Germany and provide liquidity for the world because that was the way things were done in the hours of triumph, twenty years ago. But your triumph *was* twenty years ago, memories are short. Gold is hard. The claims on your gold are already twice the amount you have, even if you remove the gold backing from your currency. When money is owed, the creditor pipes the tune. Look at England in 1964. Before you and the Boys in Basle would throw them the life preserver, you made them promise to shape up, and well you should have. A Labour Government had to put workingmen out of work. Irony."

By now my head is throbbing, and I have to repeat, "Xerox, two hundred and thirty to eighteen" to muster my motivation. Now, I know what happens in a Crisis. The Bank Rate goes to seven percent, business goes down the tube, and the stock market crumbles to powder. The Gnome now has me worried about the Crisis all right, but I still want to know the last mechanical details.

"You will hear a lot of nice-sounding phrases, and a lot of rationalizations," said the Gnome of Zurich. "Propaganda, if you will, to cover mistakes. But 1966 was the first year in which there was a *decrease* in the gold stocks of *all* the major nations. All the gold that was produced last year went into the hands of hoarders, served, of course, by the International Brotherhood of Gnomes, *Geldarbeitsgeschrei* Number Eleven. Ask the First National City Bank. They wrote it up."

"George Brown was right," I said. "There *is* a conspiracy. The Gnomes of Basle."

"Only a conspiracy of skeptics, of realists," said the Gnome of Zurich. "Now, your Treasury will never willingly devalue the dollar. But they are committed to supply gold at thirty-five dollars an ounce, and as the speculators get more and more of the gold and the Treasury has less and less, it's obvious that one day Mother Hubbard will go to the cupboard and you know what happens then. The Treasury is worried."

I demanded to know how the Gnome of Zurich knew all this, aside from being a card-carrying Gnome.

"On Mondays," said the Gnome of Zurich, "at eleven-thirty there is a tennis game."

"A *tennis game?*"

"A tennis game played on the single tennis court owned by the United States Federal Reserve."

"The Federal Reserve has a *tennis court?*"

"I thought everybody knew that. Used to have more courts, but they needed the parking spaces. The tennis is doubles, the Federal Reserve versus the Treasury. William McChesney Martin has a mean forehand drive. Every once in a while the ball is hit out of the court. The ball boy returns it. I am the ball boy, and I listen well."

By now I don't know whether to believe the Gnome or not, so I call a man on the *Washington Post* and ask him where William McChesney Martin is at 11:45 on Mondays. The reporter says that William McChesney Martin is usually playing tennis at that hour, just before he speeds up to have lunch with Henry Fowler, Secretary of the Treasury.

"If you want to check on me further—my references," said the Gnome of Zurich, handing them to me. "Call any of them. They know me."

You can call the references yourself. Maybe you know them. There is Xenophon Zolitas, Governor of the Bank of Greece, and Dr. S. Posthuma of the Bank of The Netherlands, and the Britishers Reginald Maudling and Maxwell Stamp, and so on.

"There is," said the Gnome, *"one* rabbit you could possibly pull out of the hat that would save you."

"Give up Vietnam, Germany, and foreign travel," I said.

"That's not a rabbit. The rabbit I am referring to is called *Project Goldfinger.* It is the mission of the United States Treasury to solve the gold crisis by finding more gold right here."

By this time I have just about had it with the Gnome and his James Bond shenanigans, but then there are these lingering doubts—the Federal Reserve *does* have a tennis court, and so on.

"Technology does marvelous things in this day and age," said the Gnome. "So Dr. Donald Hornig, scientific adviser to the President, was given the mission of finding more gold in the United States, preferably on Federal lands, using modern scientific techniques, laser beams for boring, infrared spectrometers, spectrophotometric determination, and I don't know what all. There may be gold in Maine, in Texas, who knows, in Central Park."

You begin to hear that James Bond music?

"The Treasury thinks *Project Goldfinger* might save you, but I don't," said the Gnome, "although it would certainly give you time. In the end, you can't keep techniques a secret, and if there is gold in Central Park there is also gold in the Bois de Boulogne. If there is gold everywhere, the problem comes back, gold sells for fifty cents an ounce. Sooner or later you have to come to reality, and stop being father to the world. Lead it, yes. Buy it. no. Fol-de-rol-de-rally-o."

The Gnome went out to play in the sandbox and I started to mull about his sermon. It is Gnome-oriented, of course. There must be another side. What about all the companies we own abroad? If the French get nasty, we remind them we own Simca, or Chrysler does. What about all the learned gentlemen in the Group of Ten, the IMF, the 216 economists in the Treasury working on this, and so on. No government—not even the French—is going to trigger off a financial mushroom cloud. And governments these days are bigger than all the speculators put together.

Or are they? How come the speculators sopped up more gold last year than all the major nations?

To cheer up, I called up my favorite roomful of gun-slingers, who were busy trading stocks to each other. I told them we better be wary of the market, there is a cloud up there no bigger than a man's hand, the transistor radios stolen from the GIs are turning into gold in London, and those Pakistan Airlines planes are carrying it right to Peking. My friend Charley said I was crazy.

"Come on down," he said. "We bought a stock yesterday that's up twenty-five percent today. Buy some, it'll make you feel better. Listen to that tape. Enjoy, enjoy."

"I just told you we were heading for a gold crisis," I said. "I have it from a card-carrying member of *Geldarbeitsgeschrei* Number Eleven, William McChesney Martin's ball-boy."

"Forget it," Charley said. "The gold-bugs have been around forever. The market still has gas. Who understands gold, anyway? And how can you worry about something you can't understand?"

20. IF ALL THE HALF DOLLARS HAVE DISAPPEARED, IS SOMETHING SINISTER GAINING ON US?

Very articulate and intelligent fellow, the Gnome of Zurich. I keep up with him from time to time. Since the conversation with the Gnome which you have just read, there have been a couple of developments. The nations of the world have gotten together and drawn up a blueprint for a kind of international currency through the International Monetary Fund. If all the congresses and parliaments ratify it, there will be special drawing rights for each country, in proportion to the deposits each country has made in this quasi-international bank. It is encouraging to see nations acting together, because together they are bigger than the speculators, or the businessmen hedging against currency problems.

But the special drawing rights are only a device which gives more time to solve the problems. The problems are still there, still unsolved. The real international currency, the dollar, still has a balance-of-payments deficit. The crisis is deepening. The devaluation of the pound late in 1967 set off some new and darker chapters. We may, if our affairs are really handled ineptly, get to the point where no American will be able to leave this country with more than $100.

Beyond this, the problem is universal. It is that governments are now held responsible for the welfare of the people. The aspirations of the people can outrun their ability to pay for them, and nobody has yet found a way to create answers to the aspirations out of thin air. What this means is that if governments have a choice between attempting full employment and defending their currencies, they will nearly always pick jobs over the worth of the currency. Currencies do not vote. In this country, the Full Employment Act of 1946 spells this out. The government

236

is committed to full employment, and if it must pump money into the economy to achieve this, and if there isn't enough money, it creates the money. Long-range inflation is the policy, articulated or not, of every country in the world.

The aspirations of the people are a noble thing and no one is against jobs. But it does seem easy to produce them with currency rather than productivity. Central governments soon learn the utility of a deficit. It is convenient to take the views of the economists who followed Keynes and spend money during recessions. There are even problems on that side of the equation, because even with the breadth of statistical reporting and with computer speed, this kind of economics is still inexact, and the central government can find itself pressing the wrong lever at the wrong time.

It is less convenient to put some of the grain in the silo during the fat years. You can always think of something else to do with it, to take the convenient part of Keynes without the inconvenient part. This country has been particularly inventive, based on a feeling of omnipotence and omnicompetence. ("Times of great crusades," says the Boston Mister Johnson, "are not times of very great reality.")

What has this to do with markets? Markets are only a tiny facet of society, but being made by mass psychology, they are a good litmus paper for what is going on. Markets only work when they believe, and this confidence is based on the idea that men can manage their affairs rationally. The longest period of prosperity in the last few hundred years came when everyone believed that the king was on the throne, that the pound was worth a pound, that God was in His Heaven, and that all these things would continue for ever and ever.

In the short run, long-range inflation must work for any kind of equity: stocks, land, antiques, real estate, works of art, and so on. If you have a $100 bond and you are getting 5 percent interest, but when the time comes to pay the principal your $100 is only worth $87, you are going to look for something else. If there is $600 billion in bonds out and $100 billion of it moves to the equity side, into stocks, the $600 billion of stocks is going to move as the incremental $100 billion swings. But as it does, capital becomes harder to raise, interest rates go up, some businesses do much worse, and some money moves back into the higher interest rates of the shorter-term bonds, and this rhythm goes on, minor eddies within the tides.

In the longer run, the actions of all the investors, individual and institutional, professional and nonprofessional, have to be based on the belief that leadership knows what it is doing and that rational men are handling the nation's business rationally. If that belief fades, then so do the markets. They do not merely dive, they dive and then they disappear. It happened here in the blight of the spirit from 1930 to 1933, and it has happened in other countries.

Can it all come tumbling down? In a paper market, based on belief, this fear is universal, no matter how deep it is buried. Sure, it can all come tumbling down. All it takes is for belief to go away. Fear is no help to functioning in the marketplace, as some of the senior generation can tell you, so it doesn't do to walk around with it every day. Most of the investment world, blazing its way through the trees, has little idea of the forest.

We all live by a thread anyway, so it may make no more sense to worry about financial H-bombs than plutonium ones.

There are those who look for Signs, and one such Sign, among those looking, was silver. I happened to be among those looking, and here is an anecdote which now seems longer ago than it was. The first stage of the Crisis has already happened. Silver came unpegged from the $1.29 price where it was carefully glued, and we are all still here. But there is more to come. Hear the story first.

Would you believe that some of the dollar bills in your wallet are worth more than the others, and the same with the fives? Well, would you believe the reason you haven't seen a silver dollar or a half dollar in a long time is that somebody has collected them all and is waiting to *melt them down?* More important, do those dollar bills that could be worth maybe two dollars, and those half dollars that aren't here any more, give you the feeling Satchel Paige warned against in his rules for survival when he said, "Never look behind you, somethin' might be gainin' on you"? Is it a sign that the Whirlwind, the Catastrophe, is that much closer? There are analysts who say simply that silver is going up, like a lot of things are going up, and then there are Prophets, who read in this event the portent that something wicked this way comes, something as wicked as 1929, the Dow-Jones average in smoldering ruins, apples on the street corners, soup kitchens.

The particular Prophet who scared me into walking over to the Fed clutching a handful of dollar bills is called James Dines. By trade Mr. Dines is a Chartist, and you know all about *them*. Preceding Mr. Dines' weekly charts is a kind of commentary with a tone very close to that of the Prophets of Israel. The Prophets of Israel, as you recall, were always displeased by the cavorting they saw before them. Always were the princes and the people straying from the path and the way, and woe, said the Prophets, the indignation of the Lord shall be visited upon you. Then in would march the Assyrians or the Scythians, and as they put everything to the torch, the Prophet, from his place upon the wall of the city, would say lo, woe, the indignation of the Lord is visited upon us.

Mr. Dines has taken himself a place on the wall of the city slightly to the right of Nahum the Elkohite. He is so pessimistic he must make up adverbs—"unmeechingly"— to describe his pessimism.

What is the date of the Catastrophe? asks Mr. Dines, and let there be no doubt that the Catastrophe lies before us. In a Catastrophe, there is wailing in the streets and lamentation upon the highways; the chariots are burned up in smoke; the bank rate goes to 7 percent or even 8 percent; the Dow-Jones average crumbles to dust; we have such trouble as has not been seen in a generation and more. Why must there be such a Catastrophe? Folly, sir, the folly of the people and their government, giving away the gold and silver, the denseness and irresponsibility of politicians, monetary problems. Never in 5,000 years has there been a government that could resist debasing its currency. And thus: Exchange your paper money for silver coins, silver certificate dollar bills, gold and silver stocks. Then wait for the collapse and the new phoenix will take shape.

Every week Mr. Dines tolls the exiting gold and the disappearing silver, the approaching doom of the pound and then of the dollar, the folly of the governments. Gold and silver are immutable and will survive, and their disappearance is a sign that the prudent people are collecting them, stashing them away against the Day of Wrath. There is even some discussion between Mr. Dines and his readers as to where the Millerite pilgrims and their money might go. South Africa is mentioned as the Land of Canaan, plenty of gold beyond the sea.

Now the price of gold is a long and complicated question, but practically everybody is agreed that silver is going up. Not so long ago some mining people came to the sage and august New York Society of Security Analysts and the only questions seemed to be when and by how much, and nobody saw it as any more a sign of the Whirlwind than copper or aluminum going up. The difference is that if silver goes up, all the old coins of the United States and some of the dollar bills in your pocket become worth more than their face value. Nobody knows what the psychological effect of this will be. Perhaps none. Perhaps—if the tolling of the Prophets gets to you—the distrust of the people toward the government increases, and the silver and gold go under the mattress, and the stock market goes into a cave to wait for spring.

One day when the market was making like those Messerschmitts in *Twelve O'Clock High*, spiraling down and belching black smoke all the way, the words of the Prophet got to me, and I canvassed the gunslingers' table at Oscar's for the dollar bills that say "Silver Certificate" on them. There weren't very many. Most ones and fives say "Federal Reserve Note" on them. There are $440 million that say *"This Certifies That There Is on Deposit in the Treasury of the United States of America One Dollar [or Five Dollars] in Silver Payable to the Bearer on Demand,"* so you'd think they'd turn up more often, but they don't. With nineteen one-dollar bills I marched to the fortress—like the Federal Reserve Bank of New York. Everybody talks about the Fed, but who ever goes there? There I am, nineteen dollars in hand, saying Pay the Bearer in Silver on Demand, footsteps echoing in the money cathedral. I tell the guard I am the Bearer, ready to Demand. I want to see if the government of the United States means what it says on the dollar bills. The guard motions me downstairs.

Why shouldn't the government Pay the Bearer on Demand? One day it won't, because it won't have the silver, so say the Prophets. Every year the world consumes 100 to 200 million ounces of silver more than it mines; photography, photocopying, electronics—Eastman Kodak alone uses up more than comes out of the mines. Normally with free market play the price would rise to the point of equilibrium for supply and demand. But the price of silver is maintained at an artificial price by the U.S. Treasury, which will sell its silver to all comers at $1.29 an ounce. The Treasury is feverishly minting those red-edged things for coins because if the price of silver goes over $1.38 the silver content is worth more than the face value and theoretically there aren't any coins left; they have all gone into the neighborhood smelters; everybody will be throwing their quarters in the oven and rushing to Eastman Kodak with the lump. The Treasury still has 620 million ounces of silver, but 440 million are for the dollar bills and 165 million are for the strategic stockpile, so the mints are white-hot grinding out the nonsilver coins. At some point, the Treasury has to stop selling silver. It takes the lid off. Zap! The coinage of the United States, 1.85 billion ounces, goes into the vat, or up on the wall with a frame around it. Already you can get fifty-three cents for a half dollar, maybe more.

So I find myself standing before a window, and to my left is a cage. I can see bales of silver certificates there behind the wire. The man in front of me opens his bag, marked The Bank of Tokyo, and the clerk counts out something like $100,000 in tens. Then I step up, with my speech about the Bearer, and I say I would like nineteen silver dollars for my nineteen paper ones that say there is silver in the treasury behind them. The clerk laughs feverishly. I figured he would, because the Gov'mint is keeping the few silver dollars it has left, but I want to get my silver anyway. The clerk sends me to the Federal Assay Office on Old South Street. First I ask him what happens to all those silver certificates in the bale. We burn 'em, he says.

The Federal Assay Office is a white desert outpost, Fort

Zinderneuf, on the river hard by the fish market and parking lots and pizzerias, in the very shadow of Wall Street. I explain my mission to the two guards at the door. I am the Bearer and I Demand. They look at each other: Another one of the nuts. Up to the big window, where the clerk spreads out the nineteen one-dollar bills. This time there is no nonsense. There is a big bag of white sand and scale that says: Maximum Weight 300,000 Ounces.

"Nineteen bucks," says the clerk, "gets you just short of fifteen Troy ounces. Pure silver."

"That's the stuff, huh," I say. White sand!

"That's the stuff," the clerk says, measuring it out like it was hamburger. "One or two of you birds in every day, don't know what you do with it." Classic Irony: Those closest to the Eye of the Whirlwind do not feel it. The clerk is measuring out the silver, 100 percent pure, none of your sterling, sterling is only 92.5 percent, and he is pouring it into—wait a minute—a plastic bag.

"Just a minute," I say. "The United States Government redeems its currency in *Baggies?*"

"Whatsamatter with a Baggie?" says the clerk.

"If you're going to give me this dust, at least give me a bag with an eagle on the side," I suggest.

"They say we have to give you the silver. They don't say we have to give you a bag," the clerk says.

Well, for a while it is okay, walking around Wall Street with a Baggie full of silver, explaining the wisdom of getting silver at $1.29 an ounce when sometime it is going to $1.50 or $2.50 or $3. But there is no action in a Baggie full of silver. We know of our need for action because Our Lord Keynes wrote it in the original *illumine*. I have gone through the whimsical exercise of getting the silver, but now the dust is just sitting in the Baggie and there are threats it is going to end up in the sandbox. I decide to sell my silver, another whimsical exercise, if you will. The handiest market is Handy & Harmon, the great refining and marketing firm. Every day Handy & Harmon quotes the price of silver. The price is the same every day, $1.293, because that's where the Treasury is maintaining it. I call Handy & Harmon and am swiftly given to a Mr. Wemple when I explain I am a seller of silver. Mr. Wemple is a director and the treasurer of this vast corporation. Mr.

Wemple says he will be delighted to buy my silver. In what form is the silver, bullion?

"It's in a Baggie," I say. "United States Government silver, one hundred percent. Buy now, price going up soon."

Mr. Wemple begins to slow down. "How much silver are we talking about?" he asks.

I tell him just short of fifteen ounces, and Mr. Wemple says, "Fifteen thousand ounces is a bit small for us; usually we like units of fifty thousand ounces; but—" and then I explain, *fifteen* ounces, in a Baggie. Now Mr. Wemple is beginning to wonder why his secretary let the call go through, but he is a good sport and says Handy & Harmon can't buy fifteen ounces of silver—the bookkeeping costs would be greater than that—but he's going to switch me to Mr. Jacobus. Mr. Jacobus is in the Old Silver department and they deal in smaller amounts.

Mr. Jacobus starts giving me the same thing about the bookkeeping costs for fifteen ounces of silver, how much it would cost to cast it, why don't I save up and get 1,300 ounces of silver, that way I could have it in bar form. And what I want to know is, here I have this metal that is good as money and vice versa, and I could starve to death carrying it around in its Baggie. How do I trade it back for the money? Mr. Jacobus says Handy & Harmon usually pays sixty cents or seventy cents for old silver that people bring in; if I'll do some other business with him he might give me one dollar an ounce. But one dollar an ounce is a loss of twenty-nine cents an ounce on the whole thing, so naturally I refuse. I warn Mr. Jacobus the Treasury is running out of silver, the price is going up.

"Going up it is, so they say." Mr. Jacobus is quite cheerful about it. "And in India they don't have bank accounts; they wear three ounces of silver on each wrist. When the price goes up, off comes the silver. That's eight hundred million wrists, and I haven't even started to talk about Mexico."

I ask Mr. Jacobus if he isn't worried about all the coins being melted down, and Mr. Jacobus says cheerfully that Handy & Harmon is in business to refine and market silver and the demand for silver goes up every year and *he* doesn't think people will even notice when the silver is gone from the coins, except the birds who are going to make a thing of it and bid up each other's coins. If the Whirlwind is coming, Handy & Harmon will be out there, flying a kite.

So I have a Baggie full of silver and I am waiting for the Day of Wrath, but I have stopped saving silver certificates. When the subway fare was fifteen cents, the authorities warned the public it wouldn't do them any good to stock up on tokens; they would change the tokens if the fare went up. The fare went up and they didn't change the tokens. Sometime the price will go up again but nobody is squirreling away tokens. The warnings about smoking go on and there are more smokers every year. The gold is exiting and the silver is disappearing, but even if the Prophets are right, it is just too much trouble to heed them, and in the end, well, Amos was banished, Jeremiah jailed, and Isaiah was sawn asunder.

I still have the Baggie full of silver. The Prophets, as you know, were right. They were right, and they were not quite right. One evening in spring, after the close of the market, the Treasury announced that it would only sell silver to qualified buyers and that no more could be exported. The next day there was such a scramble that you couldn't buy silver anywhere; silver futures went up the limit in about ten seconds and were shut down for the day.

Within the next week, silver went from $1.29 to $1.50 and then to $1.75, and finally the Treasury announced it would sell all its remaining silver at auction and ads in the paper appeared like this one:

WANTED
SILVER
CERTIFICATES
$1 · $5 · $10
PAYING 40-55% OVER FACE VALUE
10 Convenient Street
level redemption centers.
Out of Towners transfer arranged
thru your local bank.

So the entire silver coinage of the United States is headed for the vat, the collector, or the museum. You don't find silver certificates among your dollar bills any more, the silver dollars and silver half dollars are all gone, and the quarters are going. They have been replaced by non-silver coins, and nobody seems to mind much. The Prophets were right about the price of silver, but not quite right about the reaction to it. It is only a Sign if you believe the same thing will happen to gold, and then the Catastrophe will be upon us only if the rocketing price of gold upsets everyone so much that they stop believing. The folly of governments can produce a rise in gold, and that can produce Catastrophe if the folly becomes more real than the trust in governments. If everyone continues to believe, then gold and silver can go where they will, and it will be no more significant than copper and aluminum following supply and demand, except that speculators will make money on the moves. If belief fades, it is not even necessary for gold to go up—or down.

The cause of belief isn't helped when the United States Treasury says one thing and does another, or when it says the price of silver will hold for twenty years at $1.29 and it doesn't. The price of gold may stay at $35 an ounce forever, but there are more skeptics than there used to be. Even the skeptics, though, hope the believers are right.

V

VISIONS OF THE
MILLENNIUM:

Do You
Really Want
to Be Rich?

21. THE PURPOSIVE INVESTOR

Do You Really Want to Be Rich?

The wheel is about to come full circle. We have seen some of the rules of the Game, and some of the players, and some of the reasons the players play. The reasons are not entirely, as we have seen, the ones we learn as catechism in the religion we grow up with, which is the sanctity of property. The most profound reason the players play is in the essence of capitalism, and we will get to it in one moment.

It is part of the ethos of this country that you *ought* to be rich. You ought to be, unless you have taken some specific vow of poverty such as the priesthood, scholarship, teaching, or civil service, because money is the way we keep score. This feeling has been a long time in the making. It goes away sometimes in depressions, when briefly wealth becomes suspect and poverty is not dishonorable. The rest of the time, poverty is very close to criminal. The worst crimes a man can commit, other than the crimes of violence which for one with property would have to be considered irrational, are crimes against capital. A man can break most of the Commandments with impunity, but please, let him not go bust, that will get him ostracized faster than lying, fudging on his income taxes, cheating, adultery, and coveting all the oxes and asses there are.

In times of prosperity, the old feeling that you ought to be rich is very much in the air. It is not new. In a previous period of prosperity, just before the turn of the century, one of the most popular lectures in the country was Russell Conwell's "Acres of Diamonds." Those diamonds were wealth in your own backyard, and "every good man and woman ought to strive for it," thundered Conwell. "I say, get rich! Get rich!" In the same era,

William Graham Sumner, a famous professor of Yale, wrote: "There is no reason, at the moment, why every American may not acquire capital by being industrious, prudent, and frugal, and thus become rich." And Bishop Lawrence, the doyen of the Episcopal Church, really did say, "In the long run, it is only to the man of morality that wealth comes. Godliness is in league with riches. Material prosperity makes the national character sweeter, more Christlike." So it is no wonder that when John D. Rockefeller was asked how he came by his vast fortune, he answered, "God gave me my money."

If God is truly on the side of the biggest bank accounts, there will be some who will be offended by the very idea that the management of money is a Game, even though Game these days has been dignified by game theory, mathematics, and computeering. Money, they would say, is serious business, no laughing matter, and certainly nothing that should suggest sport, frolic, fun, and play. Yet it may be that the Game element in money is the most harmless of all the elements present. Is it always to be this way?

Let us go back to the Master who gave us the aphorism, John Maynard Keynes, Baron of Tilton, and leave aside his revolutionary doctrines. For our purposes Keynes is not the Master because he changed the course of economic history. He is the Master because he started with nothing, set out to become rich, did so, part time, from his bed, as a player in the Game, and having become rich, had some thoughts that must be integral to any study of the Game. For what follows, we must acknowledge Keynes' own *General Theory* and *Essays in Persuasion,* and also the stimulating works on Keynes of Sir Roy Harrod and Robert L. Heilbroner.

Even second hand, through his biographers, a certain *joie de vivre* emerges. (None of the biographers mention Keynes' subterranean relationship with Lytton Strachey, and perhaps his proclivities are as irrelevant here as the later uses made of his theories.) Here was an economist and a Cambridge don, yet a man in the center of the Bloomsbury set that included the lights of English art and letters, who married the leading ballerina of Diaghilev's company. At the same time he was the chairman of a life insurance

company and the darling of the avant-garde. He disdained
inside information. Every morning he gathered his income
statements and balance sheets and phoned his orders, using
only his own knowledge and intuition, and after his phone
calls he was ready for the business of the day. He not only
made himself several million dollars, but he became Bursar
of Kings College in Cambridge and multiplied its endowment by a factor of ten.

> He was a pillar of stability in delicate matters of in-
> ternational diplomacy, but his official correctness did
> not prevent him from acquiring knowledge of other
> European politicans that included their mistresses,
> neuroses, and financial prejudices. He collected mod-
> ern art long before it was fashionable to do so, but
> at the same time he was a classicist with the finest
> private collection of Newton's writings in the world.
> He ran a theater, and he came to be a Director of the
> Bank of England. He knew Roosevelt and Churchill
> and also Bernard Shaw and Pablo Picasso. He played
> bridge like a speculator, preferring a spectacular play
> to a sound contract, and solitaire like a statistician,
> noting how long it took for the game to come out
> twice running. And he once claimed that he had but
> one regret in life—he wished he had drunk more
> champagne.

(Mr. Heilbroner, who wrote that paragraph, is obviously
another admirer.) And what did the Master think of the
Game? All purposeful money-making impulses come from
the thousands of years of economic scarcity. But wealth
is not pursued solely as an answer to scarcity. "He that
loveth silver shall not be satisfied with silver; nor he that
loveth abundance with increase," wrote Koholeth, the
Preacher, Ecclesiastes. What does the purposive investor
seek? "Purposiveness," said Lord Keynes, "means that we
are more concerned with the remote future results of our
actions than with their own quality or their immediate
effects on our own environment. The 'purposive' man is always trying to secure a spurious and delusive immortality
for his acts by pushing his interest in them forward into
time. He does not love his cat, but his cat's kittens; nor,

in truth, the kittens, but only the kittens' kittens, and so on forward for ever to the end of cat-dom. For him jam is not jam unless it is a case of jam tomorrow and never jam today. Thus by pushing his jam always forward into the future, he strives to secure for his act of boiling it an immortality."

You know, in the end, that so deep-seated an impulse could not be merely the amusement that comes with a Game. The compounding of wealth, like the building of the City, is part of the much older game of life against death. The immortality is spurious because that particular wheel is fixed; you do have to lose in the end. That is the way the senior game is set up: You can't take it with you.

In a remarkably prophetic essay, "The Economic Possibilities for our Grandchildren," Keynes has some remarks that would seem to make him the king of the hippies, if hippies could read Keynes, the Master of the flower-children as well as of speculators. He said the problem of the future would be how to use the freedom from pressing economic cares "which science and compound interest will have won . . . to live wisely and agreeably and well." In this millennium, he wrote, "I see us free, therefore, to return to some of the most sure and certain principles of religion and traditional virtue—that avarice is a vice, that the exaction of usury is a misdemeanor, and the love of money is detestable—

> that those walk most truly in the paths of virtue and sane wisdom who take least thought for the morrow. We shall once more value ends above means and prefer the good to the useful. We shall honour those who can teach us how to pluck the hour and the day virtuously and well, the delightful people who are capable of taking direct enjoyment in things, the lilies of the field who toil not, neither do they spin.

In this millennium, wealth will no longer be of social import, morals will change, and "we shall be able to rid ourselves of many of the pseudo-moral principles which have hag-ridden us for two hundred years, by which we have exalted some of the most distasteful of human qualities into the position of the highest virtues. We shall be able to afford to dare to assess the money-motive at its true value:

> The love of money as a possession—as distinguished from love of money as a means to the enjoyments and realities of life—will be recognised for what it is, a somewhat disgusting morbidity, one of those semi-criminal, semi-pathological propensities which one hands over with a shudder to the specialists in mental disease.

There. Now that you know, do you really want to be rich?

In defense of the players, we must note that when Keynes had a heart attack in 1937, he gave up all of his activities but the editorship of the *Economic Journal*—and his daily half-hour of trading. He stayed a player.

"Beware!" he said, after his vision of the millennium. "The time for all this is not yet. For at least another hundred years we must pretend to ourselves and to every one that fair is foul and foul is fair; for foul is useful and fair is not. Avarice and usury and precaution must be our gods for a little longer still. For only they can lead us out of the tunnel of economic necessity into daylight."

Now that you know some of the things as they are and not as they ought to be, perhaps you will know whether to take the Game or leave it alone. You have to make your own choice, and there are many other and more productive outlets for time and energy.

Until daylight, I wish you the joys of the Game.

About The Author

"*The Money Game*, written by one who signs himself 'Adam Smith' (and who some believe is Harvard-and-Oxford-trained George J. W. Goodman), is a modern-day classic. Like many modern paintings, the book looks simple. But as W. Somerset Maugham said about an unforgettable Mondrian abstraction: 'It looks as though you had only to take a ruler, a tube of black paint and a tube of red, and you could do the thing yourself. Try!' "—Professor Paul A. Samuelson, First American Nobel Prize Winner in Economics.

"Everyone who is anyone in U.S. investment already knows about 'Adam Smith,' " wrote *Newsweek*. 'Adam Smith' is also the author of *Supermoney* and *Powers of Mind*.